Biblical Bible Translating

**The Biblical Basis for Bible Translating
With an Introduction to Semantics
And Applications Made to
Bible Translation Principles and Problems**

This book is affectionately dedicated to my wife,
Mary Lou Crockett Turner.

Biblical Bible Translating

The Biblical Basis for Bible Translating
With an Introduction to Semantics
And Applications Made to
Bible Translation Principles and Problems

By

Dr. Charles V. Turner, Ph.D.

Sovereign Grace Publishers, Inc.
P.O. Box 4998
Lafayette, In 47903

Biblical Bible Translating
Copyright © 1988, 2001
by Dr. Charles V. Turner, Ph.D
All Rights Reserved
ISBN 1-58960-302-8

Second Edition 2001

Library of Congress Catalog Card Number:

88-90221

Dewey Decimal Catalog Number:

268.6

*All biblical quotations are from
the 1769 King James Version.*

*Printed in the United States of America
By Lightning Source, Inc.*

About the Author

Charles Vernon Turner was born in Greenville, South Carolina, in 1934. Because of the ministry of the Marcus Hook Baptist Church in Linwood, Pennsylvania, he was born again by the Spirit of God in 1951.

Charles received his training for the ministry at Marcus Hook Baptist Church. His pastor, Rev. Jack Ludlam, taught him many helpful lessons. His fellow members at Marcus Hook Baptist, Adolph Beck and Leon Downs also had a major impact on his life. Evelyn Congleton and Harold Noden also held Bible classes that helped him very much.

In 1953, Charles began preparing for missionary service at Columbia Bible College in Columbia, South Carolina. At Columbia, Charles earned a Bachelor of Arts degree in Biblical Education in 1957. Charles further prepared for missionary service by taking linguistic training at the Summer Institute of Linguistics at the University of Oklahoma in 1957 and 1958. Two more years of training were taken in Primary Missionary Training (Boot Camp) and Secondary Missionary Training (Linguistic School) at New Tribes Institute in 1958 and 1959. He later earned a Master of Arts degree in Missions at Columbia Graduate School of Missions in 1965 and 1971. In 1990, Charles earned a Ph.D. degree in Linguistics at Great Plains Baptist College in Sioux Falls, South Dakota.

In 1960, Charles was ordained to the ministry and sent by the Marcus Hook Baptist Church as a missionary to Papua New Guinea. There he worked for twenty years among the Sinasina people who live in the Simbu Province. He translated the New Testament, Genesis and Exodus and other books on general education into the Sinasina language. Charles and his co-workers planted several churches and trained Sinasina pastors.

Charles is currently the Executive Director of Baptist Bible Translators Institute in Bowie, Texas. There he works with the sponsoring church of Baptist Bible Translators Institute, which is Central Baptist Church. During the last nineteen years at Baptist Bible Translators Institute, Charles has trained missionaries in Linguistics, Ethnology, Language Learning, Bible Translation, and Cross-cultural Communication.

Preface

Biblical Bible Translating is for people who are concerned about faithful Bible translation. There is a great deal of misunderstanding about what constitutes faithful Bible translation. This book will give the reader a clearer understanding of the principles and problems involved in producing a faithful translation of the Bible. Biblical Bible Translating was developed slowly during 21 years of teaching it to hundreds of students. It began during 2 years of teaching at New Tribes Institute in Camdenton, Missouri and it came to completion at Baptist Bible Translators Institute in Bowie, Texas.

Chapter 1 explains how the inspiration of the Bible is similar to the virgin birth of Christ.

Chapter 2 asserts that we are to work hard to communicate the gospel, but it also reminds us that our success is "Not by might, nor by power, but by my spirit, saith the LORD of hosts." (Zechariah 4:6)

Chapter 3 presents the biblical definition of a nation. This definition shows that the need for Bible translation is every Bibleless nation.

Chapter 4 shows why there is a great need for training in Bible translation principles. The missionary's identity and place in the local church are also biblically defined.

Chapter 5 deals with the problem of theological bias and how it affects Bible translation.

Chapter 8 is a device to teach Bible translation principles.

Chapter 9 presents a reasonable answer to the critical problem that the many English versions of the Bible have caused.

Chapters 10 through 13 are an introduction to Semantics, with applications made to Bible translation principles.

Chapter 14 offers the tool of Componential Analysis for interpreting the meaning of difficult verses of Scripture. This tool, when used with the principles of Semantics that are taught in this book, can help solve the problem of verses that are difficult to interpret.

Chapter 15 begins a section dealing with problem areas of translation that continues to Chapter 29.

Chapters 30 through 33 present a tried and proven method for developing the vocabulary that is needed to translate Scripture into the Bibleless languages of the world.

Chapters 34 and 35 present a way to check the accuracy of a Bible translation.

Who Will Benefit Most From This Book?

People who read these chapters, and apply the principles of cross-cultural communication taught in them, will improve their communication skills.

A preacher who reads this book will be a better preacher if he understands and applies the principles of interpretation and semantics taught in it.

The material in this book will help missionaries who are preparing to do Bible translation work and it will help those who are already involved in Bible translation.

Because interpreters in foreign languages are, in fact, instant translators, they too will profit by reading this book. Those who will be translating tracts and other Christian materials into other languages will also find it helpful.

It is hoped that the thoughts on these pages will challenge Christians to take up the work of planting New Testament Baptist churches by translating God's Word into over 3,000 languages of the world that have no church and no Scripture.

-Charles V. Turner,
Baptist Bible Translators Institute, Bowie, Texas

Translation it is that openeth the window, to let in the light; that breaketh the shell, that we may eat the kernel; that putteth aside the curtain; that we may look into the most holy place."
--The Translators to the Reader, the King James Version, 1611.

Chapter 1

The Living Word and the Written Word

The miraculous inspiration of the Bible is much like the miraculous birth of Jesus. Both are revealed in Scripture as facts for us to believe even if we cannot fully explain them. The Lord Jesus was born because of cooperation between the Holy Spirit and a human being: Mary. Mary was the human instrument used by God to bring Jesus into the world. However, Mary was not the mother of God. Jesus, being God, had already been in existence for all of eternity. She was not the mother of His Deity. She was the mother of His human body. The entire process of the conception, birth, and preservation of Jesus was miraculously superintended by the Holy Spirit. God used human beings to bring the living Word of God into the world. He also used them to protect Jesus from being killed by King Herod.

Although the Holy Spirit used a human being to bring about the entrance of Jesus into a human body, the whole process was done in such a way that human sin and error was not involved. Jesus was in no way contaminated by the sinful nature of Mary or the sinfulness of any other human being. Matthew was careful to emphasize this when he wrote Matthew 1:20 "that which is conceived in her is of the Holy Ghost." Matthew placed the word *Holy* last in the New Testament Greek sentence in order to emphasize that the birth of Jesus was in every way a *holy* birth.

Human sin did not in any way defile the Son of God or make Him anything less than the Holy, Son of God. Matthew wanted us to know that the birth of Jesus had occurred because of the work of God the *Holy* Spirit and was therefore holy in every way.

In the same manner, "holy men of God spake as they were moved (carried along) by the Holy Ghost." (2 Peter 1:21) Just as the Holy Spirit superintended the miraculous birth of the living Word of God into the world, so He also superintended the miraculous entrance of the written Word of God into the world. In the same way that the living Word of God was not defiled by human sin, so the written Word of God was not defiled by human error. As the living Word of God was protected at His birth from those who would have destroyed Him, so the written Word of God was protected from those who would have destroyed it. Just as the living Word was conceived, born, and protected by the miraculous power of the Holy Spirit who used godly people, so God used holy men who were miraculously controlled by the Holy Spirit to conceive, write and protect the written Word of God.

Jesus became the living Word through whom God revealed the truth about Himself to mankind. The Bible, likewise, became the written Word by which God has revealed his final and complete revelation of truth about who He is and what His will is for people.

The coming of the living Word into the world, and the inspiration of the written Word are both miracles wrought by the power and infinite wisdom of God. Because the inspiration of the Bible is a miracle performed by God, it is not, therefore, a matter to be totally understood by the human intellect. It must be accepted by reasonable faith.

It is impossible to fully explain how the Holy Spirit conceived the Lord Jesus. It is equally impossible to explain how God's thoughts were transmitted to the minds of men, who wrote those thoughts in the Bible. The same kind of miracle that the Holy Spirit performed in the body of Mary to bring about the birth of the living Word was also used in the minds of the writers of the Bible to bring into being the written Word. Because the inspiration of Scripture is a miracle performed by the power of God, it cannot be totally comprehended by the human intellect. However, some insist that the miracle of biblical inspiration can be totally comprehended by the human intellect. This matches human knowledge as equal to God's infinite knowledge. Therefore, some people think they are adequate judges of what words should be in the Bible and what words should not be. This is a wrong assumption. It is this false premise that is largely the reason for the many perversions of Scripture. Biblical textual critics assume that the human mind is capable of deciding which words of Scripture are valid and which ones are not. This is a wrong assumption.

This is exactly the mistake one makes when he becomes a critic of the biblical text. Biblical textual criticism is based on the false presupposition that human beings are smart enough to comprehend the miraculous method that God used in inspiring and preserving the Bible. Of course, when one assumes this, his first step must be to delete the miraculous from his premise because the miraculous cannot be comprehended by human reason. Secondly, one who takes this view must bring God's wisdom and miraculous power down to a level that he can comprehend. He must humanize God and purge the Bible of all that is miraculous. He must bring all that Jesus said and did down to a level that can be comprehended by the human intellect. This results in the humanizing of God and makes miracles impossible. It also makes God an intellectual concept that has been created by man's own intellect instead of a fact that is revealed in Scripture to be accepted by reasonable faith.

This is the Gnosticism of the First Century dressed up to be respectable intellectualism in the Twenty-First Century. It makes the judgments made by human beings superior to judgments based on God's miraculous revelation. God's revelation should be accepted by reasonable faith. However, the humanist-intellectual does not accept that God's power and wisdom are superior to his own ability to reason. He begins with the supposition that his own ability to reason is either equal to God's wisdom or superior to it. He will accept only that which he can "prove" by scientific empiricism. However, he does not stop to realize that there is no such thing as totally proven scientific empiricism. Empiricism is impossible because no human being was alive to witness all that took place in the past thousands of years. Furthermore, no human has lived long enough to discover all the facts that can be known or will be known in the future.

Bible Inspiration and Textual Criticism

It is impossible to be an empiricist of biblical textual criticism simply because one will not live long enough to read every manuscript of the biblical text that exists. Biblical manuscripts number over six thousand and are located in places far apart under conditions controlled by many governments and religious sects. The time it would take to acquire them and compare them to each other would be equal to that of several life times. No one will ever live long enough to do it. Therefore, an empirical study of the biblical manuscripts has never been made and will never be made. Even if one did live long enough, one would still be biased in his research. No one is totally objective and free from biased presuppositions. Since this is true, are we to be Agnostics who say we cannot know anything or should we be Gnostics who say we can know everything? We should not be either. We should be Bible believers, not Bible know-it-alls. We do not need to know it all, even if that were possible. We have enough revelation from God in the Person and words of Jesus to have a reasonable faith that accepts the Bible for what Jesus said it was—God's Word.

Jesus accepted that fact and lived accordingly. Nowhere in Scripture do we see Jesus being a textual critic of the Scriptures. Jesus, in His wisdom, knew that one should believe God's Word and obey it. If the Son of God, the wisest and holiest God-Man to ever live, took this view of Scripture, why should we take the view of the textual critic that only leads to confusion, doubt, and despair? We should not. It is better to say, "I do not know the answers to all the doubts about some of the texts of the Bible, but I am confident that when the true, unbiased facts of pure empirical study are known, these facts will agree exactly with what Jesus said two thousand years ago." This is the only reasonable position for a Bible believing Christian to take.

Implications of Biblical Inspiration for Bible Translators

1. Because the Holy Spirit inspired the Bible, it is, therefore a holy Book. We have it because of the power and wisdom of God and the work of the Holy Spirit in holy men of God. Therefore, the Bible translator should handle Bible translating with a respect consistent with the holiness that is inherently a part of translating the Holy Scriptures. Since holy men of God wrote the inspired Bible, only holy men of God can adequately translate it.

2. Because the Holy Spirit inspired the Bible, the person who would translate that Bible should live under the control of the Holy Spirit. Ephesians 5:18 says that Christians should be filled with the Spirit. To be filled with the Holy Spirit is to be controlled by the Holy Spirit. As the Bible translator translates God's Word, he should be under the control of the Holy Spirit. A person who is unregenerate and therefore does not have the Holy Spirit controlling him should not be a Bible Translator. The power and work of the Holy Spirit must be operative as a controlling factor in the translator's life. If it is not, the translation he produces will not have the mark of the Holy Spirit upon it. The translation will not be living water drawn from the well of salvation. It will be polluted water drawn from the well of human intellectualism.

3. Although the Holy Spirit should control the Bible translator, this does not mean that the Holy Spirit will inspire his translation in the same way that He inspired the original writers of Scripture.

His Bible translation will be inspired by the Holy Spirit only insofar as he translates accurately what the Holy Spirit said in the originally written biblical texts.

4. The inspiration of the Bible also implies that the original text of the Bible exists in the Textus Receptus Koine Greek text of the New Testament and the Masoretic Hebrew text of the Old Testament. In spite of what the textual critics say about the Bible being corrupted, God did not withhold His pure, inspired Word until 1881 when the first text produced by the textual critics appeared. From the First Century until now, God has used His churches to protect His pure, inspired Word in the many faithfully copied manuscripts. These manuscripts are the same as the original autographs. Upon being collated, they became the Textus Receptus Koine Greek text and the Masoretic Hebrew text. Therefore, these two texts should be the standard to follow as one translates the Bible into the languages of the world. Because the modern, critical texts produced by textual critics are biased, subjective, and based on flawed intellectualism, they should be rejected as the basis for translating the Scriptures into the languages of the world.

John F. Kennedy's famous Berlin Wall speech was hailed as a masterpiece. However, those with even an elementary knowledge of German had to laugh heartily when President Kennedy reached the climax of the speech by stating: "Ich bin ein Berliner." Instead of dropping the indefinite article to say that he was a Berliner, he announced to all that he was a jelly doughnut."

Chapter 2

A Biblical Philosophy for Bible Translation

The purpose of this chapter is to establish a biblical philosophy for Bible translation principles. In the work of Bible translation, it is important to be trained in linguistics and ethnology, but it is even more important to be a Spirit-regenerated, Spirit-controlled person. There can be no trusting in one's own wisdom and learning. The Bible is uniquely the Book of the Spirit of God. He who would translate it must do so in the power of the Spirit of God. This truth is the philosophy upon which all that is written in this book is based. One's study of Bible translation principles will need to be brought continually to this foundational truth. It is critical to keep this biblical view in mind as one applies Bible translation principles to translation problems.

Four Biblical Principles to Follow

1. People are God's Method.

Romans 10:14 says, "and how shall they hear without a preacher?" The man of God is crucial to any situation in the work of God. Every part of God's work stands or falls depending on those who do that work. God uses people as His method, but He uses them in relationship to the local church that sends them. "And how shall they preach, except they be sent?" (Romans 10:15) Although this book is concerned with teaching a methodology for developing faithful and effective Bible translation, it should be emphasized that ultimately God's method is to use His man as His principle method. The methodology developed in this book will not be the decisive factor in evangelism, Bible translating and church planting. A man of God, filled with the Spirit, will always be the decisive factor in any missionary situation. (I am using the word "man" in the generic sense that means people, both male and female. Ironically, the best "man" for doing God's work on the mission field has often been a woman!)

E.M. Bounds put it this way: "God's plan is to make much of the man, far more of him than of anything else. Men are God's method. The church is looking for better methods. God is looking for better men."[1]

2. God's Work is done Supernaturally.

God's work is to be done by supernatural energy. The Spirit gives life. The flesh profits nothing. (John 6:63) Andrew Murray has said, "as soon as any man trusts to natural abilities, learning or skill in language, he gives himself up to certain delusion. He has sold his birthright in the Gospel state of Divine illumination to make a noise with the sounding brass and tinkling cymbals of the natural man."[2]

The opposite of God's work being done by supernatural power is for it to be done by human ability. Almost every Christian would say he does not believe in secular humanism. Yet, he often denies what he says by what he practices. For example, a prayerless Christian is a Christian who practices humanism. He does not depend on God by asking Him for his needs in prayer. He is prayerless because he feels no need to pray and depend on God's power. He believes, in practice, that he can do it himself.

The four beliefs of naturalism[3]

1. Man's ability to reason is the ultimate judge of truth.

2. Because there is no such thing as the supernatural, anything that cannot be explained by reason is not true.

3. Everything in man's experience can be explained based on natural laws.

4. Therefore, knowledge of these natural laws through education is the ultimate need of man, causing man's highest good, as he becomes able to predict and control these natural laws.

This philosophy is the same Gnosticism that Paul fought against. Paul warned us to "Beware lest any man spoil you through philosophy and vain deceit, after the tradition of men, after the rudiments of the world, and not after Christ." (Colossians 2:8)

3. All Truth must be subject to Christ.

All truth must be subject to Jesus Christ who is the truth. (John 14:6) The Christian may inquire into any legitimate discipline of study as long as he does so with faith in the word of the Lord Jesus. Jesus said that his words would not pass away. We should believe what He said. Contrary to what higher or lower biblical criticism studies may set forth, Jesus said that we would have His word without any loss of it. We should believe the word of Jesus regardless of what critics say.

The Bible-believing Christian knows that the Lord has a higher knowledge than his own and that when all the facts are finally known, the word of the Lord will prove to be exactly as He said it would be. Therefore, the Christian yields his mind to Him who is truth and who has all the treasures of wisdom and knowledge in Himself.

The Christian does not consider any area of life without submitting it to Jesus Christ. Failure to do so leads to a practical denial of Christ's wisdom and knowledge and to an acceptance of a humanistic philosophy.

The Christian should subject all things claiming to be truth to the living Word of God, Jesus Christ, and to the written Word of God, the Holy Scriptures. All information must be "brought into captivity to the obedience of Christ." (2 Corinthians 10:5) When a Christian studies any phase of science, he takes any truth in that science that is subject to consistency with the teaching of Christ. What is not, he rejects. He does not do so blindly. He does so in full view of the One who knows all the facts, and when all the facts are finally known, the Lord Jesus will always prove to be the final source of all truth.

4. We must work together with God.

God does His part and we must do ours if people are to hear the Gospel, understand it, and believe it. "But ye shall receive power, after that the Holy Ghost is come upon you: and ye shall be witnesses unto me." (Acts 1:8) One must understand his relationship to the Spirit of God, who indeed reveals the gospel to a person and converts him. However, one must also understand his responsibility to communicate that gospel to people clearly and effectively. God's Spirit reveals the Gospel to people but we must understand our responsibility to make the Gospel as clear as possible.

Three Ways to Relate to God

In the work of preaching the Gospel, a Christian may relate himself to God in three ways.

1. The Miraculous Relationship

If a Christian has only a miraculous relationship to God, his only responsibility is that of an empty channel. One does nothing but yield to God, who does all the work himself. God can and does work miracles to reveal his message of salvation this way. Yet, we are forced to conclude by the scarcity of such working that this is not the usual way God has chosen for us to bear witness to people. Normally we must diligently study the language of the people we want to talk to before we can tell them about Jesus. However, God has at times bypassed this as he did at Pentecost when "every man heard them speak in his own language." (Acts 2:6)

2. The Religious-Magic Relationship

People sometimes presume that God wishes to use a miracle to do His work, when in fact He does no such thing. If one ignores certain natural laws of communication, such as learning the people's language, and presumptuously asks God to work a miracle, he is dealing with God and man based on "religious magic." This is the arena where Roman Catholicism often operates. "Hocus Pocus" is a phrase that was derived from the Latin mass where the priest, by religious magic, supposedly changes the wafer and wine into the actual flesh and blood of Jesus. Such belief is not faith in the word of Christ. It is dealing with God using a religious magic ritual.

A Pentecostal missionary told me that he was trusting God for a miracle to take place in the hearing of the Yagaria people, even though he did not speak their language. He said that since God had not given him the ability to speak the language, God would open the ears of the Yagaria people to understand his garbled speaking. This is a "religious magic" relationship to God. It is as phony as a three-dollar bill.

3. The Supernatural-Natural Relationship

This is how God usually reveals His Gospel to people. This has been true since God first created the world, humankind, and all the natural laws that govern man's existence. Genesis 1:28 says, "And God blessed them, and God said unto them, Be fruitful, and multiply, and replenish the earth, and subdue it: and have dominion over the fish of the sea, and over the fowl of the air, and over every living thing that moveth upon the earth." This verse is clearly a command from God for man to subdue and have dominion over all the natural laws that govern his existence.

God has put us into a world governed by natural laws. If one does not believe this, he may try defying the law of gravity as he jumps from the fifth floor of a building. This would prove that God's law of gravity is still in effect.

God has chosen to do His work within the boundaries of these laws. God can, however, choose to bypass these laws by doing a supernatural work. This is what a miracle is.

These natural laws apply not only in the physical realm. There are also laws that govern the mind, the body, and the soul. Again, God usually works within the boundaries set by these laws. Man is to subdue and dominate these laws, and thereby bring his environment under his control to the glory of God.

Even the work of Bible translation and communicating the Gospel through the written Word of God is controlled by the bounds set by these laws. In Romans 10:17 Paul says, "So then faith cometh by hearing, and hearing by the word of God." Paul does not mean that faith springs up in a person's heart by merely allowing the sound waves of spoken words to vibrate his eardrums. He also does not mean that faith springs up in a person's heart by merely reading words on a page of the Bible. Paul meant that faith is a result of a person clearly understanding the spoken or written message of the gospel and acting to obey that message.

We should not believe that God converts a man whether he understands anything or not. The Bible clearly teaches a reasoned, decision-oriented conversion, involving the total person. A person's mind and will must be involved if he is to be saved by faith. (Romans 10:9,10)

As Christians, we are responsible to preach and teach in such a way that the sound waves coming from our speech cause vibrations in the listener's eardrums that stimulate the desired word meanings in his brain. Christians must apply all their mental, physical, and spiritual capacities to bring the natural laws of communication under their control.

God has set very definite laws of communication. One has only to read a descriptive analysis of any language to realize that the dominant theme of all language is that it is *structured* by reliable phonological and grammatical rules. To violate this structure is to cause confusion, for meaning depends on the manipulation of language structure. Therefore, the structure of language, including its sound system, word structure, sentence structure, and semantic system, must be mastered if one is to translate the Bible in such a way that it communicates God's Word to human beings who are bound by the natural laws of communication.

In recent years, there has been an information explosion. Ninety percent of all research scientists are living today. They are churning out material on the natural laws of the universe in such great proportions that libraries can no longer keep up with the flood of new books. Should the Spirit-controlled man of God apply himself to using this information? Since God works in a supernatural-natural way, there is no question but that he should. William Carey would agree with this. Concerning how the world should be evangelized, he said, "By prayer and effort. The prayer must be fervent, it must be definite, and it must be united. But we must not be contented with praying without exerting ourselves in the use of means for the obtaining of those things we pray for."[4]

Building as a Wise Masterbuilder

Paul spoke of being a "wise masterbuilder." (1 Corinthians 3:10) This verse implies careful preparation, planning, and hard work. If businesses were operated on the same basis as some missionary work, they would soon be bankrupt. No business can successfully operate exclusively on tradition and a haphazard work ethic. Often in the guise of working under the control of the Spirit, Christian workers do substandard work that is the result of a lack of discipline. It is not the Spirit's work at all. It is only an excuse for shoddy work. Countless missionary hours and lives are wasted, and millions of dollars are foolishly spent because not enough careful planning and diligent research have gone into missionary projects and methods.

The missionary should avail himself of information on the natural laws of communication that have a bearing on the effectiveness of his Bible translation and preaching work. The missionary must study every area of knowledge in dependence on the Holy Spirit who shows him the truth in such knowledge.

One must continually yield his mind to Christ. After one has brought all information to the touchstone of the Word of God, he may apply himself to any valid field of learning. If one follows this rule, he can be assured that the Lord will give understanding in all things. (2 Timothy 2:7) However, the exposing of one's mind to teachings that are anti-Christ is a forbidden field of learning for the Christian.

Ignorance Versus Intellectualism

Having seen that a state of ignorance is not bliss, what about intellectualism? While some are not applying themselves to the information available to them, others are so wrapped up in the information that they cannot see the trees for the forest. Intellectualism is just as bad as a poor work ethic. Intellectualism is a pursuit of knowledge, but not considering this knowledge from God's point of view. It is a glorying in knowledge. It is a trusting in knowledge to solve one's problems. It denies God's glory by lifting up man's wisdom. It denies a need for trust in God's ultimate knowledge. It is a kind of self-sufficiency, a leaning on one's own understanding. Proverbs 3:5 says, "Trust in the LORD with all thine heart; and lean not unto thine own understanding."

Intellectualism is fond of its self-dependent scholarship because it displays its personal cleverness and it is sophisticated and popular with the academic community. However, the wisest man ever to live told us to trust in the Lord, not in our own understanding. Solomon told us to acknowledge God in all things and not to be self-sufficient. He told us to fear God and turn from evil. If we do that, he said, we would have genuine understanding. (Proverbs 3:5,6)

In spite of these words, many are trusting in themselves and in their knowledge. To these people, Isaiah 31:1 might well read like this: "Woe to them that go down to Egypt (university) for help; and stay on horses, (psychology) and trust in chariots, (cultural anthropology) because they are many; (effective); and in horsemen, (linguistics) because they are very strong; but they look not unto the Holy One of Israel, neither seek the Lord!" Intellectuals would say they are not trusting in these things, but what they do in practice, often denies what they say with words.

For thousands of years, the Egyptian people depended on the gods of their religion to control the floodwaters of the Nile. Now the gods are no longer needed. The Aswan dam controls the waters. Could it be that some Christians think they have another "Aswan Dam" in the principles of communication, cultural anthropology, psychology, and linguistics, so that the Lord is no longer needed? They would say, "Of course not." Yet, they behave as if their education were the most important factor in holding back the floodwaters of ineffectiveness in the work of God.

The Conclusion of the Matter

The Bible teaches that we should work diligently. It says that one should incline his heart to wisdom, apply it to understanding, cry after discernment, and lift up his voice for understanding. It says one should seek for wisdom, and search for it, so that he might come to understand what it means to fear God. (Proverbs 2:2) Yes, it is clear that God means for Christians to apply themselves. However, Christians are warned not to wait for "Egypt" instead of the Lord, not to take counsel from "Egypt," but from the Spirit; not to go down to "Egypt," but to ask at God's mouth. (Isaiah 30:1,2) The biblical basis for Bible translating will lead one to neither laziness nor intellectualism. If one is in reality walking in the light of God's Word, he will realize his need of moment-by-moment dependence on the Holy Spirit to enable him to preach and translate God's Word. This will lead him to humility, not pride. A right understanding of truth will cause one to live a life of faith in God's ability to answer prayer. This will result in a diligent application of oneself to master the natural laws of communication.

When Kentucky Fried Chicken entered the Chinese market, to their horror they discovered that their slogan "finger lickin' good" came out as "eat your fingers off."

Chapter 3

The Extent of the Need for Bible Translation: Every Bibleless Nation

Thousands of nations on earth do not have the Scriptures translated into their language.

The word "nation" should be defined in the sense in which it is used in the Bible. When we see how God made a nation from Abram, we understand the meaning of the word "nation" as defined by God.

In Genesis 12:2 God promised Abram, "I will make of thee a great nation." When God made this promise Abram was 75 years old and had no hope of having children. He certainly was not "a great nation" at that time. However, God promised to make Abram and his wife into a great nation. Although they were past childbearing age, God miraculously gave them a son: Isaac. Isaac had a son named Jacob, and Jacob had twelve sons who became the twelve tribes of Israel. Even so, Abram's descendents were still not a nation. Although the family of Abram had grown to become twelve large families that became twelve large tribes, twelve tribes still did not constitute a nation. The twelve tribes became a large group of people in Egypt and left that country as an unruly mixed multitude. They were by no means a nation at that time.

The Four Criteria of a Nation

Four criteria must be met before a group of people should be considered a nation in the biblical sense of the word.

1. Lineage

A nation must be a group of people who have a common lineage. Such was the case with the nation of Israel. God said to Abram, "Unto thy seed will I give this land." (Genesis 12:7) Here the word "seed" has the meaning of ancestry, descendents, or lineage. The descendents of Abram were Isaac, Jacob, and the twelve sons of Jacob who became the twelve tribes of Israel.

2. Language

A nation must speak a common language that is distinct from others. The language must identify them as a people who speak words that are intelligible to the common ancestry but, for the most part, are unintelligible to those outside the common lineage. Genesis 14:13 says, "There came one that had escaped, and told Abram the Hebrew." After Abram had lived in Hebron for several years, he became known as "Abram the Hebrew." Abram was not only called a Hebrew because he lived in Hebron. He spoke a language that became the distinctive language of the Hebrew people.

3. Laws

A nation must have common laws that express their values and govern the behavior of their people. In some nations, these laws are unwritten but are still binding for that nation. In Exodus 24:12 God said to Moses, "Come up to me into the mount, and be there: and I will give thee tables of stone, and a law, and commandments which I have written; that thou mayest teach them."

However, even with a common lineage, a common language, and common laws, the people of Israel were still not a Nation. They did not live in a land of their own.

4. Land

A nation must occupy a defined set of boundaries that prescribe the limits of their land. In Genesis 12:7, God said to Abram, "Unto thy seed will I give this land." Moreover, God said in Exodus 32:13, "all this land that I have spoken of will I give unto your seed, and they shall inherit it for ever."

However, the people of Israel were still not a nation. Only when they had a common lineage, a common language, left Egypt, received their laws from God at Sinai, entered the Land and conquered it did they become the nation of Israel. We may understand God's definition of a nation by tracing the way God made of Abram the great nation of Israel.

Implications of the Biblical Definition

1. Any group of people who recognize themselves as having a common lineage, who speak a distinct language, who have common laws (written or oral), and who live in a prescribed area of land, are a nation in the sight of God. A particular people may not be recognized as a nation because of political power struggles, because they are a small number of people, or because they are forced to leave their land. This was the case with the nation of Israel. For hundreds of years they were dispersed among other nations of the world. Israel was still a nation, although forced out of the land God had given them. This is true of other nations who have been denied their homeland for one reason or the other. They are still nations in the sight of God and deserve to be recognized as such.

2. There is a difference between a nation and a geopolitical state. Many nations live within boundaries prescribed for them by political struggles. Within the boundaries of the United States of America are hundreds of ethnic groups who meet the biblical criteria of a nation. For example, the Navajo people have a common lineage, a common language, common laws, and a common land. They are, in God's sight, a nation. The Comanche people, the Hopi people, and many other ethnic groups are also nations.

3. From the beginning of time, God purposed that by hearing and believing the Gospel of Christ all nations would be blessed. In Genesis 22:18 God said to Abraham, "And in thy seed shall all the nations of earth be blessed." God intended Abraham to be a blessing to all the nations of the world. Abraham would be this blessing in the Person of his descendent, the Lord Jesus Christ. The great missionary Paul said that God had given him grace and made him an apostle, "for obedience to the faith among all nations." (Romans 1:5) At the end of time, we have a preview of God's purpose finally accomplished. In Revelation 5:9, we read about those from every kindred, tongue, people, and nation who have been redeemed by the blood of Christ. These verses clearly show that God's priority is upon reaching the nations of the world with the Gospel of Christ. Within the boundaries of many geopolitical states live ethnic peoples who are nations in the sight of God. These peoples may be small in number, unknown, hated, and expelled from their land, but in the sight of God, these people are a nation. As

such, the God of Abraham longs to bless them through Abraham's descendant, the Lord Jesus Christ.

4. This biblical definition of a nation should dispel the myth that only large geopolitical states are important. It should help us focus on what is important to God. The people in all the nations of the world are important to God. Americans often think they are the most educated, the most powerful, and the most enlightened nation in the world. Such an attitude is offensive to the other nations of the world. Such thinking has been labeled "ethno-centricism" because every nation in the world has the tendency to think they are *the* people in the center of the world.

We should forget about the terms "people groups," "language groups," "ethnic groups," "occupational groups," and other vague terms. God is concerned about all people in all the nations who live in every geographical location on earth. In Mark 16:15 we read, "Go ye into all the world, and preach the gospel to every creature." The words "every creature" do not mean "every critter" meaning every kind of bug. They refer to every inhabited geographical location on God's creation.

5. There are not merely some 200 nations in the world as defined by membership in the United Nations. By biblical definition, there are more than three to four thousand nations in the world. About three thousand of these nations are bibleless because no one considers them important enough to learn their language and translate the Scriptures for them. Even though some of these nations number in the millions, they have been neglected because they live in a disease-plagued place or in a remote area that is dangerous for outsiders to enter.

What then is the extent of the need for Bible translation? It is nothing less than translating the Word of God for the people in every nation on earth!

When Gerber first started selling baby food in Africa, they used the same packaging as in the USA—jars with pictures of the cute little baby on the label. Later they learned that in Africa, companies routinely put pictures on the label that describe what is inside the jar.

Chapter 4

The Need For Faithful Bible Translators

Some would-be Bible translators have been so frightened by their own ignorance and the Bible injunction of Revelation 22:18, 19 (about adding to God's Word or taking away from it), that they have refused to translate the Bible at all. If a sincere Bible translator works hard and yet makes a mistake, God will not "take away his part out of the book of life." This verse is intended for those heretics who willfully twist the Scriptures in order to support their false teachings. Such deliberate, deceitful Bible changing was going on in the First Century and has continued into the present time.

On the other hand, people who are ignorant of sound Bible translation principles have also caused much confusion by their sincere but misguided attempts at Bible translating. I once visited the office of a missionary who was doing some Bible translating. He would look at a verse in his Bible and immediately proceed to translate the verse as he typed it on his typewriter. He was not using a native speaker to help him. He was not using any reference material. He was so confident of his knowledge of the language and the biblical text that he thought he could just sit and type verse after verse without consulting a native speaker or doing any exegetical work on the meaning of the verses he was translating. Some years later, it came out that when this missionary's translation of the Gospel of Mark was printed, the people who read it could not understand what the strange words meant. The publisher refused any further printing of this missionary's work because he had wasted a lot of money on a useless, confusing "translation." Does this kind of situation happen often? Yes. It happens more frequently than most people realize.

A missionary in Laos translated Psalm 23 for the Khmu people. His translation shows how a missionary, though sincere, can cause confusion. He did not have training in Bible translation principles and did not know the Khmu language and culture well. Here is his translation that appeared in the *Wichita Eagle* newspaper on January 7, 1960.

Psalm 23 Translated into Khmu

"The Great Boss is the one who takes care of my sheep; I do not want to own anything. The Great Boss wants me to lie down in the field. He wants me to go to the lake. He makes my good spirit come back. Although I walk through the valley named "Shadow of Death," I do not care. You are with me. You use a stick and a club to make me comfortable. You manufacture a piece of furniture right in front of my eyes while my enemies watch. You pour car grease on my head. My cup has too much water in it and therefore overflows. Goodness and Kindness will walk single file behind me all my life; and I will live in the hut of the Great Boss until I die and am forgotten by the tribe."

This text should convince any reasonable person that Bible translating is not for the missionary who is in a hurry. This missionary should have taken the time to learn the language and culture of the people well enough to do a faithful and accurate translation of Scripture, but he did not.

Missionaries profess reverence for the Word of God and yet many would-be "Bible translators" are doing hasty work that is merely word matching from one language to another. It makes no sense when people read it. Missionaries have mistakenly believed that Bible translation is just a matter of taking a word in one language and finding the same kind of a word with a similar meaning in another language and stringing these words together in an English like sentence structure to produce a translation of Scripture.

One sincere person wrote to someone at a Bible Society and asked if they would send him a dictionary of the words of a particular language. He wanted to find the English translation of the native words and use these native words to translate the Bible into that language. Unfortunately, this is the concept in many people's minds about Bible translating. They do not realize that merely stringing words together is not sufficient to make a faithful Bible translation. Taking the meaning of a message in one language and producing the nearest formal equivalent meaning of that message in another language is the most complex mental exercise known to the human race. It requires training equal to that of a brain surgeon.

Faced with such reality, I am amazed by people who call Baptist Bible Translators Institute and say they want linguistic training but they do not have time to come to B.B.T.I. to take the course. They want to know if they can watch a thirty-minute video or attend a seminar. They are about to leave for a mission field that has a language and culture that will present them with great complexities. However, they go to the field with little or no training in the very thing they are going to the mission field to accomplish—the communicating of the Gospel in a language the people can understand.

Humorous Translation Blunders

Here are some examples of translation blunders made by people, who were not aware of translation principles, do not know English culture, and do not speak the English language very well.

A sign in the lobby of a Moscow hotel across from a Russian Orthodox monastery: "You are welcome to visit the cemetery where famous Russian and Soviet composers, artists, and writers are buried daily except Thursdays."

A sign in a South African tailor shop: "Order your summer's suit. Because is big rush we will execute customers in strict rotation."

A detour sign in Japan: "Stop: Drive Sideways."

On the door of a Moscow hotel room: "If this is your first visit to Russia, you are welcome to it."

We smile at these "translations" of English. However, these are the very same kind of blunders we English speakers make when we try to speak Russian, Chinese, Japanese, Spanish, or some other language without putting forth the effort to learn the language and culture. Our "translations" sound just as funny as the ones quoted above. The difference is that these people were dealing with commercial situations. A missionary's work involves the eternal destiny of people.

The Missionary: His Identity and Place in the Local Church

Bible translators are usually missionaries. What is the biblical definition of a "missionary?" What is the identity and place of a missionary in the local church? What are the qualifications for a missionary? We need biblical answers to these questions.

I was surprised when I typed the word "missionary" into the search box of my computer Bible program. It did not find the word "missionary" anywhere in the Bible! Why does the Bible leave out such an important word?

Why Does the Word "Missionary" Not Occur in the Bible?

The word "missionary" is derived from the Latin word "missio." It means "the act or an instance of sending someone." The New Testament was translated from Greek, so there is no such word as "missionary" in the Greek New Testament. It uses the Greek word "apostolos" for the Latin word "missionary." The Greek word "apostolos" is usually translated as "apostle" in the New Testament, but it has the same meaning as the Latin word "missionary." However, there is a problem using the word "apostle" for the word "missionary."

There is an emotional meaning attached to the word "apostle." It sounds like some high-and-mighty person who is on the same level with the original twelve apostles. This has caused people to avoid using the Greek word "apostle" in favor of the Latin word "missionary."

"Apostle" in the New Testament has two facets of meanings to it. It means "one who is sent" and it means "one who has been given a message to deliver." Putting the two aspects together, the word "apostle" has the combined meaning of "one who is sent to deliver a message." Does the word "missionary" occur in the Bible? Yes. It occurs, but not in the Latin form "missionary." It occurs in the Greek New Testament form "apostle."

Another reason the Greek word "apostle" is a problem when used for the Latin word "missionary" is because of a failure to distinguish the difference between the twelve apostles and church-sent apostles. In Matthew 10:2 it says, "Now the names of the twelve apostles are these." They were the twelve disciples chosen by Jesus and sent by Him as the twelve apostles. Verse 5 says, "These twelve Jesus sent forth." Verse 7 says, "And as ye go, preach." Here we see the two parts of apostleship. The twelve disciples had been with the Lord and he had taught them. Now they were ready to be apostles, whom Jesus could send to teach others. These twelve were sent directly by the Lord Himself to preach His message. There were twelve apostles and only twelve. There were no successors. Revelation 21:14 tells us that, at the end of time, there will still be only "twelve apostles of the Lamb."

In contrast to the twelve apostles, sent directly by the Lord, the first church-sent apostles were recognized and sent by the church at Antioch. Saul and Barnabas were prophets (preachers) and teachers in the church at Antioch. The Holy Spirit told the congregation to set Barnabas and Saul apart for the work to which He had called them. Acts 13:3 says that the church at Antioch *sent* Saul and Barnabas *away*. Verse 4 says, "So they, being sent forth by the Holy Ghost, departed." Verse 5 says, "They *preached the word of God.*" The church at Antioch sent the church apostles, Barnabas and Saul, in agreement with the Holy Spirit. Luke writes in Acts 14:14 "Which when the apostles, Barnabas and Paul." Luke refers to Barnabas and Paul as "apostles" because they had been sent by the church at Antioch to preach the gospel in other places.

Acts 1:21-22 sets the limit of the Twelve Apostles to only those "men which have companied with us all the time that the Lord Jesus went in and out among us, beginning from the baptism of John, unto the same day that he was taken up from us." To be one of the twelve apostles, one had to be a disciple who had companied with the original twelve from the beginning of Christ's ministry until the end of it. Barnabas and Saul did not meet this qualification. They did not need to meet it. They were not following in the sequence of the twelve apostles. They were church-sent apostles to the Gentile nations. Luke, under the inspiration of the Spirit of God, calls Barnabas and Paul "apostles." In Acts 14:14 he wrote, "Which when *the apostles, Barnabas and Paul*, heard of, they rent their clothes."

In Galatians 2:8-9 Paul writes, "(For he that wrought effectually in Peter to the apostleship of the circumcision, the same was mighty in me toward the Gentiles:) And when James, Cephas, and John, who seemed to be pillars, perceived the grace that was given unto me, they gave to me and Barnabas the right hands of fellowship; *that we should go unto the heathen*, and they unto the circumcision." These verses clearly indicate an apostleship to the circumcision (Jews) by the twelve apostles and an apostleship to the uncircumcision (Gentiles) by Paul, Barnabas, and other church-sent apostles.

Defining a Church-Sent Apostle

A church-sent apostle is one who is sent by his local church, away from that local church, to cross language and culture boundaries so that he can bring God's message to the nations and plant New Testament churches among them.

The apostleship of the Twelve was primarily to Israel and only secondarily to bear witness to the Gentile nations. On the other hand, Paul and Barnabas were sent by the local church to cross language and culture boundaries so they could bring God's message to the nations.

Paul and Barnabas are not the only ones referred to as apostles. Paul also refers to Silvanus and Timotheus as apostles. In 1 Thessalonians 1:1 it says, "Paul, and Silvanus, and Timotheus, unto the church of the Thessalonians which is in God the Father and in the Lord Jesus Christ..." In 1 Thessalonians 2:6 Paul refers to these same two men by writing, "Nor of men sought we glory, neither of you, nor yet of others, when we might have been burdensome, *as the apostles of Christ.*" Paul clearly includes Silvanus and Timothy in the group of church-sent apostles.

In Philippians 2:25 Paul also referred to Epaphroditus as an apostle. "Yet I supposed it necessary to send to you Epaphroditus, my brother, and companion in labour, and fellowsoldier, but *your messenger.*" (Greek: your apostle)

In 2 Corinthians 8:23 Paul writes, "Whether any do enquire of Titus, he is my partner and fellowhelper concerning you: or our brethren be enquired of, they are the *messengers of the churches*, and the glory of Christ." In this verse, the words, *"the messengers of the churches"* in Greek is *"the apostles of the churches."*

The above verses give us the description of a New Testament church-sent apostle (missionary). He is one who is sent by the local church to take God's message to all nations. This is his identity. He is a church-sent apostle.

It is clear from the above description that the church-sent apostle was sent away from his home church. He was to go where the gospel had not gone and preach God's message about Christ's salvation in order to plant churches among the nations. The Holy Spirit sent him. The church recognized and agreed with the Holy Spirit's choice to send him. (Acts 13:1-5)

Paul called this church apostleship an "office." He wrote in Romans 11:13, "For I speak to you Gentiles, inasmuch as I am the apostle of the Gentiles, I magnify mine office." He placed great importance on his ministry as a church-sent apostle to the Gentile nations. Such ministry proved beyond all doubt that the Gospel was not limited to the Jews. Paul proved that it was for all nations in every geographical location on earth. Paul was used by God to break the bonds that self-centered Judaism had placed on the Gospel. He was also used by God to set the Gospel free from the Jewish bondage of salvation by good works. He knew that all people, including the heathen, must be saved by the *grace* of God through faith in Jesus. These two pillars of truth, the universal Gospel, and salvation by grace through faith in Christ, we owe largely to the sufferings of that despised Jew—Paul, the church-sent apostle.

We too should recognize and honor the office of the church-sent apostle in the present time.

The Identity and Place of the Church-Sent Apostle

What then is the identity and place of the missionary in the local church? His identity is that of an apostle of Christ who has been entrusted with God's message and sent by his church to take that message to all the nations on earth. What are the qualifications for a missionary? They are the same as those listed for the office of pastor in 1 Timothy 3:1-5. The missionary's place in the church is one that should be honored as any servant of God is honored in the ministry of Christ.

However, lest we church "apostles" think too highly of ourselves, we should remember what Paul said about his apostleship and that of his fellow apostles. In 1 Corinthians 4:9-13 Paul says, "For I think that God hath set forth us the apostles last, as it were appointed to death: for we are made a spectacle unto the world, and to angels, and to men. We are fools for Christ's sake, but ye are wise in Christ; we are weak, but ye are strong; ye are honourable, but we are despised. Even unto this present hour we both hunger, and thirst, and are naked, and are buffeted, and have no certain dwellingplace; And labour, working with our own hands: being reviled, we bless; being persecuted, we suffer it: Being defamed, we intreat: we are made as the filth of the world, and are the offscouring of all things unto this day."

If you are willing to be last, appointed to death, a spectacle, a fool, weak, despised, reviled, defamed, poor, with no certain dwellingplace and considered as so much trash, then welcome aboard, fellow "apostle!"

A brochure for car rentals in Tokyo reads: When passenger of foot heave in sight, tootle the horn. Trumpet him melodiously at first, but if he still obstacles your passage then tootle him with vigor.

Chapter 5

Doctrinal Persuasion and Bible Translating

A Methodist missionary was working with his translation helper and they came to the verse where it mentions "John the Baptist." The translation helper, being a loyal Methodist, suggested to the missionary that the phrase "John the Baptist" should be translated as "John the Methodist!"

At first, this incident appears humorous. However, it reveals a serious problem in Bible translation. It is the problem of a translator's doctrinal beliefs, which ultimately influence how he translates the Scriptures. Every translator would like to think he is the ideal Bible translator who has no prejudices that slant his translation toward his own doctrinal beliefs. This is, of course, erroneous thinking. Every translator is influenced by his doctrinal persuasion. This fact must be accepted as a part of Bible translating, and counteraction must be taken by having one's translation checked by someone other than the translator. This will allow for an impartial examination of the translation.

Bible translations have been and always will be affected by the doctrinal view of the translator. For example, there are many Bible translations that translate "baptism" as "sprinkle" or "pour" or whatever happens to suit the translator's own beliefs about the mode of baptism. The mode used in the New Testament was immersion into water and should be translated that way. However, Roman Catholics and Lutherans regularly translate water baptism as sprinkle. Some translators, rather than have their translations rejected by Roman Catholics and Lutherans, have accepted the translation of water baptism as sprinkle and translated it as such. One translator, in his desire to have his translation accepted by Roman Catholics, said that he intended to leave out the second commandment about not making idols: "Thou shalt not make unto thee any graven image." (Exodus 20:4) He justified this by saying that some of the fifteenth-century Reformers had translated Exodus 20:1-17 in this way. He did this in order to make his translation acceptable to Roman Catholics, who predominated among the people for whom he was translating a New Testament.

In another country, the native speakers who were used as translation helpers were modernistic Presbyterians. The translation they produced was heavily influenced by their modernistic beliefs. Consequently, the native Baptist pastors in the area rejected this New Testament. Instead, they appointed their own group of pastors who retranslated and paid for the printing of a New Testament in their language that was not slanted toward modernistic Presbyterian beliefs.

In another country, the translation of the New Testament into a native language was so slanted toward Lutheranism and Roman Catholicism that it was unacceptable to the Baptist missionaries in the area. They refused to use it. In this same country, a national language New Testament was translated predominately by Lutherans and

Catholics and was unacceptable to independent Baptist missionaries. They spent many years retranslating this New Testament.

The first edition of the Gospel of Mark in one trade language had a picture of John the Baptist sprinkling water over the head of Jesus at His baptism. This picture made it evident from the start, which way the translation would be influenced doctrinally. The independent Baptist missionaries revised this translation by correcting the doctrinal and translation problems in it.

A Native American Indian New Testament is another case in point. The Native American Baptist church in the area rejected this translation of the New Testament in their language. The Baptist church rejected this New Testament because modernistic translation helpers were used to translate it. They bent the translation toward their modernistic views. This made the translation unacceptable to the Native American Baptist pastors who refused to use it even though it was in their own language.

All of the above illustrations point out the need for Baptist missionaries to take up the work of Bible translation. We, as Baptists, claim to love the Bible and depend on it to teach us what to believe and practice. However, we are inconsistent with this belief. Independent Baptists have, for the most part, neglected Bible translation work or depended on "the experts" to do it for them. In far too many instances, the Bible translations that were done for Baptists by the "experts" have been slanted toward doctrines that are inconsistent with faithful Bible doctrine.

Many Baptist people have unsuspectingly paid for and supported Bible translations that contain a doctrinal slant that opposes what they believe. They have also supported the translation of New Testaments that have been translated from the modernistic Critical Text. The translations made from such texts leave out many verses and phrases that are part of the Word of God. Baptists would not support such work if they knew what was being done. Due to their lack of knowledge about translation work, they are uninformed about the situation and continue to rely on "the experts" to do translations for them. Our situation as Baptists is similar to the one mentioned in Isaiah 36:6, which says, "Lo, thou trustest in the staff of this broken reed, on Egypt; whereon if a man lean, it will go into his hand, and pierce it."

A sign near the elevator in a Bucharest Hotel: "The lift is being fixed for the next day. During that time we regret that you will be unbearable."

Chapter 6

The Objective of Bible Translation: Church Planting

A missionary should not only be a Bible translator, he should also be a church planter. His ultimate objective should be to establish New Testament Baptist churches. The translation of Scripture will contribute toward the establishing of these churches, but should not become an end in itself. The missionary should not only translate the Scriptures, but also preach and teach those Scriptures so that people will believe in Christ. After winning people to faith in Christ, he should organize them into New Testament Baptist churches that will reproduce themselves by planting other New Testament Baptist churches. As the missionary translates the Scriptures, he should use them in his preaching and teaching of believers. The churches that come into being because of this teaching will be founded upon the written Word of God. Their Bibles will be in the language the people understand best, their own mother tongue. This translated Word will become the rule of faith and practice for their individual lives as Christians and for their corporate life as the body of Christ.

Supporting Factors

The more closely a Bible translator involves himself in the establishing of New Testament churches, the better his translation will match the needs of those churches. The best New Testament translation always comes out of a New Testament church-planting situation. As the translator teaches the Scriptures that he has translated, the result will be a Christian experience in the lives of those who receive this teaching. From the experience of these believers there will come words to express their Christian experience. From the words used by these believers, the translator will find the vocabulary he needs for translating the New Testament. The teaching of the Word of God will result in the development of vocabulary that can be used in the translation of the Scriptures. This gives the translation process the best context in which to develop. This context is that of a living church made up of believers who begin to express their salvation experience in biblical terms they understand correctly in their own language and culture.

The Missionary Mandate

Another factor that supports the translator-preacher approach is this: the missionary command in Scripture is to *preach* God's Word. Missionaries should not only be translators of the Word, but preachers and teachers of that Word. The Scriptures do not tell us to merely translate the Scriptures and then, having done so, give it to the people and leave them to their own inclinations to understand and apply it.

In Acts 8:28-35 the Ethiopian was reading the Scriptures, but when asked by Philip if he understood what he was reading, the Ethiopian replied, "How can I, ...*except some man should guide me?*" The Bible is not a book that has religious-magical powers that will somehow communicate its meaning to people even when they do not understand it. People must understand it correctly if they are to benefit from its message. For people to understand it correctly, it must be explained correctly.

Hebrews 4:12 says, "For the word of God is quick [alive], and powerful, and sharper than any twoedged sword, piercing even to the dividing asunder of soul and spirit, and of the joints and marrow, and is a discerner of the thoughts and intents of the heart." This verse has been interpreted to mean that all we have to do is pass out Bibles to people and the Bible itself will lead them to salvation in Christ. However, this verse does not mean that the Bible, as an inanimate book made of paper and ink, is alive and does the things a human being can do. The Bible, as a book made of paper and ink, does no piercing of the soul and discerning of thoughts. Hebrews 4:12 means that the Bible is alive and powerful and discerns the thoughts and intents of the heart *when it is preached and people understand it correctly*. Only when the Bible is preached and explained does it become piercing to the soul and discerning of the thoughts.

The principle we are to follow as missionaries is given in Romans 10:14 "and how shall they hear without a preacher?" Also 1 Corinthians 1:21 says, "It pleased God by the foolishness of *preaching* to save them that believe." If missionaries only translate and distribute Scripture, they have done a good thing, but they have only done *a part* of the job that must be done. They must also preach and teach what the Bible means. By teaching the meaning of Scripture, the Bible becomes piercing to the soul and discerning of the thoughts, and this leads people to trust in Christ for their salvation.

An Objection Answered

Some people say that a missionary could not possibly be both a translator and a church planter. They say that a translator does not have time to both preach and translate. They say he must specialize in translation only. However, in the early stage of language and culture learning and the initial stage of preaching the Gospel, the translator will learn many words that he can use later in Bible translation. The Bible translator *must* be a vital part of the church-planting experience. If he is not, he will be unaware of the New Testament words that result from Christians who begin expressing their experience by using correct New Testament vocabulary. The translator must use this vocabulary in the translation of the New Testament.

The words "correct New Testament vocabulary" were carefully chosen. It is possible for a translator to be working in a non-New Testament-like situation where the people are nominally "Christian" but in reality are just unsaved people who have the outward trappings of Christianity. A translator who learns vocabulary from these people will be learning words that do not express the correct New Testament experience. A translation of the New Testament made under these conditions will lead people in the direction of salvation by good works that ultimately leads, not to heaven, but to the lake of fire.

It is important for a missionary to keep Bible translation in proper perspective. Bible translation is not the ultimate goal of the missionary. The establishing of New Testament Baptist churches that reproduce themselves by planting other New Testament Baptist churches is the ultimate goal. The more the translator keeps Bible translation in the context of establishing New Testament Baptist churches, the better that translation will be for the use of those churches. It will have been developed out of the people's own genuine Christian experience in the context of a New Testament church, and it will be the vocabulary they understand best. This is why the Scriptures declare "Christ also loved the church, and gave himself for it." (Ephesians 5:25) In Acts 20:28 we read about "the church of God, which he hath purchased with his own blood." The local New Testament church is the focal point of all that God is doing in the world. The Bible translator *must* be involved in the planting of a local New Testament church if his translation is to be a faithful one.

An Important Statement of this Book

One must be an accurate exegete of the Bible if one is to translate it accurately. By "exegete," I do not mean that one is to put his personal interpretation of Scripture into his translation. I mean the very opposite. The translator must avoid his own biased interpretation of Scripture and discover what the original author of the book meant when he wrote the passage under the inspiration of the Holy Spirit. If a translator interprets a verse of Scripture wrongly, he will translate it wrongly. The translator must carefully discover the meaning of the words as used by the author who wrote them. One cannot translate a passage of Scripture without understanding what the author meant by the words he wrote. It is impossible to translate a verse of Scripture if one does not know the meaning of that verse. It is also impossible to translate a verse if one will not make a decision about what one honestly believes the verse to mean. If the translator does not know what a verse means, it is impossible for him to explain to his native translation helper what the verse means. If the translation helper does not know what the verse means, he cannot express it in his language.

There are a few instances in the Bible where a verse is ambiguous as to its meaning, but these instances make up less than 0.1 percent of the Bible. For example, 2 Corinthians 5:14 says, "For the love of Christ constraineth us." Does this verse mean that we are constrained because Christ loves us, or does it mean that we are constrained because we love Christ? The verse could be understood either way. A verse like this should be interpreted in one of two possible ways or both ways. It should be translated in such a way as to allow the reader to choose one of the two possible interpretations or both. In any case, the translation of even an ambiguous verse requires interpreting the verse and understanding the two possible meanings of it.

Romans 6:3 says, "Know ye not, that so many of us as were baptized into Jesus Christ were baptized into his death?" Why did the King James Version translators transliterate the word *baptize* instead of translate it? They transliterated it because Paul clearly intended a double reference in the word *baptize*. The word *baptize* has the meaning of "to cause one to become united with the element into which one is immersed." In the case of water baptism, one is immersed into water, becoming united with that element. The King James Version translators transliterated the word *baptize* because they understood this word with the double reference that Paul intended. By transliterating the word, they indicated both the Christian's spiritual union with Christ in heaven and water baptism, which unites one with the local church on earth. By transliterating the word, they correctly allowed the word to indicate both of the meanings intended by the author. This is an example of how faithful translators will translate, or in this case, transliterate. In a situation like this one in Romans 6:3, they should translate in such a way as to allow the double reference of "baptize" that was intended by the author.

The King James Version

For nearly four hundred years, the King James Version of the Bible has proven to be the best translation of the inspired Word of God in the English language. Sometimes I will suggest ways that the meaning of verses in the King James Version could be restated. I do not intend that these restatements must be the way the verse should be translated into another language.

For instance, I suggest that the meaning of the words in John 10:11 "I am the good shepherd" could be stated as "I *myself* am the *good* shepherd." Whenever I do this, I am not suggesting that the verse be translated in this way. I am trying to show how the verse should be *understood correctly*. After one understands the meaning of a verse correctly, the Textus Receptus Greek text, the King James Version, and the grammatical structure of the particular language into which one is translating should determine the way one translates the verse.

Another example of this is found in 1 Thessalonians 1:3 which says, "Remembering without ceasing your work of faith." I suggest that this verse could be stated as meaning, "Remembering without ceasing how you believed and as a result you work for Him." I do not intend that this statement of the meaning of the verse must be adopted as the way it should be translated.

It is often necessary to make a written statement of the meaning of a verse. This helps one to understand the meaning of that verse. By taking the time to write out the meaning, one is forced to think clearly about how to state that meaning. The process of writing down the meaning of a verse is helpful in bringing out the meaning of that verse. When one clearly understands the meaning of a verse, he is in a better position to translate that verse accurately. Therefore, each time I make a restatement of a verse, please do not think that I am suggesting that the King James Version is wrong and needs correction.

I am also not suggesting that my restatement of a verse should be the basis of your translation. The only legitimate basis for your New Testament translation is the Textus Receptus Greek text and the King James Version. When a restatement of a particular verse is suggested in this book, it is for exegetical purposes only.

Other Objectives of this Book

One objective of this book is to help students learn the many principles, problems, and solutions of Bible translating. I hope this will enable them to translate the New Testament into one or more of the 3,000 Bibleless languages of the world. There is no need for each missionary to learn about Bible translating the hard way. He may learn from others who have already had experience in Bible translation. This will save him many wasted hours of frustration.

Another objective of this book is to provide a biblical basis for Bible translation principles and practices. This will be done by constantly seeking examples of how translation was done in the King James Version. What we find there will become the Bible translation principles and practices advocated in this course of study.

Another objective of this book is to help students gain a more accurate knowledge of the Bible translation process. This should help them be supportive of a translator and be able to offer constructive criticism of the translator's work. If one understands the problems involved in translating, one will be less of a hindrance to a Bible translator and more of a help to him. One will not be so unreasonably critical of the translator's work.

Another objective of this book is to motivate students to become Bible translation consultants. The main job of a Bible translation consultant is to train other Bible translators. As Bible translation consultants, they will also be able to check the translation work of others and offer help with verses that are difficult to translate.

A Definition of Bible Translation

In Hebrews 11:5, we read about the "translation" of Enoch. "By faith Enoch was translated that he should not see death; and was not found, because God had translated him." Enoch was taken from this earth and transported directly to heaven. He was removed from the realm of mortality to the realm of immortality. He was taken out of one place and transferred to another. In Colossians 1:13 we read, "Who hath delivered us from the power of darkness, and hath translated us into the kingdom of his dear Son." God has moved us out of the realm of the power of darkness and has moved us into another place—the kingdom of his dear Son.

This is what translation is. It is the moving of something out of one place and into another place. Enoch was taken out of the realm of the mortal and placed into the realm of the immortal. He was still the same person but he had been changed from a mortal man to an immortal man.

Bible translation is similar to this. Bible translation is transferring the meaning of the words in the Bible into the nearest formal equivalent meaning of words in the target language in a written form. The translator should be primarily concerned about transferring the meaning of words in one language into the same meaning of words in another language. Paul reminds us that we should be concerned about meaning. In 1 Corinthians 14:8-9 Paul wrote, "If the trumpet give an uncertain sound, who shall prepare himself to the battle? So likewise ye, except ye utter by the tongue words easy to be understood, how shall it be known what is spoken? for ye shall speak into the air."

We should be concerned about the meaning of the words in the source language text, the Bible. We should also be concerned about the received meaning of those words as understood by the reader of our translation. The above definition of Bible translation implies that our first concern is to determine the meaning of the words of the source language text as the author intended them to be understood. We are equally concerned about the meaning of words experienced in the mind of the receiver when he reads or hears our translation. When the intended meaning of the author's words in the source text has been translated into the nearest formal equivalent meaning in the words of the target language, faithful Bible translation has been done.

Homework

Without referring to the notes in this chapter, write your own definition of Bible translation. Afterwards, check your definition with the one in the notes.

A second-language speaker of English, describing how she lay in bed worrying about intruders: "I was sure there was something wrong; I could hear all the dogs in the neighborhood barfing."

Chapter 7

Requirements for a Bible Translator

First Requirement

A Bible translator should be a person who has been regenerated by the Spirit of God. If he is not regenerate, he will not understand the Bible that he translates and will therefore not do a good job translating it. 1 Corinthians 2:14 "The natural man receiveth not the things of the Spirit ... neither can he know them, because they are spiritually discerned." However, even though one may be a Christian, there are other requirements before one should begin translating Scripture.

Second Requirement

A Bible Translator should be thoroughly trained in Linguistics. Linguistics has four basic parts: phonetics, phonemics, morphology, and syntax. Phonetics prepares one to hear any sound made by the human voice in any language. It enables one to say that sound just like a native speaker and symbolize that sound with a symbol taken from the chart of International Phonetic Symbols.

These phonetic symbols of sounds become the basis for doing a phonemic analysis of the sound system of a language. By doing a phonemic analysis of the sounds found during the study of the phonetics of a language, the missionary can discover which of these phonetic sounds need to be symbolized in the native language and which ones do not. This is especially helpful for missionaries who are reducing a language to a written form for the first time. This enables them to make an alphabet based on phonemic principles rather than just guesswork. Phonemic analysis is critical for Bible translation. If one does not know how to arrive at the alphabet of a language, he must construct an alphabet based on guesswork. This results in confusion when the people are taught to read an alphabet that does not fit their language sound system. When the translation of the Bible is put into print using a non-phonemic alphabet, it makes it difficult to learn how to read and often causes him to be confused by what he reads.

A course in morphology enables the missionary to discover and describe the word structure of any language in the world. By understanding the word structure of a language, one can fully exploit the grammatical features of the language to translate the meaning of Scripture.

A course in syntax enables the missionary to discover and describe the sentence structure of any language in the world. This helps the translator to discover and exploit all the grammatical features of the language to translate Scripture.

These four studies in phonetics, phonemics, morphology, and syntax cover the basic principles of language sound systems and language grammatical systems. A missionary who has not had linguistic training is likely to cause a lot of confusion by the alphabet he produces. He will also not be able to exploit the full power of the grammar of the language because many of the grammatical features of the language will not be discovered without linguistic analysis.

Third Requirement

The translator should thoroughly understand the receiver's language and culture. This means that he must become fully acquainted with the people for whom he will be translating. He will need to know the grammatical features of their language. This will enable him to use the grammatical features of the language as the vehicle for translating the meaning of the Bible text into the meaning of the people's language. This will include learning both the referential meaning and the connotative meaning of the people's words. The referential meaning of their words will be those words that *refer* to specific things, events, abstractions, and relationships.

For example, the Sinasina people in Papua New Guinea use the word *maiyam* (blood) to refer to the red liquid in the veins. We refer to it in English with the word symbol "blood." However, this is only the referential meaning of the word. We need to know the emotional meaning of the word as well. The emotional meaning of the word "blood" is very strong in the minds of the Sinasina people. When a Sinasina person cuts someone, either by accident or deliberately, he must pay for the blood that was shed. People who have been cut by someone will let the blood dry and be careful not to wash it off until proper payment has been paid for the shedding of blood. When a person is killed, either by accident or in war, a relative will often scoop up some of that person's blood from the ground and eat it. This is, to a Sinasina person, one of the ways to express extreme grief. In addition, one of the most volatile curse words involves the use of the word "blood." When this curse word is uttered, it causes an immediate angry response.

These situations give one some idea of the emotional meaning behind the word "blood" in the Sinasina language.

If one is to translate into another language, he needs to understand the referential *and* the emotional meaning of words in that language. The referential meaning of words can usually be observed by noting the material objects to which the words refer or to the action the word represents.

The emotional meaning behind those objects or actions is more difficult to understand. The emotional content of words must be learned by the context surrounding those words. The context of words is the people's way of life, their culture.

The translator must learn the referential *and* connotative meanings of words in their cultural context. The only way the translator can know the cultural context of words is for him to make a thorough study of the culture of the people for whom he is translating. He must know not only the meaning of biblical words, but also what the biblical words mean when they are expressed using the words of the native language. It is critical that he knows both the biblical meaning of words *and* the native language meaning of words.

Fourth Requirement

Learning a people's language will also involve learning the generic and specific meanings of their words. For example, in English we have a generic word that covers many kinds of household articles. The general word is *furniture*. This word covers a wide area of meaning such as chairs, tables, beds, lamps, and sofas. The word *chair* specifically means one kind of object that could be covered by the more generic term *furniture*. We do not say to people, "Sit here on this furniture." Instead, we use a specific word and say, "Sit here on this chair." The word *chair* can be made even more specific by saying, "Sit here on this folding chair." In a similar way, we will need to know the ethnic language well enough to know what is a specific word and what is a generic word.

People who speak other languages divide or categorize their vocabulary differently than we do in English. For example, we think of a beetle as a bug or insect. The Sinasina people do not. They put beetles into the same category as a pig or dog. To them, it is not an insect. It is an animal. To the Sinasina people, the general terms *animal* and *insect* are covered by the same word *kabe* meaning *meat*. However, the Sinasina people also have specific words for the different kinds of animals, such as a pig (pig-kabe) or a dog (dog-kabe). They also have specific terms for spider, beetle, and grasshopper, but all these are considered by the Sinasina people to be *kabe*, meaning *meat* or *animal*.

The translator must become aware of the generic words and the specific terms in the language he is learning. He must also learn how the people categorize their vocabulary. What might be an insect to him may be an animal in the people's vocabulary. What might be an inanimate object to him may be an animate object in their thinking.

Fifth Requirement

The translator must clearly understand the Source Text (the Scriptures). For example, if one begins translating the Gospel of Mark, he should be thoroughly acquainted with that book. He should know something about the author and the historical and cultural context in which that book was written. By reading the book several times, he should become acquainted with the purpose and writing style of the author. The meaning of words and grammatical constructions used in the book will need to be understood as well.

All these matters will involve some use of either the Greek text or the English text of the New Testament. The use of commentaries, lexicons, Bible dictionaries, and other aids will help one make a grammatical analysis of the text. Such study will help one understand the meaning of the text in the way intended by the author. If one cannot use the Greek text, he must rely upon a careful analysis of the English text of the King James Version. By carefully studying the English text, one can arrive at the meaning intended by the original author.

If one does not arrive at a clear understanding of a verse of Scripture, it will be impossible to translate such a verse correctly. If one does not make a decision about what a verse of Scripture means, it is also impossible to translate such a verse correctly. Therefore, it is necessary that one do a sound grammatical and exegetical study of a verse of Scripture if one is to translate it accurately.

Sixth Requirement

The translator should understand the principles of Bible translation. As in any job, there are "tricks of the trade."

Each missionary can learn the hard way by blundering along on his own, or he can learn the principles of Bible translation from experienced translators who have already translated a New Testament. By learning from the experience of other translators, he will avoid some of the pitfalls others have fallen into. It is hoped that he would not make the same mistakes and that his translation would profit from the work of those who have gone before him.

He should also learn where to go for help when he comes up against a particular problem in Bible translating. There are many helps available to speed up the work of translation and make it more efficient. If one is not aware of these helps and how to use them, a lot of valuable time can be wasted.

Seventh Requirement

The translator must learn to use a native speaker of the language as his translation assistant. The translator should not translate without the presence of a native speaker of the language to guide him. The skillful use of a translation assistant is essential to the production of a good and faithful Bible translation. The translator who trusts only his own knowledge of a native language and culture is not wise.

Some translators become good bilingual speakers of a language, but almost none become bicultural speakers of a language. To be both bilingual and bicultural one must be born and raised in the native environment. Very few missionaries meet this standard. Therefore, Bible translators must depend upon native speakers of the language to help them with correct usage of native language grammar and understanding of the cultural context of words used in the translation.

Eighth Requirement

Before the translator begins translating, he should analyze several hundred pages of language text material. Text material consists of any spontaneous language utterances spoken by a native speaker. Text material is not obtained by asking questions about how to say a certain phrase, but by letting the native speaker say what he wants to say in his own way. By recording these utterances, whether long or short, and analyzing them, the translator will develop a "feel" for a written style of the spoken native language. This written style should reflect, as closely as possible, the spoken language style. Text material will become an objective check on just how well the written style of the translator matches the spoken style of the people. If the written style of the translation is very different from the spoken style of the people, the translation will seem foreign to them and will, most likely, not convey the meaning of God's Word to them.

Ninth Requirement

The translator must have the ability to stick at the job of translation hour after hour, day after day, year after year. Bible translation work is not for the "quick fix" person. If one does not have the patience to work over an extended period, he will not be a good translator. A translator need not be brilliant, but he must have the determination to keep at the job.

William Carey, that great Baptist Bible translator of India, had a motto that guided him in his work. His motto was, "I can plod."

The ability to plod along day after day, doing a few verses a day, is a necessary quality for a Bible translator. However, this does not mean that if you are not happy with long, tedious hours of work that you should not be a Bible translator. No one likes long hours of hard work. However, someone must make the sacrifice of working tedious hours if people are to have God's Word in their language.

Tenth Requirement

There is a correct orientation necessary for a faithful Bible translator. He must be oriented to producing a nearest formal equivalent translation. He should not be oriented to producing a dynamic equivalent one. During the last forty years, those who advocate "dynamic equivalence" translating have heavily influenced the translation of Scripture into ethnic languages. "Dynamic equivalence" means that a word meaning in the Bible should be translated by a culturally equivalent meaning in the ethnic language. The American Bible Society's Eugene Nida and Wycliffe Bible Translators' founder Cameron Townsend have both been advocates of this approach to translation.

The Errors of Dynamic Equivalence

1. In a dynamic equivalence translation, the goal is to use those ethnic words that would maximize conformity of Bible thought to the ethnic cultural equivalent. This often leads to a translator pressing the issue to such an extent that he makes Bible vocabulary conform to ethnic culture thought. He does this by choosing words that maximize ethnic language meaning over biblical language meaning. This often results in the decreasing of biblical meaning. This is translation based on thought for thought translation and not on word for word translation. This is not faithful Bible translating.

The nearest formal equivalent words used in a Bible translation should not always conform to the reader's cultural thought. In dynamic equivalence translation, the reader's cultural worldview is too often made to override the Judeo-Christian cultural worldview in which the Bible was written. Dynamic equivalence translation gives the false impression that what one is reading happened in one's own culture rather than in the Judeo-Christian culture.

2. The goal of dynamic equivalence translation is to translate in such a way that it maximizes conformity of the translation to the understanding of the unregenerate person. This approach sounds like it would be commendable but it is a serious mistake. Bible translation should not be excessively influenced by the dynamic equivalence philosophy that advocates that a Bible translation should be made in such a way as to maximize the comprehension of it by unregenerate people. It assumes that unregenerate people can understand the vocabulary used in the Bible. This is experientially impossible.

One who has never had the experience of being born again will never understand what being born again means. After having been born again, he will understand it and be able to describe it in terminology that a regenerate person would use. The nearest formal equivalent words used in faithful Bible translation may or may not conform to the non-Christian reader's understanding. In many cases, biblical vocabulary will be contrary to the non-Christian's understanding.

Since vocabulary is developed through experiential knowledge of the subject, the unsaved person cannot adequately speak about that which he has not experienced. Therefore, any vocabulary he produces about biblical subjects is open to serious question as to its validity. Paul explained this principle when he wrote, "But the natural man receiveth not the things of the Spirit of God: for they are foolishness unto him: neither can he know them, because they are spiritually discerned. (1 Corinthians 2:14)

3. In dynamic equivalence translating, the equivalence desired between Bible words and ethnic words is achieved by choosing words that conform to the understanding of the reader who *must* understand what he is reading. If the reader does not understand the translation, it is considered a wrong translation. This is a commendable goal but it is going too far. The nearest formal equivalent words used in a Bible translation may or may not conform to the understanding of the reader. He may not understand what he is reading until a teacher of God's Word explains it to him. This is exactly what happened with the Ethiopian in Acts 8:31-35.

Bible translation should go hand in hand with Bible teaching and church planting. If it does not, a translator may be pressured to resort to dynamic equivalent translation in order to make sure his readers understand the Bible. The problem with this is: the reader may understand what the translation says, but what he understands may not be what the original writer of Scripture wrote.

Instead of dynamic equivalence translating, this book advocates formal equivalence translating. The formal equivalence approach to translation seeks to find words in the native language that are the nearest formal equivalent to the words in the Bible. The word "formal" means that the words chosen for the translation conform to the formal grammatical patterns and meaning of the language used in the Bible. The word "nearest" means that one continually strives to find words that change the understanding of the ethnic reader to that understanding advocated in Scripture.

The formal equivalence translator resists the pressure to always conform biblical words to the ethnic language cultural meaning. Those native language words that conform to the nearest formal equivalent of biblical words are sought. For example, 1 John 3:17 says, "... and shutteth up his bowels *of compassion* ..." The word σπλαγχνα (splankna) in the Greek New Testament, meaning "bowels," is accurately translated by the King James translators. They preserved the formal equivalent of the Greek text that used the word "bowels" even though this would not be equivalent to what English people would say. This is nearest formal equivalent translation. However, the translators added the phrase "*of compassion*" to help the English reader understand the meaning of the Greek word "bowels." The translators put the words "*of compassion*" in italics to show that these words were added to the text. This allowed the English reader to know what word was used in the Greek New Testament and at the same time allowed him to understand the Greek word in the way intended by the original author.

The Jolly Green Giant translated into Arabic means "Intimidating Green Ogre."

Chapter 8

Adding To and Taking Away from Scripture

"For I testify unto every man that heareth the words of the prophecy of this book, If any man shall add unto these things, God shall add unto him the plagues that are written in this book: And if any man shall take away from the words of the book of this prophecy, God shall take away his part out of the book of life, and out of the holy city, and from the things which are written in this book." (Revelation 22:18-19)

A Good Fear to Have

Because of the above two verses, most Bible translators have a well-founded fear of adding their own ideas to the Scriptures as they translate them. This is a fear every translator should have. Every Bible translator should work hard to keep from adding his own personal interpretation to the Word of God. Most Bible translators try very hard *not* to add to God's Word. However, some Bible translators forget that the above verses not only warn us not to add our own thoughts to Scripture, they also warn us not to take anything away from the Scripture.

It is equally serious that we not take away from Scripture, as it is that we add nothing to Scripture. As Bible translators, we are not to add our own words to the Scriptures. If we do, we could be saying things that God has not said. We are also not to translate in such a way that our translation is inadequate because it does not say all that God has said. By producing an inadequate and faulty translation, we may be guilty of taking away from God's Word. The Bible translator must translate in such a way that his translation says exactly what God said, nothing more and nothing less. He must neither add to God's words nor take anything away from them.

Taking Away from Scripture

How is it possible that a Bible translator could take away from God's Word? One who translates in such a way that his translation does not convey the meaning intended by the words that God inspired is taking away from God's Word. Such a translation misrepresents what God said. It says less than what God intended when he caused the words of the Bible to be written.

A lie is saying less than the truth. This applies to Bible translation as well. A Bible translator who does not do a good job of translating all that the original author intended is taking away from the Word of God. This is just as bad as a translator who adds his own thoughts to Scripture.

Ignoring Grammar

A translator may take away from God's Word by ignoring what his translation means to the native speakers of the language. He may know what the biblical words mean, but make little or no effort to assure that this meaning is carried over into the native language translation. He may translate with little or no regard for what the verse means in the grammatical structure of the native language. A translator who does this is most likely taking away from the words used in the Bible. His translation will most likely misrepresent God's message.

If a translator does not make sure that the meaning in the Bible is the same meaning the people have in their mind, it is possible that they will understand something different from what the authors of Scripture intended. If a Bible translator does this, he is guilty of taking some of God's Word away from those who read his translation. If people read his translation and think it means something other than what the original words of the author intended it to mean, this translator has taken away from the Word of God.

How the Mind Works

A Bible translator may also take away from God's Word by producing a translation that is confusing to those who read it. People do not read a poorly translated verse of Scripture and simply ignore it. God has made the human mind in such away that it will make some kind of sense out of a translation that is nonsense. The reader will decide what a verse means even if the verse he reads makes no sense to him. In his mind, there is no neutral ground. The mind has been programmed by God to work in an orderly way. It will automatically try to make sense even out of nonsense. If a Bible translator has not taken care to translate in such a way that his readers are not confused by his translation, this Bible translator may be guilty of taking away from the Word of God. His translation will say something to the reader other than what the original writer intended by the words he wrote.

Who Is at Fault for Confusion?

Some would object to this conclusion and say that the confusion of the reader of a Bible translation is not the fault of the translator. He would say that it is the fault of the reader. To some extent, this is true. If the translator has done all he can do to avoid confusing the readers of his translation, he is not at fault. However, if he has not, it is his fault that the readers are receiving a message that was not intended by God. How much is a Bible translator responsible for what the readers of his translation understand? A Bible translator is primarily responsible for what his readers understand by the words he uses in his translation. If he pays little or no attention to the grammatical structure of the original words used in Scripture or the grammatical structure of the native language, his translation will likely both add to and take away from the Word of God.

It is not enough to merely take a word count to ensure that the same number of words in the Bible is the same number of words in one's translation. This is word matching, not translating. It inevitably leads to misrepresenting what God has said in His Word.

Can Teaching Compensate for Inadequate Translating?

Some have suggested that by teaching the right meaning later, an inadequate translation could be explained. This is a needless risk. It is possible, at the time of translating, to incorporate in the translation itself the meaning intended by the original Author. In addition, the opportunity may never come when teaching can be given to correct the confusion caused by an inadequate translation. The people reading the translation may be so far removed from the location of the translator that he might never have an opportunity to correct his flawed translation by teaching. There will be no one there to teach correctly, what the translation communicated incorrectly.

A Translation or a Commentary?

When I use the words "incorporate in the translation itself the meaning intended by the Author," I do not intend to imply that a translation of Scripture should be a commentary that explains everything said in the Bible. However, I do intend to imply that a translated verse of the Bible should contain enough information in it to allow the reader to understand the verse, as nearly as possible, in the way the Author intended it to be understood. If the translation does not communicate this, it is an inadequate translation, and the translator is guilty of taking away from the Word of God. This is equally as serious as adding to the Scripture. Both adding to Scripture and taking away from it is undesirable.

An Unwise Choice

What is a translator to do then? Many missionaries have faced this dilemma, and rather than take the risk of adding to or taking away from the Bible, they do not translate any Scripture at all. These missionaries take away more of God's Word from the people than anyone else! They do not give them any portion of God's Word. To do no translating is not the answer.

A translator who has done his best to study the meaning of the Bible and learn the native language and culture will not be adding to Scripture or taking away from it. He can rest assured that he will receive a "Well done" from the Lord. Those who willfully distort the Word of God are the ones who should be concerned about the warning given in Revelation 22:18-19. However, one may distort God's Word either through a deliberate attempt to distort it or by not learning the native language and culture well enough to do a faithful translation. Either way, the result is the same. The translation is misleading the reader to think the translation says something that it does not say.

Translators are Human

All translators have made translation mistakes. That is, they often fail to translate all that the author intended by the words he wrote. Translators are only human. It is not this kind of a problem that Revelation 22:18-19 addresses. These verses apply to the willful corruption of Scripture either by false cults like the Jehovah's Witnesses or the lazy missionary. The one perverts it to prop up his false doctrine. The other perverts it because he has not applied himself to learning the native language and culture thoroughly. Either way, the Word of God is distorted.

If a Bible translator has not worked hard enough to learn exactly what a Bible passage means, both in its original context and in the context of the reader's culture, that translator may be adding to *and* taking away from the Word of God. If he has not worked hard to learn the native language and culture well enough so that he can convey in that language exactly what the original author meant, that translator may be adding to and taking away from the Word of God.

In Taiwan, the translation of the Pepsi slogan "Come alive with the Pepsi Generation" meant "Pepsi will bring your ancestors back from the dead."

Chapter 9

A Device for Teaching Bible Translation

One of the best ways to learn Bible translation principles is to do some Bible translating. Many people have strong opinions about how Bible translation should be done. However, their opinions are usually not based on experience and therefore are often invalid. If one does some Bible translation, he becomes more sympathetic of those who are engaged in Bible translation work.

One of the most common Bible translation experiences is that of Bible college students who take a course in New Testament Greek. By translating from the Greek New Testament into English, they are doing Bible translating. It is for this very reason that New Testament Greek is a part of the curriculum at Baptist Bible Translators Institute. Teaching New Testament Greek not only provides our students with a tool to use in their interpretation of the New Testament, it also gives them some experience in Bible translating. They translate Greek New Testament verses into English and English sentences into New Testament Greek. This is often their first experience at Bible translating.

It is difficult to tell someone what translation is, but if they do some translating themselves, they soon realize what translating is and how to do it properly.

This is the purpose of the following exercise. We want you to learn some New Testament Greek grammar so that you can translate verses from the Greek New Testament yourself.

Koine Greek Present Active Indicative

Greek sentences that have present active indicative first person singular verbs are common in the Greek New Testament. Verbs in the present tense express events that are happening in the present time. However, the Koine Greek speaker would be thinking more about the continuation of an action than he would about the action as occurring in the present time. To the Koine Greek speaker the present tense signifies continual action more than it does present time.

The word *active* means that the subject is the one doing the action of the verb. He is the one performing the action, not the receiver of the action. *Active* is the opposite of passive.

The word *indicative* means that the sentence is a declarative statement. An action is occurring, in contrast to an imperative statement that would be commanding someone to perform an action.

"First Person Singular" means that the subject of the verb is the first person singular "I" in contrast to the first person plural "We."

The Greek Verb

λυω

luow

For the purpose of this exercise, we will transliterate Greek letters with letters from the English alphabet. Greek accent marks will not be used. The

Greek verb λυω will look like this: *luow*. The Greek verb *luow* is made up of the following morphemes (parts of words):

lu- This is a verb root meaning "to release" (any person or thing that is tied or fastened). The hyphen after the root indicates that suffixes may be added following the root.

-ow This is a verb suffix meaning *I am*. It indicates that the verb "to be" is in the present, active, indicative mode, first person singular. The hyphen before the suffix indicates that it may be added following the verb root.

Translate **luow** into English:

lu- "to release"

-ow "I am" (singular)

Notice that the verb root *lu-* comes first in Greek and then the suffix *-ow*. This suffix indicates the singular-person, the present tense, the active voice, and the indicative mood. Therefore, the Greek verb *luow* should be translated as "I am releasing."

The Greek verb

λυεις

lueys

Translate *lueys* into English:

lu- *"to release"*

-eys *"You are"* (singular)

The Greek verb *lueys* should be translated as "You are releasing." Notice that it takes three words in English to translate what is a single word in Koine Greek. This should make it obvious that word-for-word matching is not always possible between languages. What is a single word in Greek *must* be translated by using three words in English.

The Greek verb

λυει

luey

Translate *luey* into English:

lu- *"to release"*

-ey *"He is"*

The Greek verb *luey* should be translated as "He is releasing." Notice again that it takes three words in English to translate what is a single word in Greek.

Translate

λυω προβατον

luow probaton

We know that λυω (*luow*) means, "I am releasing." The word *probaton* is made up of the word root *probat-* and the suffix *-on*. The word root *probat-* means "a sheep." The suffix *-on*, when added to the root *probat-*, means that the word *probat-* "sheep" is singular. There is only one sheep. The suffix *-on* also means that the word *probat-* is the receiver of the action of the verb *lu-* (to release). The suffix *-on* is a singular object indicator. It tells us that the word *probat-* (sheep) is the receiver of the action of the verb *lu-* (to release). It also tells us that the receiver of the action of the verb is singular, meaning that there is only one sheep. Therefore we should translate *luow probaton* with the English words, "I am loosing a sheep."

Notice that it takes five English words to translate two Greek words. It is not possible to translate this Greek sentence by using a single word in English for every single word in Greek. It would not be correct English to say, "Loosing sheep." The two Greek words would have to be translated by five English words, "I am loosing a sheep."

Translate:

λυειs προβατον

lueys probaton

lu- "to release"

-eys "you are" (singular)

probat- "a sheep"

-on Object indicator. It marks the word as the receiver of the action of the verb. It also marks the object as singular in number.

Your translation of the sentence *lueys probaton* should be "You (singular) are releasing a sheep."

Notice again that it took five English words to translate two Greek words. If we were translating *lueys probaton* from the Greek New Testament into English, we would leave out the bracketed word (singular) unless we were teaching a class on Greek grammar. Since a Bible translation is not intended for teaching Greek grammar, we would translate *lueys probaton* with the nearest formal English equivalent, "You are releasing a sheep."

This would still require us to use five words to translate what are two words in Greek. Although Old English had a way to indicate a difference between singular "you" and plural "ye," we do not have a way to indicate the singular or plural of the word "you" in modern English. That meaning is lost in the modern English translation.

Translate:

λυει προβατον

luey probaton

Your translation of the sentence *luey probaton* should be: "He is releasing a sheep." Notice that the word order of the Greek sentence is first the verb **lu-** (to loose), and the suffix **-ey** (He is, present active indicative, third person singular) and then the noun *probat-* (a sheep). The suffix *-on* means that the word *probat-* is the singular receiver of the action of the verb.

If we were to translate the Greek word order literally into English, the translation would be "Loosing, he is, a sheep." This would be an incorrect English translation. Correct English would dictate that we change the word order to, "He is loosing a sheep."

The three Greek sentences we have learned to translate are:

lu-ow probat-on

I am releasing a sheep.

lu-eys probat-on

You are releasing a sheep.

lu-ey probat-on

He is releasing a sheep.

Our vocabulary of the Greek language consists of the following morphemes (parts of words):

lu- to release

-ow I am

-eys You are

-ey He is

probat- a sheep

-on marks the word "sheep" as a singular object of the verb.

Let us apply what we have learned to some other Greek verbs.

The Greek verb

γραφω

grafow

The verb root is **graf-**, meaning "to scrape marks" (to write).

The verb ending **-ow** means "I am."

The nearest formal English equivalent of **grafow** would be "I am writing."

What does this Greek sentence mean?

γραφω βιβλον

grafow biblon

The word *biblon* is made up of *bibl-* meaning "the inner bark of the papyrus reed." The papyrus reed was used to make a rather crude kind of paper that was used to write on and so it came to mean, "a book." The *-on* that is suffixed to the word *bibl-* is the indicator of singular objects that we already know. Therefore, we could translate *grafow biblon* into its nearest formal English equivalent as, "I am writing a book."

Notice, again, that two Greek words are translated by five English words. What does this tell us about the translation process? It tells us that matching one English word for one Greek word would not be the best way to translate Greek into English. Suppose we wanted to force the issue and say that we *must* use only one English word for each Greek word. If so, our English translation of *grafow biblon* would be, "Write book." This would leave out some information that is in the Greek sentence *grafow biblon*. The words "Write book" do not tell us who the subject of the sentence is. We would be guilty of not translating *all* that the author said. By forcing the sentences to have the same number of words, we would be taking away from the meaning of the words of the Bible.

The two-word translation is also misleading because "Write book" sounds like baby talk. This would not be proper English. It would be interpreted to mean, "*You* write a book," which is a command. A command was not what *grafow biblon* was intended to mean. Now we are in more trouble. Not only have we taken away from what the author said, we have also misrepresented what he intended to mean by the words he wrote. The author made a statement that we have translated as baby talk meaning a command, "Write a book!" Therefore, a word-for-word English translation of *grafow biblon* is not an adequate translation.

What are we to do then? We should translate *grafow biblon* into its nearest formal English equivalent, "I am writing a book." Although the two Greek words cannot be matched by only two English words, the five English words translate the two Greek words accurately. This is faithful translating. An accurate translation always conveys the meaning intended by the author. Word matching would not convey that meaning.

Translate:

ανθρωπος γραφει βιβλον

anthropos grafey biblon

The Greek word *anthropos* is made up of a word root *anthrop-*, that means "face." This is the most prominent part of a person and so the word has come to mean "man" in the general sense of mankind, and in the specific sense meaning "man" (a male human being).

The suffix -*os* on the end of *anthrop-os* is a subject indicator that tells us that *anthrop-* is the subject of the sentence and that it is singular. The meaning of *anthropos* would be: "a man."

The verb *grafey* is familiar to us already. It is made up of *graf-* (to write) and -*ey* meaning "he is."

The word *biblon* is made up of *bibl-* (book) and -*on* (singular object indicator). Therefore, we could translate *anthropos grafey biblon* as, "A man, he is writing a book." That would be a correct English translation but it is not normal English speech. To translate it that way would not be the nearest formal equivalent in English. It would be better to translate this sentence as, "A man is writing a book."

Suppose we still believe that, we must be as close to the original Greek sentence as we possibly can and so we translate the sentence word-for-word. We want it to be a literal word-for-word translation. We translate it as, "Man he writes book." This would sound more like Indians speaking on the old Lone Ranger radio serial and would not be the nearest formal equivalent English translation of the Greek sentence. "A man is writing a book" would be correct English usage and faithful translating.

Translate the Greek sentence:

αποστολοι διδασκουσι

apostoloy didaskousi

This sentence is made up of a noun, *apostol-* meaning "apostle," and the suffix -*oy* meaning "plural subject indicator." The suffix -**oy** is used to indicate who or what is the subject of the sentence. It also shows that the subject is plural. The word *apostoloy* therefore means "apostles." The word *didask-* is a verb root that means "to teach." The suffix –*ousi* means "they are." The sentence would therefore mean, "Apostles, they are teaching." If we put this in better English we would say, "The apostles are teaching."

Add Two Words to the Greek Sentence:

αποστολοι διδασκουσι τον λογον

apostoloy didaskousi ton logon

The word *ton* is a Greek word that means, "the." The word *logon* is made up of *log-* and -*on*. The word *log-* is the Greek term meaning, "word." The suffix -*on* is the singular object indicator that we have already learned.

Therefore, what does *apostoloy didaskousi ton logon* mean in English? Literally, it could be translated, "The apostles, they are teaching the word." In better English we would say, "The apostles are teaching the word." In this case, it takes only six words to translate the four Greek words. This is a closer correspondence between the number of words in Greek and the number of words in English, but the number of words in each language still does not match.

Translate John 10:11:

εγω ειμι ο ποιμην ο καλος

egow eymi ho poimen ho kalos

egow is a stand-alone word that means, "I."

eymi is a verb meaning, "I am."

ho means "the" (singular-subject) and modifies the next word *poimen*, which is made up of two parts: *poim-* meaning "a shepherd," and *–en*, which is a singular subject indicator. The word *ho* is the same word as the other *ho*, meaning "the" (singular-subject). However, this time *ho* modifies the adjective following it, which is *kalos*. The word *kalos* is made up of *kal-*, meaning "good," and the suffix *-os*. The suffix *-os* means that *kal- (good)* modifies the singular subject of the sentence, which is the word *poim-* meaning *shepherd*.

From this information let us translate John 10:11 from the Greek New Testament into English. Literally the sentence could be translated, "I, I am the shepherd, the good one." The Koine Greek speaker used reduplication of words to show emphasis. The double "I, I am" is intended to say emphatically, "I!" This information is difficult to translate into English since we do not use the reduplication of the word "I" to emphasize the subject of our sentences. We could translate the double "I, I am" by saying, "I am myself" or "I myself am." Therefore, we could translate it as, "I am *myself* the shepherd, the good one." That sounds a little better, but the phrase "the good one" is still too awkward.

We are striving to reflect the Koine Greek language in our English translation. When a Koine Greek speaker wanted to emphasize an adjective like the word *kalos* (good), he would use the word *ho* (the) twice. He would put it once before the subject and once before the adjective, and in effect would be saying that the adjective was being emphasized. Therefore, we should include this bit of information in our translation.

We could further modify our translation to read, "I am *myself* the *good* shepherd."

Jesus is saying that he *himself* is the shepherd and that he is the *good* one. Other shepherds were hirelings who, when not paid, left off caring for the sheep. This was not true of Jesus. He cared for his sheep even when the only pay he received for it was death by crucifixion. Other shepherds were bad shepherds in that they looked after the flock only when there was something in it for them. When there was no monetary return, they proved to be false shepherds and left the flock to the wolves. That is why Jesus said, "I am *myself* the *good* shepherd!"

We often have to settle for the nearest formal equivalent meaning in English, even though that meaning does not contain the total meaning of the Greek sentence. The emphasis on the word "I" in the Greek sentence is lost in the English translation. The emphasis on the word "good" in the Greek sentence is also lost in the English translation. Sometimes it is not possible to say in English *all* that the Greek sentence means. Therefore, we are forced to settle for the *nearest* formal equivalent meaning in English.

Translate Matthew 1:18.

εν γαστρι εχουσα εκ Πνευματος

Αγιου

en gastri   exousa ek Pneumatos Hagiou

The word *en* literally means "in." However, in this sentence, it is a Greek idiom meaning "by means of." The word *gastri* is made up of the root word *gastr-* that means "stomach" and the suffix *-i* indicates that "stomach" was the means used by the subject of the sentence. The subject of the sentence is the Holy Spirit. The word *exousa* is made up of the verb root *ex-*, meaning "to have" and the suffix *-ousa* indicates that the word is a present active participle. The word *ek* is a stand-alone word meaning "the source of or the cause of." It indicates the cause of the participle *ekousa* (to have). *Pneumatos* is made up of *Pneumat-* meaning Spirit, and the suffix *–os,* which means that *Pneumat-* is the singular subject of the sentence. *Hagiou* is made up of *Hagi-* a root word meaning "Holy," and the suffix *-ou* which means "belonging to." It modifies the word "Spirit" to mean "Spirit, the one that is holy." Because the word "holy" is placed last in the sentence, this position of the word emphasizes that the Spirit was the *Holy* Spirit, not an unholy or immoral spirit.

The phrase *en gastri ekousa ek Pneumatos Hagiou* is a Greek idiom that literally means, "by means of stomach having, from the source Spirit, Holy one." This literal English translation of the Greek words means very little in English. Idioms are not intended to be understood literally. The sum total of the individual words in an idiom is not intended as a word-for-word meaning. The Greek idiom "by means of stomach having" is a euphemistic way of saying "pregnant."

Here in Matthew 1:18, Matthew purposely used an idiom to soften the insensitive word "pregnant." His idiom would sound much like the way the King James Version translators translated it. They used the euphemistic form, "with child." Matthew is also careful to add the words, "from the source Spirit, the *Holy* one." He wants everyone to know that the conception of a child by Mary had come from a *Holy* source, namely, the *Holy* Spirit of God.

It is difficult to say in English all that this Greek idiom means. For instance, the emphasis on the word **Holy** in the Greek idiom is lost in the English translation. The English translation of "by means of stomach having" is translated as "with child." This is a good translation, but actually there is no word for child in the Greek idiom. Does that mean the translators are adding words to the Scriptures? No. The English language makes it necessary to add the words, "with child." This is not adding to Scripture. It is translating exactly into English what the Greek idiom, "by means of stomach having from the source Spirit, Holy one" means.

Translate Matthew 1:6b

Before you translate the Greek words from Matthew 1:6b, put your Bible away. Do not peek to see how the words were translated in the King James Version. After you have translated it by using the information below, check the King James Version to see if you have translated it properly.

Δαβιδ δε ο βασιλευς εγεννησε

τον Σολομωντα εκ της του Ουριου

Dabid de ho basileus egenneyse

ton Solomonta ek teys tou Ouriou

The information to translate Matthew 1:6b is as follows:

Dabid "David" (masculine subject singular)

de "and" (a conjunction joining Matthew 1:6a with 1:6b)

ho "the" (masculine subject singular, modifying the word *Dabid*) *basileus* "king" (subject singular modifying the word *Dabid*)

egenneyse "to beget, or to generate" (The verb tense is an event which happened in the past as an action that occurred and can be translated as "He begat.")

ton "the" (masculine object singular). It modifies the word *Solomounta*.

Solomounta "Solomon" (masculine object singular)

ek "out of" (denoting origin or source)

teys "the" (feminine possessive singular)

tou "the" (masculine possessive singular)

Ouriou "Urias"

The literal word order of this sentence in the Greek is, "David and the king he begat the Solomon out of the the Urias." The words "the the" are not a typographical mistake. That is exactly the order in which the words occur in the Greek sentence.

Now write out what you believe to be the correct translation of this verse. Do not check your translation with the King James Version until after you have made your own translation of the verse using only the information provided above. Do not read the remainder of the next paragraph until you have attempted to translate the verse yourself.

Matthew 1:6b has some words that were added by the translators. The King James Version translators added the words, "that had been the wife." Does this mean they added words to the Bible? No. They are translating the word *teys* that means "the." However, the word "the" is in the feminine possessive case and would have the meaning of "the female person who belonged to Urias." This means that she had been the wife of Urias.

It would be nearly impossible to translate this verse literally. If we translated it literally, it would read, "David and the king begat the Solomon out of the the Urias." This would not be good English. The translators were correct when they added the words, "that had been the wife." They added nothing to the words of the Bible. They were simply translating the Greek idiom into the English language.

Translate 1 John 3:9a

Do not check your Bible to see how the verse was translated until after you have translated the verse from the Greek.

πας ο γεγεννειμενος εκ του θεου

αμαρτιαν ου ποιει

pas ho gegenneymenos ek tou Theou

hamartian ou poyey.

pas "all" (masculine subject singular)

ho "the" (masculine subject singular, modifying *pas* "all")

gegenneymenos "to be born" (The tense of this verb-like word is that of the perfect tense. Perfect tense indicates an event that has happened in the past with the results of the event continuing into the present time.)

ek "out of " (denoting origin or source)

tou "the" (masculine possessive singular, modifying the word "God")

Theou "God" (masculine possessive singular)

hamartian "sin" (singular object, modifying *poyey* "he is doing")

ou "not" (negative) modifies *poyey* "he is not doing")

poyey "he is doing" (present active indicative third person singular. The action of this verb is that of continual action in present time with the prominence placed on the continually repeated action rather than the time it occurs.) The literal word order of the sentence in Greek would be "All the born out of the God sin not he is doing." The translation in the King James Version is, "Whosoever is born of God doth not commit sin."

I hope you can see from this exercise that translation is not simply replacing one word in one language with one word in another language. There are many important literary principles to understand and apply correctly before faithful translation can be done.

Homework

1. Is it always possible to translate a verse of Scripture literally? If your answer is yes, explain why you think so. If your answer is no, explain why you think it is not.

2. What is an idiom? Write a definition of the word "idiom" and write an example of an idiom that is used in Scripture.

Pennsylvania Dutch sentence structure allows one to say, "Throw the horse over the fence some hay" and "Throw me down the stairs a towel."

Chapter 10

Why the King James Version?

The Preservation of the Bible By Faithful Churches

The New Testament in English is the result of translating a Greek text into English. However, there are several different Greek texts, each one different from the other. Which one is the translator to use as the basis for his translation into another language? The 1973 edition of the United Bible Societies Greek text by Aland, Black, Martini, Metzger, and Wilgren is very different from the 1881 Greek text of Westcott and Hort. The Westcott and Hort text is different from the American Bible Society Greek text by Nestle, and the Nestle text is different from the Greek text by the Trinitarian Bible Society.

The many Greek texts are represented by many different English translations. There are over two hundred translations of the New Testament in the English language. Each one has different translations of the same verses. Which one is a translator to use as the basis for his translation into another language?

The Need for a Standard

Someone has wisely said that a man who owns one good watch knows what time it is, but a man who has two watches is never quite sure. If a person has set his watch by a reliable source and buys another watch, he now has two standards. Which watch is right? This is similar to the problem with translations of the Bible. Because there are so many translations of the Scriptures, all claiming to be God's Word, many people are not sure "what time it is." They are not sure which translation is truly God's Word.

There was a time when there was a translation in the English language that was accepted as *the* Bible. It was the King James Version. When we wanted to know what God had said, we went to our Authorized Version and read there the words of God. Now there are many "Bibles" all claiming to be the words of God but each differing from the other. Which one of them is authoritative? They cannot all be authoritative because they each differ from the other. Now that there are so many "authorities," this has resulted in no authority at all.

The reason we have so many translations is due largely to the amount of money to be gained by publishing catchy, clever, and trendy translations of God's unchanging Word.

Why do people who speak English need over two hundred translations when there are over 3,000 ethnic languages that do not have one word of Scripture? The money that should have been used to publish God's Word in these languages has been used on English-language readers who want their ears tickled by yet another trendy translation. Such a situation reflects a serious sickness in the spiritual condition of those who "need" many translations of the Bible when thousands of language groups have no Bible at all.

The Erosion of Authority

An even more serious issue is the matter of authority. The authority of God's Word in the English language has been eroded because of these many translations. They all claim to be God's Word. Who decides which one is Correct? The answer to this question is, you do. You choose which one you believe to be the Word of God. However, who put you in charge of deciding which translation is the Word of God? If one translation does not suit your prejudice, you can probably find one that will. God's Word no longer has authority over you. You have, due to your picking and choosing of translations, become the authority over God's Word! When there are two or more authorities, the result is that there is no authority at all.

The many translations have robbed the Word of God of its authority and left man's intellect in charge of deciding whether he would have this version or that version to rule over him. The situation is similar to that one mentioned in Judges 17:6 "In those days there was no king in Israel, but every man did that which was right in his own eyes." This is the deplorable state of modern man. Each person becomes an authority unto himself, and confusion reigns.

There Can Be Only One Authority

Because of the controversy and confusion caused by so many English translations, the King James Version stands out more than ever as the one authoritative Bible in the English language.

We do not accept the King James Version as our standard because of some sentimental connection to its Elizabethan English, nor because it is the oldest translation. We accept it as the only standard because it is the most accurate and reliable translation in the English language.

There are very good reasons for accepting the King James Version as the standard for English speaking people.

The King James Version is the only translation of the New Testament that is based entirely on the faithful Textus Receptus Greek text. All other English language translations since 1881 have followed modern "scholarship." They have based their translations on Greek texts that came from the poisoned wells of textual criticism. The Textus Receptus is the only Greek text of the New Testament that has not been subjected to the false presuppositions of modern intellectualism. Modern Greek scholars have, because of the criteria they set up themselves, deleted verses, phrases, and words from the original Greek text.

Examples of deletions

The last part of Matthew 6:13, reads, "For thine is the kingdom, and the power, and the glory, for ever. Amen." In all Greek texts, except the Textus Receptus, these words are deleted. If a translator were to translate from any other text but the Textus Receptus, he would leave these words out of his translation.

Colossians 1:14 says, "In whom we have redemption through his blood, even the forgiveness of sins." The words "through his blood" have been deleted in every text except the Textus Receptus.

In Romans 8:1 the words "who walk not after the flesh, but after the Spirit" have been deleted in all the Greek texts except the Textus Receptus. There are many other such deletions. The Textus Receptus is the only text that has not been mutilated by such deletions. All the other texts have grown shorter and shorter over the years as "scholars" took their lead from the rationalism of Lachmann and whittled away more and more of the New Testament Greek text. This deleting of more and more of the New Testament Greek text is not genuine scholarship. It is prejudiced rationalism working under the disguise of textual criticism.

The Development of Textual Criticism

When the books of the New Testament were originally written at the hand of Luke, Paul, and others, they became the precious possession of local churches. These churches recognized the writings as different from commonly written communications. The churches recognized the apostolic books and letters as the inspired Word of God. The books and letters of the New Testament were hand copied and passed around to other churches in the first, second, and third centuries. Of course, in the copying of these books and letters, there were small errors made in the copying. They were much like the typographical errors we make while typing. In addition, the copies were worn out with constant use, resulting in the words nearer the edge of the parchment or papyrus being worn off the page. Sometimes, especially in the first and second centuries, false teachers deliberately changed the text in an effort to support their false teachings. However, it was always a simple matter to correct an errant text by comparing it with the faithful, inerrant copies held in trust by many faithful churches. This brought the errant copies back to the standard set by the original text. The only thing the churches had to do was check with other churches and find out what the reading was in the other church copies. By doing this, the churches made sure the texts were valid, and by this means, the text was preserved in its original form.

Identifying the Correct Text

This process continued down through the centuries. Faithful churches would decide the validity of the Greek text by consulting the church copies of the particular text under question and would judge its validity based on the copies held in trust by the other churches. If one church had an erroneous copy, the six or seven valid copies that were kept in trust by faithful churches soon corrected the erroneous copy. The six or seven correct copies that all said the same thing were judged the correct reading. This reading was used to correct the deviating copies.

The Biblical Basis for Textual History

2 Peter 3:15-16 says, "Even as our beloved brother Paul also according to the wisdom given unto him hath written unto you; As also in all his epistles, speaking in them of these things; in which are some things hard to be understood, which they that are unlearned and unstable wrest, as they do also the other scriptures, unto their own destruction." In these verses, Peter clearly considers the words of Paul on the same level as "the other scriptures." Peter believed the words of Paul to be the inspired Word of God.

Peter wrote this in a time when there were those who did "wrest" the Scriptures; that is, those who took some words in Paul's letters and wrested them. The word *wrest* has the meaning of "to put on the torture rack" in order to force the Scriptures to say what their torturers wanted them to say. This clearly shows that the early churches were on the lookout for those who would pervert their copies of the Scriptures. The early churches were aware of this problem and took great care to avoid the twisting of their Scriptures by false teachers who would deliberately try to change the original reading. Peter warned the Christians to watch out for this very thing.

The Churches Circulate Scriptures

Colossians 4:16 says, "And when this epistle is read among you, cause that it be read also in the church of the Laodiceans; and that ye likewise read the epistle from Laodicea."

This verse shows that there was a sharing of copies of the Word of God from church to church. Because such a prominent leader as Peter considered the words of Paul as Scripture and said that he knew about those who would wrest the Scripture, is it not evident that the churches would take even greater care to watch over these Scriptures? This is obviously the case because the early churches, led by the Holy Spirit, rightly concluded that the words of Paul were the inspired Word of God. They took every precaution to watch over these Scriptures by comparing them with faithful copies held in trust by other churches.

When the first Greek New Testament was collated and printed in 1516, the readings, which varied with the majority of the other texts, were disallowed and the readings of the majority were accepted. This is how the churches had preserved the Word of God for 1,516 years. By this simple but accurate method, the Word of God was watched over by the Holy Spirit, who worked through the churches who were faithful custodians of the Scriptures they cherished.

Karl Lachmann the Rationalist

This process of preserving the pure Word of God through faithful local churches continued without interruption until 1831 when Karl Lachmann, a German rationalist, began to apply to the New Testament Greek text the same criteria he had used in editing texts of the Greek classics. Lachmann had studied such Greek classics as Homer's *Iliad*. These Greek writings were mere stories, but Lachmann tried to get back to what Homer and other Greek authors had originally written. The Greek classics had been thoroughly altered over the years. So many alterations had been made that no one was sure what the original author had written. Lachmann wanted to know what the original text had been, so he developed a textual criticism process whereby he tried to sort out the original text from the badly corrupted modern text.

Someone got the "bright idea" that Lachmann's process should be applied to the New Testament. Lachmann had set up a series of presuppositions and rules for arriving at the original text of the Greek classics that were hopelessly corrupted. He now began with these same presuppositions and rules to correct the Greek New Testament.

He began with the primary presupposition that the Greek New Testament was as hopelessly corrupted, as were the Greek classics. This was a glaring mistake. A similar process in the copying of the Greek classics did not match the loving and reverent care given to the copying of the Word of God by faithful churches. The Greek classics were hopelessly corrupted but this was not true of the New Testament.

Extremely careful scribes took great pains to copy New Testament manuscripts. These scribes knew the exact number of words and letters that were in the original copies. They counted the words and letters each time a new copy was made to ensure that nothing had been added or deleted. In addition, faithful churches carefully guarded their precious copies of Scripture to protect them from heretical changes that may have been inserted in other copies of the text.

The Greek New Testament

Long before Lachmann, a Dutch theologian named Desiderius Erasmus published the first printed edition of the Greek New Testament in 1516. Erasmus collected all the available manuscripts of the Greek New Testament books and decided which variant reading was the original one based on the reading in the majority of the texts. He followed the same method that had been used by the churches through the centuries; namely, correcting an errant reading by the reading in the majority of the texts that had been preserved by the churches. The Greek text collated by Erasmus became known as the Textus Receptus. The words *Textus Receptus*, are Latin words for Received (Accepted) Text. When Erasmus published it, the churches accepted it as the only valid text of the Greek New Testament. Even though the text of Erasmus was slightly revised in later editions, there still were no rival texts that claimed to be based on better scholarship and better manuscripts, until Lachmann came along in 1831.

Pandora's Box Opened

Following Lachmann's lead, B. T. Westcott, and F. J. A. Hort produced their first textual critical edition of the Greek New Testament in 1881. It was based almost entirely upon the same presuppositions of Lachmann's textual criticism. These men used most of Lachmann's rules of textual criticism and came up with a few of their own. They applied these rules to the Greek text of the New Testament as produced by Erasmus and came up with a different Greek New Testament based on the scholarship of Lachmann and their own. The point of departure had been made. No longer were the majority of manuscripts preserved by faithful churches the basis for recognizing the original reading. From now on, the learned professors would deliver the Christian world from their "ignorance" and, by their expertise, would deliver to the churches a purer text of the New Testament. Dr. Gresham Machen, the greatest Greek scholar and theologian in American history, called this kind of scholarship "the tyranny of the experts."[1]

Just before his death in 1892, Charles H. Spurgeon preached his final sermon at the Pastors College Conference. It was entitled "The Greatest Fight in the World." In that sermon, he refers to textual critics. He calls them "correctors of Scripture."

In his final sermon at the Pastor's College, Spurgeon said, "We have given up the Pope, for he has blundered often and terribly; but we shall not set up instead of him a horde of little popelings fresh from college. Are these correctors of Scripture infallible? Are we now to believe that infallibility is with learned men? Now, Farmer Smith, when you have read your Bible, and have enjoyed its precious promises, you will have, tomorrow morning, to go down the street to ask the scholarly man at the parsonage whether this portion of the Scripture belongs to the inspired part of the Word, or whether it is of dubious authority. We shall gradually be so bedoubted and becriticized, that only a few of the most profound will know what is Bible, and what is not, and they will dictate to all the rest of us. I have no more faith in their mercy than in their accuracy: they will rob us of all that we hold most dear, and glory in the cruel deed. This same reign of terror we shall not endure, for we still believe that God revealeth himself rather to babes than to the wise and prudent, and we are fully assured that our own old English version of the Scriptures is sufficient for plain men for all purposes of life, salvation, and godliness. We do not despise learning, but we will never say of culture or criticism, 'These be thy gods, O Israel!'" [2]

Machen had it right and so did Spurgeon. Textual criticism is drawn from the wells of infidelity by a horde of little popelings who by their assumed infallibility have the impudence to tell us what is God's Word and what is not. Such is the tyranny of the experts.

After Westcott and Hort, the Pandora's box had been opened and all the evils of German rationalism began to tear at the Foundation of the Faith, the Holy Scriptures. This has continued until the present day in both the higher and lower forms of textual criticism. Today the situation involves almost as many different texts of the Greek New Testament as there are scholars. Each scholar decides for himself what he will or will not accept as the Word of God. Consequently, each new edition of the Greek New Testament has led to a smaller and smaller New Testament. If Satan has his way, this will continue until *all* of the New Testament ceases to exist.

1, 881 Years Without the Experts

Until 1881, the churches accepted one text of the New Testament, the one preserved by faithful churches in the majority of the manuscripts. Since 1881 and the Westcott and Hort text, there has not been a text accepted by all Christians. Since 1881, there has been controversy and confusion (which, by the way, is reflected in the many modern translations all claiming to be the Word of God and all different from each other). Some say that the United Bible Society's Greek text and the English translation of it is God's Word. Others say that the Nestle Greek text and the English translation of it is God's Word. Now it comes down to the tyranny of the experts. What do the scholars say? Each scholar says something different. This leaves the King James Version standing like a lighthouse on the storm-swept shore, for it is the only English translation of the New Testament based entirely upon the text that has been passed on to us by faithful churches.

It comes down to two choices: Accept the text handed down by faithful churches for two thousand years or accept the findings of modern textual critics, no two of which fully agree. If we go with the scholars, there is no text that is accepted by all of them. Confusion reigns. There is no standard. We are left like a ship at sea without a rudder.

Since 1881, all the critical texts of the Greek New Testament are a little shorter than the one published before it. Westcott and Hort had a few hundred variant readings. Metzger's edition has three to four thousand variant readings, many of which he has deleted from the text without even a footnote to indicate it was deleted. The modern critical texts have steadily become shorter and shorter. This is clear indication that there are some "snakes in the woodpile somewhere."

Rules of Modern Textual Criticism

These textual critics have rules they follow in deciding if a word, phrase, or sentence should be allowed in or taken out of Scripture. To give you an idea of some of the rules, here is one of them:

"In general, the more difficult reading is to be preferred, particularly when the sense appears on the surface to be erroneous, but on more mature consideration it proves itself to be correct."

This statement is very vague. It says, "In general," which means sometimes this rule applies and sometimes it does not. Who decides when the rule applies and when it does not apply? On what basis is such a decision made? We are not told.

Then it says, "The more difficult reading." Who decides when a reading is more difficult than another one and on what basis? Again, we are not told. Then the rule says, "Particularly when the sense appears on the surface to be erroneous." Who decides when this "sense" or that "sense" is "on the surface" and "erroneous?" The scholars do.

Then it says in a question-begging statement "on a more mature consideration it proves itself to be correct." Who decides which consideration is the mature one? Naturally, the same self-appointed scholars do. This "rule" allows a textual critic to read the Greek New Testament variants and decide which reading is the more difficult, which sense is the surface meaning, and which consideration is the mature one. Somehow, these experts get down into a "deeper knowledge" that allows them to include or exclude a verse of the Greek New Testament.

Their decisions to include or exclude words and verses from the Bible are based on what the scholars think. It is no longer the Word judging them. Because of their self appointed "superior" scholarship they can now judge the Word. This is nothing more than the old first-century Gnosticism, which feeds on the pride of man in his intellect and leads to the destruction of the faith that was once delivered to the saints.

Another rule followed by textual critics says:

"In general, the shorter reading is to be preferred."

If a textual variant is the longer reading, then choose the shorter textual variant as the most valid one. Who says so? The scholars do. In textual criticism, you can make up your own rules and follow them to your own predetermined conclusions.

Another rule of textual criticism says:

"That reading which involves verbal dissidence is usually to be preferred to one which is verbally concordant."

This vague language means that one should choose the variant reading that clashes most with the grammatical structure of the book rather than the reading that is most in harmony with its grammatical structure. This meaningless jargon allows each scholar to choose whatever he wants.

Therefore, it comes down to accepting what the scholars say or accepting what the majority of the manuscripts say. One can ask the scholars which variant is the right one and they will say, "Well, for certain reasons the few manuscripts with the variant reading are the right ones." They base their decisions on the "external evidences" and "internal probabilities" developed by German rationalism.

This is not the right way to go about deciding the text of the Holy Scriptures. The textual critic is flying into the face of thousands of years of history when the text of the New Testament was preserved, not by scholars, but by faithful churches. For nearly two thousand years, the churches never applied these vague rules of textual criticism in order to determine what the correct reading of Scripture was. Faithful churches preserved accurate copies of the New Testament that had been passed on to them. Eighteen hundred years later, the scholars came along and said, "No, your text is as corrupted as the Greek classics. In addition, you cannot determine the right reading based on the majority of the manuscripts. You must now determine the correct reading on the basis of scholarly principles."

No Two Greek Scholars Agree

So now, the correct reading is "up for grabs." One Greek scholar says one reading is right, while another says it is not. There is mass confusion, much like the ridiculous uncertainty of modern art.

That is how the situation came to be, but that is not what it should be. God is not the author of confusion. God inspired the Scriptures by causing them to be written by holy men of God who were controlled by the Holy Spirit. (2 Peter 1:21)

Moreover, after God inspired His Word, He did not abandon it to be protected by mere man's scholarship. Through faithful churches, He watched over the transmission of the Scriptures from one century to the next. True, this transmission was done by copyists who made mistakes in their copying, but there was always the checking of manuscripts with those of other faithful churches to ensure that the text was transmitted without error. God not only took great care to inspire men to write the Scriptures, He also took great care to preserve those Scriptures through faithful New Testament believing churches.

When God sent His Son into the world as the living Word, He did not abandon Him. God preserved His life until it was time for Jesus to die on Calvary. Even then, He raised Him from the dead to triumph over all His enemies. Similarly, God did not send His written Word into the world and abandon it. He watched over His written Word to preserve it just as He preserved His Son, the living Word. Without the preservation of Scripture, the inspiration of Scripture would be in vain. God guarded His Word through faithful churches. These churches carefully checked their copies of manuscripts with those of other churches. The result is that today there are over 5,000 manuscripts of various books of the Greek New Testament and some complete New Testaments, all of which, in the majority of manuscripts, agree. If we need to decide what is the right text, we can go by what the reading is in the majority of the manuscripts.

Because of the extreme care taken by Scripture copyists and the reverent care of faithful churches over their Scriptures, God has preserved a text in the majority of the manuscripts that is the same as the original Greek New Testament!

Which Books Are Canonical?

Churches formally affirmed the canon of the New Testament in AD 397. However, all the books of the New Testament had been judged by faithful churches to be authentic long before that. The churches rejected other books as not being Scripture. Those rejected books were the unauthenticated books that claimed to have a special vision of God's truth. These apocryphal books were rejected by the churches as not being drawn from the "wells of salvation." There was no mark of divine inspiration on them. Under the leadership of the Holy Spirit, the churches decided the issue of which books were a part of Scripture and which books were not.

Therefore, since God, through the churches, took great care to determine which books should go into the New Testament, it also follows that he certainly preserved, through faithful churches, which words should go into that New Testament. Since we know that the books of the New Testament were preserved when the churches decided which books should be a part of the Canon of Scripture, we also know that God preserved the words of each book of the New Testament. God preserved every word of the New Testament by preserving the majority of the manuscripts that were without error and by using the churches to correct the few erring manuscripts by the majority of correct ones.

The Majority of Manuscripts Agree

At the scene of an accident, if nine people witness it and report it accurately to the police, but one person says it happened differently, the account given by the nine is considered the true one. This is especially true when the witnesses are reliable and have no reason to falsify the facts. The same thing is true of over 5,000 Greek manuscripts of New Testament books that exist today. They are reliable and have no reason to falsify the facts. The overwhelming majority of these manuscripts agree as to what a variant reading should be. Faithful churches for over 1,900 years have accepted this evidence as final. So should we.

What Did the Author of the Book Say?

More important than these reasons is the word of the Lord Jesus on the matter. In Matthew 4:4 Jesus, quoting from Deuteronomy 8:3, says, "Man shall not live by bread alone, but by every word that proceedeth out of the mouth of God." In this verse, Jesus sanctions every word of Scripture. He says that *every word* "proceedeth out of the mouth of God," not only out of men's minds. In Matthew 24:35 Jesus said, "Heaven and earth shall pass away, but my words shall not pass away." He declared that His words would not pass away. We have His promise on it. We may believe Jesus or the textual critic whose basic assumption is that the New Testament is hopelessly corrupted. In Luke 16:17 Jesus said, "It is easier for heaven and earth to pass, than one tittle of the law to fail." In Matthew 5:18 Jesus said, "For verily I say unto you, Till heaven and earth pass, one jot or one tittle shall in no wise pass from the law, till all be fulfilled." Jesus was speaking of the Old

Testament but what He said is equally applicable to the New Testament because He is the Author of both. In these verses, Jesus declares that it is easier for heaven and earth to be destroyed than it is for the smallest part of a letter of Scripture to be destroyed. The jot and tittle are small marks that go under a letter. Jesus said that not even these would be lost. His argument is that if the smallest part of Scripture (the jot and tittle) would be preserved, then certainly the larger parts (the words) would be as well.

In John 10:35 Jesus bases His argument on a single letter in a word. The whole argument is based on the difference between *theos* (God) and *theoi* (gods). The difference is the last letter being an *-s* or an *-i*. The suffix *-s* indicates singular and the suffix *-i* indicates plural. The Lord based His argument on the single letter *-i*. Jesus was conscious of the fact that the words of Scripture were preserved without error. He was also conscious of the fact that the very letters and even the small jots under the letters were preserved without error. If Jesus bases an argument on a single letter in Scripture, and He says that not even a part of a letter will be destroyed, this shows us that Jesus had complete confidence in the words and even the smallest part of words in the Scripture.

Should We Believe the Scholars or Jesus?

One can accept the vague thinking of scholars or the clear words of Jesus. Jesus said that God would preserve His Word, and that is exactly what has happened. God not only inspired holy men to write His Word, He used faithful churches to preserve that Word even unto the present day. We have God's unerring Word in the Textus Receptus, because it is based on the majority of manuscripts preserved by the churches.

Since 1881, much of Christendom has followed Westcott and Hort into error. Even many of the major Bible societies have fallen into this error. As for Baptist Bible Translators Institute, we stand with those faithful churches that have preserved God's Word through the centuries. We stand on the Word of God in the King James Version, because it is the only translation in the English language that is free from the presuppositions of modern Gnosticism. There is no reason for us to move into the Gnostic camp, where it is a matter of one opinion versus another. We must not follow anyone's opinion. If we do, we will be shifting constantly and every man doing that which is right in his own eyes—the deplorable state of modern man.

The Conclusion of the Matter

God has preserved His Word through the centuries down to our present day. We have thousands of manuscripts that have been preserved by God through His faithful churches. It is a simple matter of reading them and finding what is the correct reading in the majority of the manuscripts. We accept it on that basis. God has seen to it that faithful churches have by this method preserved these manuscripts and kept them pure through the centuries unto the present time. Therefore, we can know beyond a shadow of doubt that we have the Scriptures down to the very word, to the very letter, and to the smallest part of a letter. The Lord Jesus said we would. Whom do you believe?

"I know that you believe that you understood what you think I said, but I am not sure you realize that what you heard is not what I meant."

Chapter 11

An Introduction to Semantics

Because meaning is the primary part of language that is translatable from one language to another, any study of the principles of Bible translation should contain an introduction to meaning. I use the word "introduction" because this book will not exhaust all that one needs to know about semantics. Therefore, I am dividing the next few chapters into two parts. The first part is a study of semantics (meaning) with applications made to Bible translation. The second part is a study of Bible translation problems and principles with applications made to translating the Old and New Testament Scriptures.

Why Study Semantics?

Every missionary must struggle with linguistic and cultural barriers. To be the most effective missionary possible he must learn the language of the people to whom he has been sent. Along with learning the language, the missionary must learn the culture of the people. Their culture is the context in which their language is spoken. Words only have meaning in terms of the cultural context in which they are spoken. A study of meaning will help missionaries understand the various ways words are used and what they mean in their linguistic and cultural contexts.

This is especially true where the missionary is dealing with linguistic and cultural contexts that are radically different from his own. The frontier across which the missionary must probe into the thinking of people in another language and culture is narrow and difficult. The result, all too often, is misunderstanding by both the missionaries who are confused by the people's culture and the people who are confused by the missionary's message. A missionary who does not understand the language and the culture of the people with whom he works, is like a blindfolded man working on an engine he has never seen before.

In Mark 12:30 Jesus said, "Thou shalt love the Lord thy God with all thy mind." This means that we should diligently apply our minds to study subjects that will help us do a better work for Him. Some would just "let the Spirit lead," but all too often "letting the Spirit lead" is just a cover-up for laziness. If one truly loves the Lord with all his heart, he will love the Lord with his entire mind as well. This is what I have tried to do in this study of semantics.

While I worked for twenty years among the Sinasina people in Papua New Guinea, I tried to test and apply each of the semantic principles I present in this course. If a missionary understands these semantic principles and applies them in a missionary situation, they will make his work a lot less frustrating and a lot more effective.

Understanding in the Way Intended

Someone has estimated that only 80 percent of what is communicated in English is understood in the way intended by the speaker. This is among literate people who speak the same language and have a common culture. This percentage drops to 50 percent or less when communication takes place between people of a different language and culture. An understanding of some facts about languages and the basic elements of the communication process will be helpful to missionaries.

Some Facts About Languages:

1. There Are No Primitive Languages.

Some well-meaning people have said that it is not possible to translate the Bible into many of the world's languages, because these languages are not sufficiently complex for the Scriptures to be translated into them. These people have mistakenly thought that the faulty use of a language by a missionary was all the capacity the language had. Just because a missionary did not study a language well enough to discover its complexities is no indication that the language is not complex enough for the Scriptures to be translated into it. The fault lies not in the language but in the missionary's inadequate mastery of the language. As someone has well said, "God don't make no junk." This is certainly as true of God's creation of human beings as it is of God's creation of languages. God did not create languages that are inadequate to express complex meaning. The speakers of any language on earth can use their language to say whatever they have a need to say. Missionaries often make a statement something like, "There is no word for *love* in this language." What they should say is that they have not yet discovered or developed a word for *love* in this language.

To say there is no word for this or that concept in a language is like saying that there are no snails on a certain island. How can one be sure there are no snails on the island unless he has diligently searched every inch of the island and found no snails? It is like that with a language. We cannot say that a language does not have words for this or that concept unless we have exhausted all that there is to know about that language. A missionary who talks as if the language he is studying is deficient of vocabulary is showing, not the supposed deficiency of the language, but his own ignorance.

God has never created a human being with a primitive language of just a few grunts and squawks. Every language that has ever been diligently studied has proven to be adequate for the people who use it to say anything they need to say.

If a native speaker of a language of the jungle sees an airplane for the first time, he is able to express this new experience in his own language. Not only can he express the experience; he also has the capacity to develop ways for describing new experiences precisely.

The Comanche Code Talkers used a very complicated code to transmit information from one part of the battlefield to another. This code was so complicated that during World War II the Germans never broke it. The Code they used was their own Comanche language. The Comanche men were located in different places on the battlefield and were able to relay information to other Comanche men at other places. They described German tanks using the Comanche words for "big turtles," which Comanche men understood perfectly. The Germans never caught on and so were never able to break the Comanche "code" language. The Comanche language was more complicated than any code that could have been devised by the United States Army Signal Corps!

No language is locked into a narrow range of meaning that cannot be expanded. No language is in any sense primitive. Many languages that were thought to be "primitive" are among the most elaborate and complex languages in the world.

The Zulu language spoken in South Africa is one of the most precise languages in the world. All word roots in Zulu must have a prefix that marks the word as belonging to one of several word classes. Zulu words are classified as animate, inanimate, concrete, mass, individual, or collective. This results in Zulu having about twenty-three kinds of nouns with a complicated verb system as well.

Since there is no such thing as a primitive language, the missionary will not need to waste time and effort forcing his own grammatical patterns onto the native people's language to make up for some supposed deficiency in their language. The language of the native people can express any meaning any other language can express. However, the missionary must discover all of the grammatical features of the language he is studying. If he does, he is in a good position to fully exploit these features to express the meaning of words in the New Testament. Along with learning the grammatical features of language, one must learn the culture of the people if one is to know the true meaning of the words as used by the native speaker.

2. Language and Culture Are Inseparable.

An ethnic language expresses meaning in terms of the cultural context in which it is spoken, and an ethnic culture is expressed through its language. The language of a people and the culture of a people are mutually interrelated. The language expresses their way of life, and their way of life affects the meaning of words used in their language.

The Sinasina people use a sentence meaning, "He pays a bride price." Translated literally, this sentence means, "He puts a stone axe on a rain cape." Today stone axes and rain capes are no longer made or used in the Sinasina culture. However, the sentence used to express "He pays a bride price" is still the old idiom that literally means, "He puts a stone axe on a rain cape." Many years ago, the major part of a bride price was a large stone axe. The blade of the axe was made of obsidian and was valuable. It took months of work to rub the stone blade against another stone to make the axe blade smooth. In recent years, steel axes and plastic sheets have been acquired, and both stone axes and rain capes have disappeared from the Sinasina culture. Even though much of the material culture has disappeared, the material culture of the past still determines the words used in the phrase, "He pays a bride price." Literally, it still means "He puts a stone axe on a rain cape."

The words one will use in his translation will have meaning only in terms of the cultural context in which these words are used. To learn the meaning of ethnic-language words one will have to find out the various situations in the culture where the words are used and how people respond to them in each situation. How words are used in cultural contexts and how people respond to them, reveal the meaning of the words. The missionary must know how the words he uses from the native language are understood in the native culture. After that, he will be able to use the ethnic-language vocabulary correctly in his translation. It is impossible to claim that one has learned a language if one has not painstakingly studied the culture of the people as well.

3. There Are No Perfect Languages.

No language has grammatical constructions for all possible verb tenses, and all the actions that could be expressed by a verb. All languages have strengths and weaknesses. One language will have great power in expressing one thing, while another may be weak in that area but strong in some other aspect of expression.

The English language has no single word that expresses we (inclusive) or we (exclusive). We (inclusive), includes the speaker along with those to whom he speaks. We (exclusive), excludes the speaker from those to whom he speaks. Many ethnic languages make these distinctions by using different words or affixes to precisely identify who is included or excluded in the word "we." If one wants to include others, he uses the inclusive form of "we." If one wants to exclude others, he uses the exclusive form of "we."

We should not force English grammatical structure or even New Testament Greek grammatical structure onto an ethnic language by making it conform to a supposedly "superior" language. Neither English nor New Testament Greek is a perfect language. For example, the New Testament Greek language uses prepositions in an indefinite way. The Greek preposition *en* can be translated "in," "within," "on," "at," "by," "among," and other meanings. Many ethnic languages have a more precise way for expressing such words. The word *igal* in Sinasina means "inside," and that is the only thing it means. Other words are used to express "on," "at," and "by."

Ethnic languages will have grammatical features that will enable one to express meaning just as precisely as one could if he were using Greek or any other language. There is no need to reconstruct the ethnic language in order to make it conform to Greek or English.

4. Every Language Can Express Any Meaning Any Other Language Does.

In years past, the Sinasina people did not have a sentence to describe a twin-engine airplane. They had never seen one before 1945. Upon seeing one, they generated an equivalent meaning in their own language by saying, "The sky-animal (airplane) attaches two noses (engines)." They know that this means, "The airplane has two engines."

The translator does not need to borrow words excessively from the national language in order to express the nearest formal equivalent New Testament meaning in the ethnic language. Any meaning expressed in the national language can just as precisely be expressed in the ethnic language. One should also forget the myth that one language is somehow superior to another.

5. All Languages Borrow Words.

No language is 100 percent pure in the sense that it uses no words or grammatical constructions from other languages. Fifty percent of English-language vocabulary is not English at all. It has been borrowed from other languages. We may think the word "chocolate" is surely an English word. In fact, it is an Aztec word. Such a common English word as "hamburger" is a German word. The word "garage" is

French and the word "thug" is Hindustani. The word "atoll" comes from the language spoken on the Maldive Islands south of India.

Borrowed words may be used in Bible translation, but caution should be used in doing so. There should not be an excessive use of borrowed words. All people borrow words, but one should be sure the people themselves have borrowed the words. It should not be just the bright idea of the translator. Any borrowed word should be checked to find out if it means what is intended. The meaning can only be identified by the way native speakers use the word, not by how it is used in the national language. In Venezuela, the Spanish word "santo" means "holy," but to many Indians it means "an image in the Catholic Church." One must not take for granted that a word borrowed from the national language will mean the same thing in the ethnic language.

6. Every Language Has Different Grammatical Features.

Just as the meanings of words in a particular language are distinct to that language, so also the grammatical features of a particular language are unique to that language.

New Testament Greek grammar uses passive constructions such as in Matthew 5:4, "They shall be comforted." Many ethnic languages do not have a passive grammatical structure. Instead of a passive voice, many ethnic languages use the active voice, and the subject and object of the verb is an obligatory part of the grammatical structure. Instead of saying, "They shall be comforted" (passive voice), the ethnic language uses the active voice, "God (obligatory subject) shall comfort them (obligatory object)." One could invent some concoction of a passive voice in the ethnic language, but it would only cause misunderstanding.

The distinctive grammatical features of an ethnic language will have to be discovered by the translator if he is to take full advantage of them for use in his translation. Any language will have grammatical features available to it to express any meaning desired. The translator must discover these features if he is to use them. In many cases there will be no grammar books written for him. He must find out how the grammar of the language functions. If a particular grammatical feature of the language is not discovered and understood fully by the translator, he has one less feature of the grammar to use as the vehicle for expressing the meanings of New Testament words.

7. There Are No Total Synonyms Within Languages or Between Languages.

People's experiences with words differ widely; therefore, the meanings they associate with those words also differ widely. Total synonyms are at variance with the law of language efficiency. If two words meant exactly the same thing, one of them would not be needed and would disappear.

To a Roman Catholic the word *Catholic* means the Roman Catholic Church ruled by the Pope in Rome. However, to some people the word "Catholic" means simply the church made up of Christians from all over the world. The words "dog" and "canine" both refer to a four-legged animal, but the meanings are not the same. Even the word "dog" means different things to different people. The meaning one has for the word "dog" depends on what one's experience with dogs has been. If one has had pleasant experiences with dogs, the word "dog" means a pleasant thing to him. If a dog has bitten one, the word "dog" means a frightening thing to him. The responses each of the two people will make upon hearing the word "dog" will be very different. The word "dog" has a similar referential meaning to both people but the connotative meaning is different for each person.

If there are no complete synonyms within the same language, then certainly one should not expect to find complete synonyms between different languages. This is especially true when the cultures of the two languages are entirely different. Realizing this should deliver the translator from trying to translate by matching a word in the New Testament with a 100 percent formal equivalent word in the ethnic language. This does not mean that one does not strive for 100 percent formal equivalence. He does. However, in many instances one must be satisfied with the *nearest* formal equivalent.

8. All Languages Have Vocabulary Focus.

People talk about what is important to their survival in the environment in which they live. Naturally, they will develop a vocabulary about those things that are important to them, and conversely, they will develop fewer words for things of secondary importance.

The Eskimos have eight words for different kinds of snow that are used for different important parts of their life. They have a certain kind of snow that is best for melting to make drinking water. They have another kind of snow that is for making igloos. They have a well-developed vocabulary for snow, but they do not have a word for a crocodile. Crocodiles do not exist in their environment so there is no need for the word. The Iwam people on the Sepik River in Papua New Guinea have many words pertaining to crocodiles, but they do not need a word for snow. This is not to say that they cannot develop a word for snow. They could talk about snow if a need occurred where it was important for them to do so.

The vocabulary of any language will be focused on matters that are important in the environment of that particular people. However, the vocabulary focus of a language can be widened to include words that refer to new experiences that are not usually a part of the local environment.

Language focus indicates that a translator can concentrate on vocabulary in the language that will be useful for translating New Testament words. He need not occupy himself with exhausting the entire vocabulary in a language. That would take a lifetime and still would not be complete. Instead, he should concentrate on words that are useful to him for translating New Testament words. What does it matter for a Bible translator if the Sinasina people have two hundred words for the different varieties of sweet potato? One need not occupy large amounts of time with remembering two hundred words for the varieties of sweet potato.

The Elements of Communication

To understand some of the problems involved in the process of Bible translation, it is helpful to understand some of the basic elements in any communication between two people. The five basic elements of the communication process are as follows:

The Source of a message

The message given

The receiver of the message

The feedback resulting from a message

The cultural context of the message

Symbolizing the Communication Process

S = **S**ource of message

M = **M**essage

R = **R**eceiver of message

f = feedback

The communication that takes place between two people could be symbolized by the following illustration:

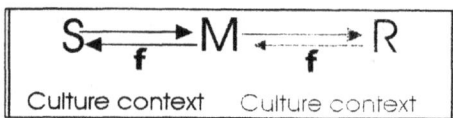

The red color symbolizes the culture of the Source who encodes his message in terms of his culture. The green symbolizes the culture of the Receiver who decodes the message of the Source in terms of his own culture. The feedback is in green and red because the Receiver will respond in terms of his own cultural context, and the feedback from the Receiver will be interpreted by the Source in terms of his cultural context.

The Source is the one who speaks to a person. The one spoken to is the **Receiver**. The **Message** is given by the **Source**. The Receiver also sends feedback to the Source. When we add the elements of **Feedback** (F) and **Cultural Context** (CC), then our symbolizing of communication between two people will look like this:

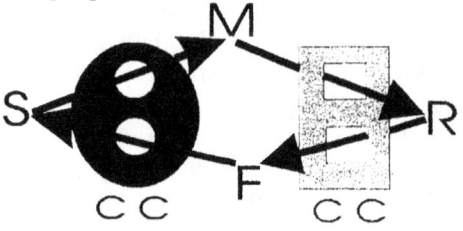

Applications of the Communication Process

As a Source of the Message, a missionary will be communicating with a Receiver of that message through two cultural contexts: his own culture and that of the Receiver.

This would imply that the original Message as given in the Bible could be modified by his own cultural bias, and thus a corrupting of the original message could occur. The original message was given in a Semitic context. Our own Cultural Context is not a Semitic one and we are many years removed from the time when the original communication was given. The possibility that our own Cultural Context can distort the Message is ever-present.

This would also imply that the original Message as given in the Scriptures could be modified by the cultural bias of the Receiver as well.

The process of communication as symbolized above would imply that there must be a change in the form of communication if the meaning of the message is to be understood by the receiver in the way intended by the source. The source must change the form of his speech sounds and grammar to that of the receiver's speech sounds and grammar if the receiver is to understand what the source meant by the message he presented to him.

These symbols of the communication process also imply that it is important for the source to check feedback from the receiver to see if his message was understood as he intended. The receiver will always receive some kind of message when spoken to by the source, but will the receiver understand the message as it was intended by the source? Feedback that comes from the receiver to the source will enable the source to know if his message was understood by the receiver as was intended. If the receiver does not understand the message of the source, adjustments can be made to help the receiver understand the message that was intended by the source.

These symbols also imply the importance of the source being receiver-oriented. The source must put his message into words that the receiver understands in the same way the source does. If the source uses words that he knows to mean certain things, but the receiver has other meanings for the same words, confusion results.

This further implies that the source must understand the cultural context of the receiver. If the source is to know whether the receiver understands his words as intended, the source must understand the cultural context of the receiver. The cultural context of the receiver determines the meaning of the words he understands. The source must use words the receiver understands in the same way the source does. If he does not, the receiver will misunderstand what the source intended to say.

This further implies that a receiver will understand a message given by a source in terms of his own cultural context and not in terms of the cultural context of the source. The source must not take it for granted that the receiver will understand his words in the same way he intended them. It is not enough for the source to know the meaning of his words. The source must also know what meaning is stimulated in the mind of the receiver by the words he uses.

Conclusion

All of these elements of the communication process are important to our understanding of the principles of Bible translation. Bible translation is similar to any communication between two people. When a missionary preaches the Gospel to people, he has a message that he wants to give them. Preaching the Gospel in a foreign language is somewhat like rapid Bible translating. One must choose words almost instantly. The preacher hopes he is choosing foreign-language words that are the nearest formal equivalent to what he means. Due to the rapid choice of words, it is unlikely that this will happen all the time.

This is also the case when using an interpreter. The interpreter is asked to make rapid choices of words. Unless careful preparation is made ahead of time, the interpreter may choose words that mean something other than what the source intended.

However, in the process of written Bible translating, the words chosen to communicate the meaning can be done slowly and carefully. We can "freeze" the message in a written form that can be read by the receiver.

The first step in Bible translating is to understand clearly the message of the Bible without corrupting its message by our own cultural or theological biases. In order to do this we must learn how to exegete the meaning of the Bible verses we want to translate. All too often, we assume we know what the meaning of a verse is. Actually, we may not have studied it carefully enough to find out what the original author meant by the words he used.

The next step involves putting the biblical message into a written form so it can be read and understood by the receiver in the way intended by the original Source of the message. In order to do this, we must thoroughly understand the culture of the people into whose language we are translating. We must know what the words they use mean in their own cultural contexts. If we fail to learn this, we will be using words that most likely will not express the meaning intended by the author who wrote the verses we are attempting to translate.

Homework:

Explain the illustration below:

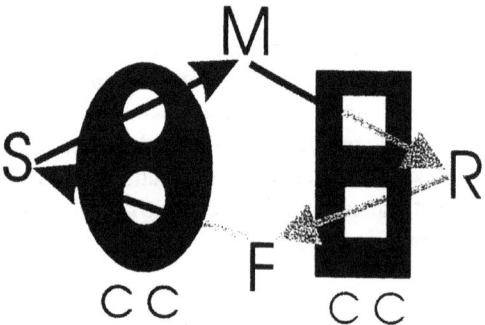

The Sinasina people in Papua New Guinea call a white man a red man and they call a black man a red black man. Therefore, a red man is equal to a white man and a black man is equal to a white black man. Got that?

Chapter 12

Some Facts about Semantics

The preceding study of the communication process will help us understand the following facts about meaning:

1. Meaning is an event, not a thing.

When one person speaks to another person, the thought in the mind of the speaker (source) is put into words by means of his nervous system, including the brain and speech organs. The sounds uttered by the source travel on the air as sound waves. The sound waves cause the eardrum of the receiver to vibrate, and he hears the sounds. The nervous system of the receiver distinguishes the sounds and places a meaning on the words he hears. The words spoken by the source have stimulated the brain of the receiver, causing meaning to occur in his mind. However, the meaning the source intended may or may not have been understood in the way intended. Because the meaning of what the source said will be interpreted in the receiver's own mind, the receiver may or may not understand the message of the source as he intended it.

This process of communication may be illustrated by the following illustration:

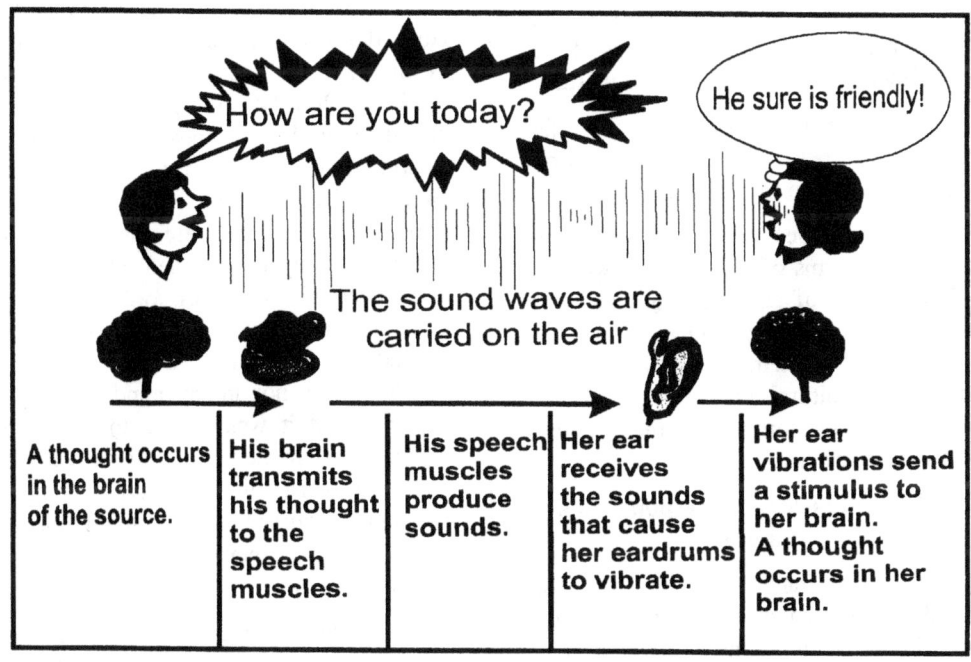

If I were to say to you, "I was in the Boot Heel area of Missouri recently; I worked on a farm there and helped to repair the tin roof on the barn." Would you understand my words in the same way I understand them? Most likely, the meaning you understand by these words would not be the same as I intend you to understand them. You may not know where the Boot Heel area of Missouri is or what it is like. You would not know that land in the Boot Heel is flat. You may be thinking of the farms you have seen in some other place. If so, your meaning for my words would not be the same meaning I intended you to understand.

The color of the barn may occur to you as red, but in the Boot Heel area, barns are made of gray, unpainted Cypress wood. Because the meanings for words occur in the minds of both the source and the receiver, those meanings may not be the same. Each person will attach meanings to words in terms of the experience he has had with those words.

A French proverb says, "The spoken word belongs half to the one who speaks and half to the one who hears."

Meaning occurs in the mind of the receiver in terms of his own experience. When people of another language read our translation, the meanings, which the words signal to them, will be in terms of their own cultural experience and not necessarily in terms of the biblical cultural experience.

2. Meaning occurs in response to a stimulus.

The meanings people have for words are stored in their brain. We do not know exactly how this storage system works. We do know that it is based on the experiences a person has with those words. However, these meanings only occur when a stimulus (a spoken or written word) causes them to occur in the thinking processes of the brain.

In the Sinasina language, there is a word *kware*, which I heard often. I first heard it used when the speaker was talking about an event that took place *a long time ago*. Therefore, I took the meaning of *kware* to mean "a long time ago." I heard people say, "*kware* Yani (the Sun) and Geluwa (the moon) made the earth and people." The word *kware* clearly seemed to mean "a long time ago." Then one day I asked Bare if Milan had left to go to town and he replied, *Kware pumue* meaning, "He already went." Without ever having heard that word in this new context, I knew what he meant. I knew he meant, "He has already gone." The moment I heard the word *kware* used in this new context, I knew exactly what was meant. How did I know this was the correct meaning? I had never heard the word used this way before but my mind had already stored up a meaning for *kware* "a long time ago." In the incident with Bare, it clearly meant, "He has already gone." The new meaning for this word occurred in my mind based on my prior experience with the word *kware* that had already been stored in my brain. The second meaning for the word *kware* (already) was not in my mind's storage capacity, but it was caused to occur in my mind by the new situation in which I heard the word stimulus *kware*. The new meaning occurred in my mind rather than existing there in a particular location.

Because meaning should not be considered as existing in a certain place, and because meaning occurs rather than exists, meaning should be considered in terms of all the situations in which a word is used in daily life. The meaning of a word must be understood in terms of the events that take place in relation to that word and the way people respond to that word during those events. These events and responses are the contexts that surround a word. These contexts will indicate the meaning of that word. Therefore, the translator must understand the meaning of the people's words in terms of the situations in which they use those words in their own cultural setting. As the translator knows this, he can use the people's words correctly and be able to predict what the words will mean to them when they read them from his translation.

3. One cannot tell another person the meaning of a message.

The missionary cannot tell people the meaning of his words. He can only transmit verbal stimuli (words) by which the people will tell themselves the meaning of his words in terms of their own cultural experience. When one speaks to someone else, it is impossible to transmit meaning to that person. One can only transmit verbal stimuli that have been shaped by his nervous system and speech organs into word symbols. These word symbols, carried on the air as sound waves, will stimulate the mind of the receiver, who will place his own meaning on the words he hears. When a source has spoken words that stimulate his intended meaning in the mind of the receiver, the receiver understands the message of the source correctly.

If I were to say to you, "As the farmer plowed the field, he spoke to the mule saying, 'Gee!' and 'Haw!'" Would you know what I meant by the words *Gee* and *Haw*? I would be transmitting verbal stimuli to your eardrums that would stimulate a meaning in your mind. However, if you had never seen a man using a mule-drawn plow, you may not know what the words *Gee* and *Haw* mean. I would have been able to transmit stimuli to your ears by means of sound waves but you would have received these stimuli and placed a meaning on them according to your own experience. Therefore, I have not transmitted the meanings of the words I have in my mind to yours. I have only transmitted stimuli to your mind. Your mind will receive these stimuli and meaning will occur in your mind in terms of your own experience.

Even if you have had no experience with the words *Gee* and *Haw*, your mind will not stay blank. It will attach some kind of meaning to the words even if you have never heard them before. In this respect, one cannot tell another person a story. One can only transmit stimuli to a receiver by which he tells himself a story in terms of the meaning-experiences that are stored in his own mind.

This should make us aware of some of the reasons people do not understand the words we say in the way we intend them to be understood. They are only receiving stimuli (words) from us, and their own mind is placing a meaning on the stimuli they receive. The person who reads our translation will receive stimuli from the printed words on the page. The meanings he actually understands by these words will take place in his own mind.

4. A person tells himself the meaning of words in terms of his own culture.

This fact can be easily observed by going to Australia and standing before a group of people and innocently using the word *bum*. One will notice immediately that the people in the audience are uncomfortable. To me, the word *bum* is a person who rides boxcars and does not have a job. To the Australian the word *bum* is a vulgar term referring to the buttocks.

An American was on an international flight and innocently made a remark to a woman from England that her little girl was a "cute little *bugger*." The English woman gave him a very stern look because in British English *bugger* means, "prostitute."

The translator must know the language and culture of the people well enough to predict how the people who hear or read his words will understand those words. If he does not know how the people will understand his words, he may embarrass himself and offend the people.

5. Meaning expressed by a grammatical structure in one language may be expressed by a different grammatical structure in another.

Some languages show the receiver of the action of the verb by its syntactical position in the sentence. The position in the sentence determines where the receiver of the action occurs. In English we say, "John hit Bill." We know it was Bill who was hit because, in English, the object of the verb always occurs last in the sentence order. The order is SUBJECT (John), then VERB (hit), and last OBJECT (Bill). The syntactical positions of the words in the sentence tell us who the receiver of the action is. In the Sinasina language the syntactical word order is: "John Bill hit." The Sinasina grammatical word order is SUBJECT (John), OBJECT (Bill), and VERB (hit).

In some languages, the word order does not matter. The words can be placed in any order because the words themselves have markers on them to indicate which word is the subject, which word is the verb and which word is the object. The object is marked by an affix that indicates to the people in that language that this word is the receiver of the action of the verb. A language that uses an object indicator affix may look like this: "Bill-sa John-zo hit." The -sa suffix indicates that Bill is the receiver of the action of the verb. The –zo suffix indicates that John is the subject of the sentence. The sentence would mean, "John hit Bill."

The translator must not force either his own grammatical structure or that of the Greek New Testament onto his ethnic language translation. He should find out how the ethnic language uses its own grammatical features to express meanings that are the nearest formal equivalent of those in the New Testament.

6. Similar grammatical constructions can signal different meanings.

In English we may say, "The man is eating," meaning a man is eating food. The Sinasina language has a similar grammatical feature. One may say in Sinasina, "The knife is eating," but it does not mean the knife is eating food. It means the knife is sharp. We may say in English, "She killed a man," meaning a woman killed a man. The Sinasina language has a similar grammatical structure in the sentence, "She killed the moon," but it does not mean she murdered the moon. It means she had her monthly menstruation period. In English we can say, "He has a cold heart," meaning he has no sympathy for people. However, to say, "He has a cold heart" in the Sinasina language means, "He is not angry." All these sentences have similar grammatical structures, but the same grammatical structure has different meanings in each language.

If a translator assumes that a grammatical construction in the English New Testament must be translated by a similar grammatical construction in the ethnic language, the two similar grammatical constructions may mean something entirely different. Translators must be primarily concerned with matching meaning for meaning not necessarily grammatical construction for grammatical construction.

7. Different grammatical constructions can signal equivalent meanings.

In English, we greet a person in the morning with "Good morning." The Sinasina people greet each other in the morning with "Have you horizontaled and come?" The grammatical constructions are different but they both mean, "A greeting one uses in the morning." The English New Testament in James 1:1 uses the phrase "a servant of God." The Sinasina New Testament in James 1:1 uses the phrase "one who does water-wood work for God." This phrase means, "one who is a servant of God." The grammatical constructions are different, but they both express equivalent meaning.

Even though the ethnic-language translation may use a verbal construction to express what is a noun in English, this is still faithful translating as long as the meaning is the nearest formal equivalent. Because different grammatical constructions can express equivalent meanings, translation is possible between two different languages, but the translating must be done in terms of equivalent meanings, not necessarily equivalent grammatical constructions.

8. To translate the meaning of the source language into the meaning of the receiver language, adjustments must be made in both languages.

In the Sinasina New Testament, the phrase "born again," (John 3:3) is easy to construct literally. I used the word "again" with the verb "to be born" and the phrase "born again" was constructed. However, the Sinasina people, after understanding more of the meaning of the term "born again," added two more words: "thoughts in the inside." I adjusted the English term to Sinasina grammar by constructing the term "again to be born," and the people adjusted the term further by adding "thoughts in the inside again to be born." By adding the words "thoughts in the inside" the term means, "to be born again in the inner person."

If the translator does not adjust the source language meaning from the Greek or English New Testament to the receiver language grammatical form, he will likely communicate a misunderstanding of the intended meaning. However, the speakers of the receiver language must also adjust their grammatical constructions. They must be willing to adjust their word forms to that of the source language if they are to understand the meaning of New Testament words as intended by the Author. A completely indigenous translation would be a totally pagan one. If there were no influences on the translation from outside the native culture, the native translator would be limited only to his own cultural experience. There *must* be input from outside sources if the ethnic-language translation is to be the nearest formal equivalent of New Testament meaning.

9. The meaning of words should be considered in terms of what they mean to the receiver.

A little girl came to her mother and asked her to tell her where she came from. The mother was at first embarrassed, but after reading some books on the "birds and the bees," she took her daughter aside and carefully explained the process of human reproduction. When she finished, the little girl said, "But Mom, I still want to know where I came from. Joe said he came from Chicago and he asked me where I came from." The mother had *assumed* that her daughter meant physical reproduction by the words, "Where did I come from?" The meaning the little girl had for the words "came from" meant, "place of origin." Consequently, there was a complete misunderstanding of meaning between the mother and daughter. The mother only thought in terms of what the words meant to her. She did not stop to think what the words might mean to her daughter.

The translator must think in terms of meaning as understood by both the original source and the present receiver. He must know the meaning of New Testament words as used by the original writer, and he must put this meaning into words the receiver will understand in the way intended by the original writer. This implies three things:

> 1. The translator must know the meaning of words as used by the author of the book.

> 2. The translator must know the accumulation of meanings the people have stored in their minds.

> 3. In order to find out the accumulation of meanings stored in the people's minds, the translator will have to understand their culture.

10. The meaning of new words can only be understood in the context of old words already understood.

If I were to tell you a story using Sinasina words, you would not be able to understand the Sinasina words. For example, if I were to say, "Kabenoges usually have nice yome," the first word and the last word would make no sense to you. You cannot tell what these words mean in the sentence as it stands. If I added some words by saying, "Kabenoges usually have nice fluffy yome. The kabenoge sleeps all day concealed in a tree. He comes out at night and hops around looking like a miniature kangaroo. The Sinasina people value the kabenoge's yome for weaving purposes. They weave yome into their baby-carrying bags to make them soft and comfortable for the baby." Now, because you have related the new words to old words for which you already have meaning, you can conclude that a kabenoge is an animal similar to a small kangaroo that has some fur that is fluffy in texture.

A translation of the New Testament that uses new words must have sufficient contexts surrounding those words to indicate to the reader what these new words mean. This is based on the principle that words mutually delimit the meaning of each other. The more words there are around a particular word, the more specific is its meaning.

A mother directed her 4-year-old son to go out and get some fresh air. Perplexed, he cupped his hands and asked, "How will I bring it back in?"

Chapter 13

More Facts About Semantics

11. In living languages, the meaning of words change over time.

As people's experience with a word changes, so does the meaning they have for that word. The Sinasina people call a rich, powerful leader a *Yobal kun*, meaning "a chief." As we taught the Sinasina people about God, it was natural for them to begin referring to God as "Kun," meaning a person of great power. As the Sinasina people learned more about "Kun" from the context of Scripture, their meaning for the word changed until it became the nearest formal equivalent for the word *God*. Similarly, people who speak Spanish address either a male person or God himself by using the word *Señor*.

Because people's meanings for words can change, the translator can use the people's words in new contexts to give old words new meanings. The translator can also construct words and condition them by a context that causes them to mean what he wants them to mean.

12. In living languages, words do not have a single, fixed point of unchanging meaning.

A person uses a word in terms of his own experience. Since each person has varying experiences, the meanings people have for words vary and change according to the experiences they have with those words.

To one person the word father may mean a warm and loving person who protects the family and provides security for them. To another person, the word father may mean a drunk who is violent, beats up the family, and makes their lives miserable. One person told me that he had trouble praying to God as Father because his father had been a drunken tyrant who beat up his mother and struck fear into the hearts of the children.

The Sinasina people use the word *father* to mean biological father. However, they also use the word *father* to mean owner. They say that he is the "father" of a parcel of land, meaning he is the owner of it. They also use the word *father* to mean "leader," as in, "They are all my children. I am their father." The Sinasina people also use the word *father* for "police officer," who is spoken of as "the father of the gun."

This should illustrate that words do not have a single, fixed point of meaning. Words have areas of meaning, and these areas of meaning can change. After his experience with God expanded, the person who had a drunken tyrant for a father began to experience new meaning for the words "Heavenly Father."

The translator, realizing that words are not fixed points of meaning, will try to learn the various areas of meaning covered by a word in the ethnic language. In the same regard, one should not use a word from the vocabulary of the New Testament without finding out the various areas of meaning covered by that word in the New Testament.

13. The areas of meaning covered by a word will overlap areas of meaning covered by other words in the same language but the overlap will not be complete.

The overlap of meaning between words may look like the following illustration:

In English, we say "I love you" and "I like you." "I love" and "I like" overlap in meaning in some areas but do not overlap completely. The words "I love you" may also mean, "I lust for you."

14. Areas of meaning in a word will overlap areas of meaning in a word of another language, but the overlap will not be complete.

The translator must find the words in the ethnic language that cover the areas of meaning that are the nearest formal equivalents to the New Testament words to be translated. There will be some overlap of meaning between the words in the ethnic language and the words in the New Testament, but one should not expect this overlap to be complete.

The New Testament Greek word for love is *agapao*. However, which area of the English word "love" does the Greek word overlap? Is the Greek word, *agapao* equivalent to "be fond of," "to fall in love with," "to be devoted to," or "to have benevolent concern for"? The Greek word for *love* and the English word for *love* overlap in some areas but do not overlap in others. In fact, no single English word covers precisely the meaning of the New Testament Greek word for "love." The single Greek word, *agapao* can be expressed in English with several words, such as "self-sacrificing love." Even these several words do not adequately express the total meaning of the Greek word for "love."

This fact about meaning will save us from trying to always find 100 percent equivalents between words of two different languages. We must find the word that is the nearest formal equivalent. This fact shows us that there cannot always be a 100 percent transferring of the meaning of a word in one language over into a word of a different language. In some areas of meaning, there will be an overlap of meaning, but in others, there will be no overlap.

15. The areas of meaning in a word can be established by discovering the situations in which the word is used and how people respond to it in those situations.

The word *bone* in Sinasina can mean one of the bones in the body or it can mean "strength," "power," "faithfulness," or "hard." The meaning of *bone* depends on how the word is used in what situation. If a Sinasina "asks God for bone," he is asking strength to endure trials. If he "hits bone," he is victorious in warfare. If he "bakes bone," he is faithful. If the cement "hits bone," it has become hard. The meaning of the word *bone* depends on the situation it is used in and how people respond to the word in that situation.

The translator must determine the meaning of a word by how it is used in different situations. He may personally know of these situations, or he may ask a language helper to offer some examples of how the word is used in different situations that occur in his village. Further observation and study may be necessary to find out all the areas of meaning covered by a word.

16. The dictionary meaning of a word does not always reflect all the situations in which a word is used.

A missionary in Central America wanted a dresser for his bedroom, so someone told him to buy the lumber for it and take it to the local carpenter and tell him what he wanted made. The missionary purchased the lumber, looked up the word for dresser in his Spanish dictionary, and found the word *gabinete*. Because he wanted drawers in the dresser, he looked up the word for drawers and found *calzoncillas*. Then he went to the carpenter and told him he wanted a "gabinete con calzoncillas." He intended to say that he wanted a dresser with drawers, but the word *gabinete* is usually used when one speaks of a cabinet in the government. The word *calzoncillas* he chose for drawers is usually used when one is talking about underwear. What the missionary actually said was, "I want a government cabinet with underwear."

Someone wrote a letter to a Bible society asking them to send him a dictionary of one of the ethnic languages so he could translate the New Testament into that language. This person thought he could look up the English equivalent in the ethnic-language dictionary and place the ethnic-language word in place of the English word in the Bible to translate the New Testament. You can see from the above illustration why such a procedure would not result in a faithful translation.

Even computers, which are capable of making millions of word matches almost instantly, make the same mistakes as humans when they try to translate by word matching. When a computerized translation machine was asked to translate into Russian "The spirit is willing, but the flesh is weak," it translated the phrase as, "The vodka is good, but the meat is spoiled." Word matching from one language to another is not faithful translation.

17. A single meaning can often be expressed by several different grammatical structures.

It is possible to say the same thing in several different ways. In English, we use several different grammatical structures to say essentially the same meaning. Note the following:

I did not go. It rained.

Because it rained, I did not go.

I did not go because it rained.

It rained, so I did not go.

It rained, and I did not go.

All of these sentences have the same meaning but different grammatical structures. Where one language may use one kind of grammatical structure, another may say the same meaning but use a different kind of grammatical structure.

The following sentences illustrate the possibility of translating the same meaning into seven different language structures.

Language 1:
They blamed me for the problem.

Language 2:
They blamed the problem on me.

Language 3:
They blamed me because of the problem.

Language 4:
They said that I caused the problem.

Language 5:
They said to me, "You caused the problem."

Language 6:
They accused me of causing the problem.

Language 7:
They accused me of being responsible for the problem.

It is possible to translate meaning from one language to another but it is not always possible to translate grammatical structure from one language to another. It is not necessary to always translate by matching the same grammatical structure of one language to that of the other language. The seven sentences above illustrate that the same meaning can be expressed by seven different grammatical structures.

18. Several meanings can be expressed by only one grammatical structure.

It is also possible to express several different meanings using only one grammatical structure.

In English we can say:

I ate ice cream with my wife (in her company).

I ate ice cream with my spoon (by means of my spoon).

I ate ice cream with my pie (together with my pie).

It is possible to translate more than one meaning by using only one grammatical structure. One grammatical structure can be used in several ways with different meanings resulting from the one structure. Because the same grammatical structure can express several different meanings, this should help us place priority on meaning rather than on always translating a particular grammatical structure the same way.

19. A word in one language may be equivalent in meaning to a word in another language but all the areas of meaning between the two words may not be equivalent.

If one compares the French word *marche* with the English equivalent word *march*, this results in the French word *marche* being translated by four different English words.

French Sentence:

Le bebe ne marche.

English Translation:

The baby is not *walking*.

French Sentence:

Le train marche.

English Translation:

The train is *moving*.

French Sentence:

Est-ce que ca marche?

English Translation:

Is it *working* out?

French Sentence:

Le temps marche.

English Translation:

Time *flies*.

Although the French word *marche* is equivalent to the English word "march," the English word is not equivalent to all the areas of meaning covered by the French word. The French word *marche* is used for the English word march, but the same word can also mean "walk," "move," "work," or "fly."

A translator must not think he can find an equivalent for a New Testament word in the ethnic language and use that same word as equivalent to every occurrence of that word in the New Testament. A word that is the nearest formal equivalent in one context of the New Testament may not be the nearest formal equivalent in another. The Greek word *pneuma* meaning "spirit" must be translated as "Spirit" in John 3:6, but must be translated as "wind" in John 3:8, and as "demon" in Mark 1:26, and as "human spirit" in Luke 1:47. The word *pneuma* itself does not tell you which of these meanings should be translated in every place it is used. The context in which the word occurs determines how the word should be translated. The word *pneuma* should not be translated the same way in every verse of Scripture.

20. Meaning expressed by a single word in one language may need to be expressed equivalently by several words in another.

Many languages do not use a single word to express a meaning that is expressed by a single word in English. Many single words in English become several words in other languages. The English word *carpenter* becomes in Sinasina, "He who builds houses." Many languages do not have single-word nouns as the English language does. Instead, they are more descriptive and actually describe the meaning content of an English noun by using a verbal phrase. The word "teacher" in English becomes in Sinasina, "He who strikes learning to them."

Here are some examples of one word becoming a phrase:

English: "kill"

Ethnic Language: "cause to die"

English: "bring"

Ethnic Language: "take and come"

English: "shepherd"

Ethnic Language: "one who cares for sheep"

21. A meaning expressed by several words in one language may need to be expressed equivalently by a single word in another language.

English Language	Sinasina Language
It is his pig.	Bonamwe.
He is his father.	Nomwe.
She is his mother.	Mamwe.
They are His father and mother.	Nemamwe.
It is his house.	Igemwe.

The Sinasina language is sometimes shorter than its English equivalent and sometimes longer. It takes four English words to say, "It is his pig," but only one Sinasina word, *Bonamwe*, to say the same thing. However, it takes three Sinasina words, Ige kengwa yale, (Man who habitually builds houses) to say the one English word, *carpenter*.

Homework

Is it possible for a person to transmit the meaning in his mind to the mind of another person? Explain why you think your answer is the correct one.

People in Thailand have difficulty saying English words like "clap." They tend to replace the "l" sound in the word "clap" with an "r" sound. One evening after a musical performance a Thai woman turned to some American friends and said, "Let's all stand up and crap."

Chapter 14

Semantics: Verbal Meanings

There are many kinds of meaning. The red traffic light means "stop." In some cultures, the distance people stand in nearness to one another indicates the degree of friendliness between them. If one wants to be friendly, he does not leave a wide space between himself and the one to whom he speaks. Many meanings are signaled by the cultural cues of body language. As Bible translators, we are primarily concerned with the verbal symbols that are printed in the books we translate. There are several meanings carried by verbal symbols in written form. Among these are the following:

1. Referential Meaning

All people use their language to refer to objects by using symbols to represent the objects in question. Rather than carry a stone around with us and show it to people each time we want to signal the meaning of a stone, it is more convenient to invent a word symbol, such as "stone," to refer to the object. The symbol chosen is to some extent arbitrary. In most cases, there is no relationship between the symbol chosen and the object referred to by the symbol. Anything that can be referred to is called referential meaning. When we say "running," we refer to a process of movement by using our legs. Anything that can be referred to by using a verbal symbol to represent it is considered referential meaning. We can talk about any physical object by giving the object a verbal symbol. We may also refer to things that have no physical properties. Such things as actions, processes, or things that happen rather than exist may be referred to as well. We can say, "He died," or "He is sick." We can even talk about abstract things by giving these non-physical things a verbal symbol. We can say, "He loves cats," "He is faithful," or "She is bad." Symbols like "love," "faithful," and "bad" are not physical properties, yet we can symbolize them and use the symbols to talk about them. We may also refer to relationships that exist between things or people or events. We use such symbols as "under the table," "on the ground" or "in the house." The words "under," "on," and "in" refer to spatial relationships that exist between objects.

A grocery list will contain words that have a purely referential meaning. This is also called the *primary* or *literal* meaning of a word. Referential meaning is that meaning of a word that is usually assigned to it unless the context gives it another meaning. The referential meaning of words is that meaning we learn as a child when someone gives us an object and repeats the name of it to us. They show us things and use the word symbol to represent whatever it is they are showing us.

2. Connotative Meaning

We not only use word symbols to refer to things (referential meaning), but we have emotional reactions to word symbols. Connotative meaning involves the emotional response a word symbol arouses in a person because of their feeling for the meaning of that word.

Such a word as "mother" in contrast to the word "woman" illustrates the difference between connotative and referential meaning. Both words may refer to the same person, but one has a different emotional content from the other. This emotional content of a word symbol is usually culturally conditioned.

The Sinasina people have been shown to have a high emotional response to the word *blood*. The word *blood* has less of an emotional connotation to English speakers than it does to Sinasina speakers.

The Yanamamo people in Venezuela reacted coldly to the story of the arrest, trial, and crucifixion of Jesus. Jesus surrendered without a fight. The emotional response of the Yanamamo was that Jesus must have been a coward because any self-respecting Yanamamo would have fought for far less of a provocation.

When the Sawi people of West Irian heard the same story of the arrest, trial, and crucifixion of Jesus, they reacted by considering Judas the hero of the story, not Jesus. In the Sawi culture, the art of deceit and treachery is finely honed. Every Sawi person lives for the day when he can deceive his enemy and betray him into the hands of those who will kill him. Judas masterfully accomplished such a feat. To the Sawi people Judas was the hero of the story.

To the Yanamamo, the connotation of Jesus' arrest and trial was the cowardice of Jesus who refused to fight. To the Sawi, the connotative meaning of the same incident was the tremendous accomplishment of Judas, who skillfully used treachery to have Jesus arrested and killed.

A translator must not only know the referential meaning of words; he must also know the connotative meaning.

Such a word as *Samaritan* does not have the connotative meaning now that it had in Jesus' time. To be called a Samaritan was like disgustingly calling a person a half-caste. Words like "publican" meant "thief" and "traitor" in New Testament times. The word "circumcision" meant Jewish. All of these words had a high emotional content at the time of the writing of the New Testament. When we read them in our Bibles today, this connotative meaning is largely unknown to us.

It is not enough merely to translate the referential meaning of such words. The words we use in our translation should be the nearest formal equivalent that evokes the same emotional response, as did the words written originally in the New Testament. The translator should also be aware of the connotative meaning of the ethnic-language words he uses to translate the New Testament. If he does not know the emotional response of the people to the words he uses, he may find the words are not responded to in the way he intended.

3. Contextual Meaning

It is not possible to know what a word means apart from the context in which the word occurs. The context that surrounds a word determines the meaning of that word.

What does the word *stone* mean? If the word *stone* occurred alone in a list of words, we probably would say it means a "stone that is found on the ground." I have to use the words a "stone that is found on the ground" before I can even tell you what I mean by the word "stone." If we take the word "stone" from a list and put it into a different context, the word will take on an entirely different meaning. In the sentence, "They threatened to stone him," the word *stone*, which was a noun on our list, becomes a verb, meaning "to stone someone."[1]

In the sentence, "He is stone deaf," the word that was last a verb has now become an adverb describing the extent of one's hearing ability. He hears like a stone hears, meaning "not at all." The sentence would be equivalent to saying, "He is totally deaf."

In the sentence, "He got stoned," we are not sure if it means someone threw stones at him or if he is out of his head due to drug abuse. All of these sentences show how important context is in determining the meaning of a word.

If I were to draw a small circle and ask you what it was, you probably would say, "A circle." If I were to draw another small circle next to the original circle, you would not be sure what the two circles meant. If I were to draw a nose under the two circles, the two circles begin to take on new meaning. If I were to draw a mouth under the nose, you are more certain that the original circle is an eye. Finally, if I put eyebrows over the circles, you are certain that the original circle is an eye.

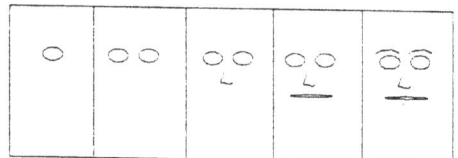

Words work in a similar way. They tend to mutually delimit the meaning of each other. Just as more and more context was added to the circle and it became obvious what it meant, so one becomes certain of the meaning of a word as it is delimited in meaning by the words around it. This is what context is.

Words have meaning only in relationship to the contexts in which they occur. Therefore, the translator must be familiar with both the context in which the ethnic-language words are used and the context in which the New Testament words are used. Only as one is familiar with the contexts in which words occur will one be able to use those words with their intended meaning.

4. Generic Meaning and Specific Meaning

Words may have either a general or specific meaning. That is, some words have a meaning that covers a large area of meaning (generic), while other words cover only a point of meaning (specific). It is important to learn this distinction in words, or one will sound rather foolish if he says, "Would you like a drink of liquid?" when he means specifically "water."

The word *furniture* is a generic word covering a number of pieces of furniture in a house. A more specific meaning of the word furniture would be "chair." One does not say, "Sit on this furniture" when he means, "Sit on this chair." An even more specific word would be "high chair," on which you would expect a baby to sit. An even more specific word would be "electric chair," which has only one specific use.

Paul says in Galatians 1:13 that he "persecuted the church of God, and wasted it." Here he uses the word *church* in a generic sense, meaning the church in general, not a specific church. We know he is using the word *church* in a generic sense in this verse because Acts 9:31 tells us that after Paul's conversion, "Then had the churches rest throughout all Judaea and Galilee and Samaria." Why did these churches in Judaea, Galilee, and Samaria (specific) have rest? Because Paul stopped persecuting the church (generic) after he was converted.

In Ephesians 5:23 when Paul says, "Christ is the head of the church," he is using the word *church* in the same way he used it in Galatians. He is using it in a generic sense, meaning that Christ is the head of the church as His institution to reach the world. A misunderstanding of the generic and specific usage of the word *church* has led to many mistaken notions about the doctrine of the church. The word *church* (generic) in "I persecuted the church" includes within it a reference to the specific "churches" in Judaea, Galilee, and Samaria in the same way that the word *furniture* (generic) includes within it the specific words *table*, *couch*, and *chair*.

Jesus said in Matthew 16:18, "I will build my church (generic)." In Revelation 1:13 Jesus is in the midst of the seven specific churches in Ephesus, Smyrna, Pergamos, Thyatira, Sardis, Philadelphia, and Laodicea. Evidently, the church (generic), which Jesus built, includes within it a reference to the churches (specific) of Revelation 1:13. When Jesus said He would build His church, He was using the generic term. When we see the Lord actually building His church, we see that He is not among a church (generic), but among seven specific churches. When Paul writes to the Ephesian church, "Christ also loved the church, and gave himself for it," (Ephesians 5:25) he is using the word *church* in the generic sense. Included within the generic word *church* (as an institution) is the meaning of specific churches in various locations.

The chart that follows illustrates generic and specific meaning:

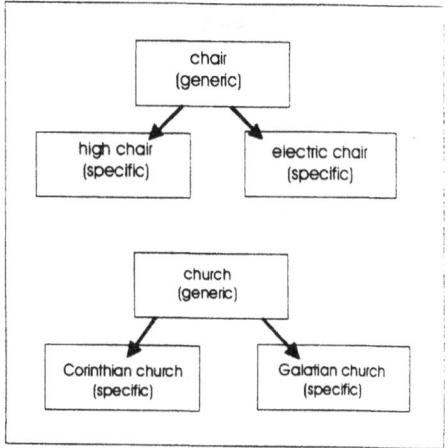

The translator must know whether the vocabulary words he uses have a generic or specific meaning. If he does not know this, he may make the mistake of saying, "Christ died for our thefts" (specific) instead of saying, "Christ died for our sins" (generic)."

I had assumed that salt would taste "salty" to the Sinasina people, but I found that the Sinasina people do not think of salt as salty in taste but "sweet." The specific word I expected was not the one that was correct. The more general word *sweet* was the one preferred by the people. The word *sweet* is used to describe the taste of food in general, including the taste of salt.

The specific-generic relationship of words makes it confusing for the missionary who would find the right word for the correct meaning. Conversely, this fact of meaning in terms of specific and generic can be helpful to him. In his search for words, a missionary may often begin by finding a general word, which will lead him to the more specific word he wants. One may be looking for the term "to blaspheme," so he begins with a generic term meaning "to criticize." Then the discussion with the language teacher can lead to finding the term for criticizing by saying bad things about people. As the discussion progresses, one may find a term meaning "to criticize a person by saying bad things about his character." Now the discussion is getting more specific and closer to the meaning of the phrase *to blaspheme*. Finally, the translator should be able to find the specific meaning of "to blaspheme God's character" from the discussion that began with the generic term *to criticize*.

5. Idiomatic Meaning

Words that have a specialized meaning are called *idioms*. The normal referential usage of the words cannot be used to determine the meaning of idioms. Referential meaning is no longer valid in words that are idioms.

Paul says, in Philemon 7, "The bowels of the saints are refreshed by thee." In this sentence, the Greek word *splanchna* literally means "intestines," hence the translation, "the bowels." However, the Greek word *splanchna* is an idiomatic usage of the word. It is a Greek idiom meaning the seat of the emotions. It is similar to our English seat of the emotions, the heart. We say, "I love you with all my heart." The King James Version translators chose to preserve the Greek idiom in English, and therefore we have the translation, "the bowels of the saints."

Idioms are usually unique to the language using them and can seldom be carried over literally into another language without causing some problems. The Sinasina people say, "He steal eats," meaning "He commits adultery." This idiom, if carried over literally into English would sound strange to an English reader. In the same way, English idioms will sound strange if translated literally into another language.

6. Figurative Meaning

A word has a figurative meaning when the usual referential meaning does not apply in the context. In a figure of speech, the literal meaning is extended to mean something other than the literal meaning of the words.

The word *fox* usually refers to a small, wild dog-like animal. However, when Jesus said, in Luke 13:32, "Go ye, and tell that fox," meaning Herod, he was using figurative language meaning that Herod had some characteristic of a fox.

When the Bible says in Isaiah 53:6, "All we like sheep have gone astray," the comparison of who is being compared to what is stated, namely, "People are like sheep that go astray." This is a figurative reference to people going astray from God like sheep go astray from the shepherd.

As idioms are usually unique to a language, so are figures of speech. The word *fox* may mean "sly and deceptive" to the English speaker, but slyness and deceptiveness may be used of rabbits or snakes in other cultures. The translator will need to know if the word he uses is a figure of speech or if it should be taken literally. He must know this in both the language of the New Testament and the language of the people. If one finds a figure of speech in the New Testament, he must find the nearest formal equivalent meaning of that figure of speech in the other language.

One must not only be able to recognize a figure of speech, but one must be able to state how the two things being compared are alike. When Jesus said, "I am the door," to what characteristic of a door was Jesus comparing Himself? How is He like a door? Usually there is only one characteristic of comparison being made. Jesus is saying that He is like a door in the sense that a door is the entrance by which one gains access to a sheepfold. Similarly, Jesus is the only way people can find access to God and heaven.

7. Grammatical Meaning

Word order is itself a kind of meaning. In English, the order of the sentence "John hit Bill" is structured meaning. The word order is a structure that means "John" is the subject because his name comes first in the sentence. The structure of this sentence also tells us that "Bill" is the object or receiver of the action of the verb "hit." The order of the words is the signal that indicates who hit whom. If we change the order of the words to "Bill hit John," the meaning is changed.

We also say, "Did you go?" and "You did go." The position the words take in a sentence make the difference in the meaning of that sentence. The meaning results from the relationships that exist between the words. Notice how the same word order can have different meanings depending upon how the words are related:

The teacher said, "The student is stupid."

"The teacher," said the student, "is stupid."

What is that in the road ahead?

What is that in the road? A head?

Not only must the translator know the usage of words, with their referential and connotative meanings, he must also know how words are related grammatically. This is true both for the English text from which one translates and the language into which one translates.

Homework

1. Choose one of the words below for a word study. Look up every reference to the word in the New Testament. Write at least one full page listing the various meanings of the word as it was translated in various contexts. The words to choose from are:

Grace

Spirit

Flesh

Sin

If you wish to study a different word, please check with your instructor before doing so. Husbands and wives must choose a different word from that chosen by their spouse.

2. Should a missionary attempt some translation work after living among a people and studying their language and culture for only one year? If you think one should, explain why. If you think one should not, explain why.

The second grade girl came home from school and said to her mother, "What is sex?" For the next half an hour, her mother explained about the birds and the bees. The little girl showed her mother a school registration card and said, "But how can I get all of that in this little square?"

Chapter 15

Semantics: Componential Analysis

There are four basic components of referential meaning. These components provide a useful tool for analyzing the referential meaning of Bible verses. This method of biblical exegesis is called componential analysis. It uses the four basic components of referential meaning (things, events, abstracts, and relationals) to analyze the referential meaning of any sentence in any language. These four components are universal to all languages.

1. Things

This component of meaning refers to persons or objects such as a dog, a house, a man, water, spirit, God, a stick, and so on. Anything that is a material or non-material reality is considered a thing. Things are the participators in events. They are the initiators or receivers of actions.

2. Events

This component of meaning refers to actions, processes, and happenings. It is what things do, such as run, jump, kill, speak, appear, grow, die, melt, freeze, and so on. An "event" is some action or process.

3. Abstracts

This component of meaning refers to the qualities, quantities, and degrees that describe things, events such as red, quickly, two, many, often, and slow.

4. Relationals

This component of meaning refers to relationships that exist between the other components of meaning such as to, between, under, in, at, around, and among.

Let us review the four components of meaning. They are things, events, abstracts, and relationals. A thing is the component of meaning that is filled by words such as "house," "persons," "stone," or any real object in the material or non-material world. For our purposes, all object-like words will be labeled "T" to indicate that it is a "Thing."

The second component of meaning is that of events. Event words are actions, such as running, walking, hitting, going, talking and such processes as melting, rotting, aging, dying and so on. Event words refer to what is done by Things. That which is done by someone or something is an event. It is an action or process that Things do. We will call all action-like words Events, even words that may be nouns in English. Such a noun word as "carpenter" is in its basic components of referential meaning an Event that someone does. A carpenter is someone who makes things of wood. Any word, which, in reality, is an action or process, will be considered an Event word. Event words will be labeled "E" for Events.

The third component of meaning is that of Abstracts. Abstracts are descriptions of Things and Events. A ball, may be described as a *red* ball. The word *red* is an abstraction. There is no physical quality that can be handled called redness, but the color is a reality and can be referred to with an Abstract word. Abstracts can be seen and described but not held in the hand like Things can be. Words like red, blue, small, strong, quick and slow are Abstracts. They describe the quality of a Thing or an Event in sentences like, "It is a *blue* house" or "His response was quick." Abstracts modify or describe how things look or how an event is done. For our purposes, all words that describe something will be labeled "A" for Abstracts.

The fourth component of meaning is that of Relationals. Relational words show relationships between Events and Things. One may say, "The ball is *in* the house." The word *in* expresses a relationship between the ball and the house. The ball is *in* the house. Words like "in," "of," and "to," all express a component of meaning called Relational words. They indicate relationships between Things and Events. For our purposes, we will label all Relational words "R" for Relationals.

How to Decide What Label a Word Should be Given

As one looks at a sentence in the New Testament, he must first decide which category each word in the sentence fits into. One must decide whether each word is, in context, a Thing, an Event, an Abstraction, or a Relational word. The context in which the word is used will be the determining factor. If we were trying to decide what label should be place under the word *stone*, we would look first at the context in which the word occurs. If we read. "He picked up a stone on the ground," we know that in this context the word "stone" is a Thing. We would put a "T" under that word. If we read the sentence. "They will stone him," we know that the word "stone" is an Event. If we read. "He is stone deaf," we know that the word "stone" is an Abstract that describes the degree of deafness. If we read, "They stoned him beside the house," the word "beside" shows the relationship between the subjects and where they were when they stoned the person. The word "beside" is a Relational word indicating where the event took place.

By using these four components of referential meaning, we can analyze the referential meaning of any verse in the Bible. Because one of the major goals of the translator is to determine the meaning of the words in the Bible, this tool of componential analysis is of great value to the translator. It will not be necessary to do a componential analysis of every verse in the New Testament. It will help primarily in the more complex verses of the Bible.

What is the Meaning of the Text?

After learning much of the language and culture of the people, the greatest problem to be overcome by the translator is this: What do the words. phrases, and sentences of the Bible mean? Very often translators assume they know what a verse means when in fact they do not know the meaning intended by the author. The meaning of the biblical text is often not fully understood by those who read it some two thousand years removed from the culture and historical context in which it was written. Nevertheless, the meaning of the text as was intended by the original author must first be clearly understood by the translator if he is to translate it accurately.

After that, he must decide what words in the ethnic language are the nearest formal equivalent to the original words that were used by the author. Once the meaning of a verse has become clear in the translator's mind, he can explain the meaning of the verse to his native-speaking language helper, who can then give him an approximate translation of the meaning in his own language. I say, "approximate" because the translator's first attempt at explaining the meaning of a verse to his translation helper will itself be faulty. Consequently, the translation helper's attempt to put the meaning into his language will also be faulty. By revising each earlier attempt, a more exact formal equivalent of the original meaning intended by the author can be achieved. However, if the translator is not clear in his own mind about the meaning of the verse, he will only convey his own confusion to the translation helper. The translation helper will not be able to offer an equivalent meaning because he does not know what meaning the translator wants him to express for the verse under consideration. The primary responsibility of the missionary translator is to explain to the translation helper what the words, phrases, and sentences of the Bible mean. Once the translation helper understands the meaning of the verse, he usually has little difficulty translating the meaning into his own language.

I learned the above lesson the hard way. While working with my translation helper, Milan, I was not clear in my own mind as to the meaning of a certain verse. I had assumed that I knew what the verse meant, but upon attempting to explain the meaning of the verse to Milan, I became confused in my explanation of it. I became agitated with him and he with me. We were both struggling to come up with a rendering of the verse, but neither one of us was sure what we wanted to say in the Sinasina language. Finally, Milan said disgustedly, "You just tell me what the verse means, and I'll tell you how to say it in the Sinasina language!" I told him to take a break and I began reading a commentary or two, analyzing the referential meaning of the verse, looking up the meaning of a word or two, and checking to see how the verse had been translated in some other languages. After a while it became clear in my own mind what the meaning of the verse was. Upon explaining this meaning to Milan he said, "That's not heavy (difficult). We say that like this," and he proceeded to give me a very good translation of the verse.

Our first goal in Bible translation, after learning the language and culture of the people, is to decide what the verses of Scripture mean. We must study either the Greek text or the English text to *decide* what the meaning of a verse is.

Often, the translator will not be absolutely certain what the exact meaning of a verse is. Even when one is not completely sure of the meaning of a verse, one must *decide* what the meaning is before one can explain it to his translation helper.

One must use every means available to find out the meaning of the text as was intended by the author. One may analyze the referential meaning of the text. One may read commentaries on the text and consult dictionaries, lexicons, and other translations of the New Testament. While studying verses that are the most difficult to understand, the translator will be desperate and use every procedure at his disposal to arrive at a clear understanding of the meaning of the verse or passage of Scripture. It is at this point that the componential analysis of a text of Scripture can be helpful.

Componential Analysis

The four basic components of meaning, which are universal to all languages, can be used as a tool to help the translator arrive at the referential meaning of a word, a phrase, a sentence, or a paragraph of Scripture.

To help us remember these four categories, we will use the acrostic T.E.A.R., or TEAR. This stands for Things, Events, Abstracts and Relational words. These four components of meaning cover all the referential meaning categories in any language and will be adequate to use in analyzing the referential meaning of any verse in the Bible. After we analyze the referential meaning of a verse, we can translate that verse into the ethnic language.

We read in 1 Corinthians 1:1, "Paul, called to be an apostle of Jesus Christ through the will of God." What does the phrase "the will of God" mean? How could I explain what it means to my translation helper?

First, let us ask ourselves which of the four components of meaning (TEAR) each of the words in this phrase represents. Is the first word, *the*, a Thing, an Event, an Abstract or a Relational word? The word *the* is an Abstract, because it describes the word *will*. It is not just any will; it is *the* will of God.

Next, what is the word *will*? It is an Event, because someone does it; namely, God. God wills to do something or wills that someone should do something.

The word *of* shows a relationship between the words *will* and *God*. Therefore, *of* is a Relational word.

The word *God* stands for a Person, so this component of meaning is a Thing.

We can reduce the above analysis to a procedure.

A Procedure for Analyzing Semantic Components

Three steps can be used to analyze the components of meaning in a verse of Scripture. The procedure involves doing at least three things.

1. Analyze the components of meaning in each word of the phrase or sentence and put the component's label under the word.

the   will   of   God

A   (T) E   R   T

Parentheses ( ) are used to enclose an implied Thing like this (T). The symbol (T) indicates an implied person who does the Event, in this case, God. An Event implies someone who performed it.

The arrow represents the relationship between *will* and *God*. God is the one who wills. God is doing the Event.

2. Make a statement of the Event or Events in each phrase or sentence.

God wills. (God wills that something should happen.)

3. Make a statement that expresses the relationships that exist between Things, Events, and Abstracts.

"Paul, called to be an apostle of Jesus Christ *because God willed it*."

Mark 1:4 "John did baptize in the wilderness, and preach the baptism of repentance."

What does "the baptism of repentance" mean?

1. Analyze the components of meaning.

The first word, *the,* is an Abstract because it describes the word *baptism*. It is *the* baptism.

The word *baptism* is an Event because it is something that someone does to someone.

There are two persons implied in the Event of baptism. One person (the subject) baptizes another person (the object). We indicate implied persons by placing the symbol (T) next to the event.

The parentheses around the T indicate that the (T) is implied by the Event. We indicate who did what to whom with an arrow. The (T) E (T) indicates that someone (T) baptized (E) someone (T).

The word *repentance* is also an Event. Someone repents or changes his mind. The word *of* shows a relationship between *baptism* and *repentance*.

However, the word *of* does not state what that relationship is. This must be discerned from the wider context of the verse.

2. Make a statement of each event.

Someone baptizes someone.

Someone repents.

Note: The order in which the events occurred is not stated in the verse. This also must be discerned from the wider context of the verse.

3. Make a statement of the meaning by stating the relationships between the Events and the Things.

The relationship between these two Events should be stated as "(John) baptized people after they repented." Alternatively, it could be stated as, "(John) baptized people when they repented." Since this "baptism of repentance" is what John preached, we could put the phrase in direct speech and state it as, "John preached, 'If you repent, I will baptize you.'" On the other hand, we could state this in direct speech as, John preached, "Repent! If you repent, I will baptize you."

From the wider context in Matthew 3:8, we know that John refused to baptize people who would not repent. So we could state the relationship between *baptize* and *repent* as a baptism that was administered on the condition that a person repented.

Mark is writing here using indirect speech to say what John said directly. John preached to people, telling them that they must repent. John told them if they repented, he would baptize them. Due to the Sinasina language structure, which does not use indirect quotes, this verse, when put into the Sinasina language would become a direct quote. John preached to people, "You must repent (turn your inside thoughts)! If you turn your inside thoughts, I will baptize you."

In Matthew 13:35 we read, "I will utter things which have been kept secret from the foundation of the world." What does the phrase "from the foundation of the world" mean?

1. Analyze the components of meaning.

the   foundation   of   the   world
A   (T) E (T)   R   A   T

2. Make a statement of the event.

Someone founded (or created) the world.

3. Make a statement of the meaning by stating the relationship between the components.

"I will utter things which have been kept secret from the time when God founded (or created) the world."

In Romans 15:33 we read, "Now the God of peace be with you all. Amen."

What does the phrase "the God of peace" mean?

1. Analyze the components of meaning.

the   God   of   peace
A   T   R   (T) E (T) ⇔ (T)

2. Make a statement of the event.

Someone makes peace between two persons who are antagonistic with each other.

Peace comes from the Greek word ειρεινε (*eireine*) and means: "to set at one again those forces that were opposed to each other." In this verse, God gives peace to people by causing people to be at peace with one another. Paul prays that God would cause them (Jew and Gentile) to be at peace with one another. See Acts 7:26, which says, "would have set them at one again, (make them at peace with each other). In Romans 15:33 the ones who are not at peace with each other are Jews and Gentiles). See Adam Clark where he explains the context of the book of Romans.[1]

3. Make a statement of the meaning by stating the relationship of the components.

"Now may God, who causes people to be at peace with one another, be with you all." (Paul implies by the expression "be with you all" that he prays that God, who causes people to be at peace with one another will be with the Jewish and Gentile Christians to cause them to be at peace one with the other).

2 Timothy 1:2 says, "Grace, mercy, and peace, from God the Father and Christ Jesus our Lord."

What do the words *our Lord* mean?

1. Analyze the components.

our   Lord
(T) A   (T) E (T)

2. State the event or events.

Someone rules us.

3. State the meaning by stating the relationship of the components.

"Grace, mercy, and peace, from God the Father and Christ Jesus, *the One who rules us*."

Ephesians 1:15 says, "Wherefore I also, after I heard of your faith in the Lord Jesus." What does the phrase "your faith in the Lord Jesus" mean?

1. Analyze the components.

```
...your     faith    in    the    Lord Jesus
 (T) A     (T)E(T)   R      A         T
```

Note: words that are underlined should be treated as a unit.

2. State the event or events.

You believed in the Lord Jesus.

3. State the meaning by stating the relationship of the components.

"Wherefore I also, after I heard about how you believed in the Lord Jesus."

In 1 Thessalonians 1:9 we read, "how ye turned to God from idols to serve the living and true God."

What does the phrase "to serve the living and true God" mean?

1. Analyze the components of meaning.

```
to serve   the   living  and  true   God
(T)E(T)     A      A           R      T
```

Note: words that are underlined should be treated as a unit.

2. State the events.

Someone serves someone.

God lives (is alive, not dead).

God is genuine (is real, not a false god).

3. State the meaning by stating the relationship of the components.

"How ye turned to God from idols to serve the God who is alive and who is genuinely God." (As opposed to idols that are not alive and not genuinely God)

1 Thessalonians 1:3 says, "Remembering without ceasing your work of faith."

What does the phrase "your work of faith" mean?

1. Analyze the components.

```
 your    work    of    faith
(T) A   (T)E(T)  R    (T)E(T)
```

2. State the events.

You work (for our Lord Jesus Christ)

You believe (in our Lord Jesus Christ)

3. State the meaning by stating the relationship of the events.

"Remembering without ceasing how you believed (in our Lord Jesus Christ) and as a result you work for him."

Romans 1:5 says, "By whom we have received grace and apostleship, for obedience to the faith among all nations."

What does the phrase "for obedience to the faith" mean?

1. Analyze the components.

```
for  obedience   to   the   faith
 R    (T)E(T)          R      T
```

2. State the events.

Someone must obey some person or some thing.

3. State the meaning by stating the relationship of the components.

"By whom we have received grace and apostleship to cause all nations (people in the nations) to obey the faith."

Note: *The faith* is defined by what is written in the Bible. Therefore, the Bible is the body of truth (*the faith*) that is to be obeyed.

1 Thessalonians 1:3 says, "Remembering without ceasing your work of faith, and labor of love, and patience of hope in our Lord Jesus Christ."

What does the phrase "patience of hope in our Lord Jesus Christ" mean?

1. Analyze the components.

patience of hope   in our Lord Jesus Christ
(T) E (T) R (T) E (T)   R A   T

2. State the event or events.

You wait patiently for someone.

You have confidence/faith in someone.

Because you confidently believe our Lord Jesus Christ will come again, you wait patiently for Him.

3. State the meaning by stating the relationship of the components.

"Remembering without ceasing your work of faith, and labor of love, and how that because of your faith in Jesus, you wait patiently for our Lord Jesus Christ (to return)."

This phrase could also mean, "Remembering without ceasing your work of faith, and labor of love, and how you are patient (in tribulation) because you eagerly expect (hope for) our Lord Jesus Christ (to come back again)."

1 Thessalonians 1:6 says, "having received the word in much affliction"

What does the phrase "having received the word in much affliction" mean?

1. Analyze components.

having received the word
(T) E (T)   A (T) E (T)

in much affliction
R A   (T) E (T)

2. State the events.

Someone preached the word to you.

You received (the word).

They afflicted you much.

3. State the meaning by stating the relationship of the components.

"Even though they afflicted you much, you received the word and became followers of us and of the Lord."

Mark 1:4 "John did baptize in the wilderness, and preach the baptism of repentance for the remission of sins."

1. Analyze components.

John   did baptize

T   (T) E (T)

in the wilderness and preach

R A T   R (T) E (T)

the baptism of repentance for the

A (T) E (T) R (T) E   R A

Remission of sins.

(T) E (T)   R (T) E

2. State the events.

People committed sins (implied).

John was in the wilderness (implied).

People went out to where John was (implied).

John preached to people.

Someone turned to God from sins they had committed. (repented)

God forgave people their sins.

John baptized people (who repented and were forgiven by God of their sins).

3. State the meaning of the verse by stating the relationship of the components.

Indirect quote: John was in the wilderness and preached that people (who had committed sins) should repent. John said that if they would repent, God would forgive their sins, and he (John) would baptize them.

Direct quote: John came to the wilderness and preached to people, saying, "Because you have sinned, you must repent. If you repent, God will forgive your sins, and I will baptize you."

Ephesians 1:7 says, "In whom we have redemption through his blood, the forgiveness of sins, according to the riches of his grace."

1. Analyze components.

In whom we have redemption through

R T T   (T) E (T)   R

his blood,

A (T) E (T)

the forgiveness of sins,

A (T) E (T) R (T) E

according to the riches of his grace.

R   A A R A (T) E (T)

2. State the events.

Someone committed sins.

Jesus shed his blood.

Jesus' blood redeems us.

God is very gracious to us.

God forgave us.

3. State the meaning.

Because Jesus shed His blood, we have been redeemed and Jesus very graciously forgives us of our sins.

Romans 1:5 "By whom we have received grace and apostleship, for obedience to the faith among all nations, for his name."

1. Analyze components.

By whom we have received grace

R   T   (T) E (T)   (T) E (T)

and apostleship,

R   (T) E (T)

for obedience   to the faith

R   (T) E (T)   R A T

among all nations, for   his   name.

R   A   T   R   A   T

2. State the events.

    God was gracious to us.

    God sent us.

    People obey the faith.

    This glorifies God's name.

3. State the meaning by stating the relationship of the components.

    The Lord (Jesus) was gracious to us and sent us. He sent us to cause all nations (all people in the nations) to obey the Bible (message of the Bible) so that His name (person) may be honored.

    Ephesians 2:8,9 "For by grace are ye saved through faith; and that not of yourselves: it is the gift of God: Not of works, lest any man should boast."

1. Analyze components.

For by grace are ye saved

R   R   (T) E (T)   (T) E (T

Through faith; and

R   (T) E R (T)   R

that   not of yourselves:

(T) E (T)   A   R   T

it is   the gift   of God:

(T) E (T) A   (T) E (T)   R   T

Not of works,

A   R (T) E

lest   any   man   should   boast.

A   A   T   (T) E

2. State the events.

    God was gracious to you.

    God saved you.

    You believed what God said.

    You did not save yourself.

    God saved you freely.

    You did not work to be saved.

    You should not boast.

3. **State the meaning by stating the relationship of the components.**

"Because God was gracious to you, He saved you when you believed. You did not save yourself. God's salvation was given to you freely. God did not save you because you did good works. Therefore, you should not boast (that you deserved to be saved because of your own good works)."

Analyze the Components of Meaning in a Single Word.

It is sometimes necessary to analyze the components of meaning in a single word.

The word *king* implies a person (thing), an event, and a receiver of the action of the event.

1. **Analyze the components of meaning involved in the word *king*.**

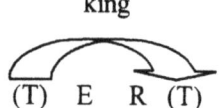

2. **State the event.**

Someone reigns over someone.

3. **State the meaning.**

A king is a man who reigns over people.

The word *centurion* has an implied person (thing), an event, an abstract, and a receiver of the action of the event.

1. **Analyze the components.**

2. **State the event.**

Someone commands 100 soldiers.

3. **State the meaning.**

One who is the commanding officer of 100 soldiers.

The word *shepherd* implies a person (thing), an event, and a receiver of the action of the event.

1. **Analyze the components.**

2. **State the event.**

Someone shepherds sheep.

3. **State the meaning.**

One who cares for sheep.

The word *apostle*

1. **Analyze the components.**

2. **State the event.**

Someone sends someone to someone to tell them a message

3. State the meaning.

One who is sent to someone to tell them a message.

The word *mediator*.

1. Analyze the components.

mediator

2. State the events.

Someone mediates between someone and God.

3. State the meaning.

Jesus mediates between God and Mankind.

The word *disciple*.

1. Analyze the components.

disciple

2. State the event.

Someone learns from someone.

3. State the meaning.

One who learns from what someone says and does.

The word *sinner* is similar to the above. It contains the components of a person (thing) and an event. A person who sins is a sinner. (T) E

The word *sanctify* implies a thing-event-thing-abstract relationship. Namely, God (thing) declares or causes (event) a person (thing) to be holy (abstract).

The word *justify* implies a thing-event-thing-abstract relationship. Namely, God (thing) declares (event) a person (thing) to be righteous (abstract).

The word *Jesus* when it needs to be translated, instead of being used as a name, implies a thing-event-thing relationship. Namely, God (thing) saves (event) people (thing). The word *Jesus* could also be considered as a thing, event, thing, relational, abstract, and event relationship. Namely, God (thing) saves (event) people (thing) from (relational) their (abstract) sins (event).

Homework

1. Analyze the components of meaning in 1 Thessalonians 1:3. State the events and then state the meaning by stating the relationship between the components. Do not consult your notes until after you have first done this yourself. Then consult your notes and make any corrections necessary.

2. Analyze the components of meaning in the words that follow. State the events and the meaning of each word. Consult your notes afterward and correct where needed. The words to be analyzed are below.

repentance

mediator

apostle

"A critic on the sacred text should be Candid and learn'd, dispassionate and free; Free from the wayward bias bigots feel, From fancy's influence and intemperate zeal; For of all arts sagacious dupes invent, To cheat themselves and gain the world's assent, The worst is—Scripture warped from its intent."

--William Cowper

Chapter 16

Interpreting the Biblical Text

A componential analysis of every verse in the New Testament will not be necessary. However, an awareness of the components of meaning (Things, Events, Abstracts, and Relationals) will help the translator apply this method of verse analysis in an informal way as he translates.

Even though much of the New Testament will not require componential analysis, some verses will. Verses like Ephesians 1:7-12 and 2 Thessalonians 1:3-10 should be analyzed more carefully than some other passages.

In order to arrive at a clear understanding of verses like Ephesians 1:7-12, it may be necessary to write out a componential analysis of each verse and make statements of the event words and state the relationships which exist between the events. A componential analysis of the passage will enable the translator to break up long, complicated sentences into shorter, more manageable units. The translator can then manage these smaller units with less difficulty. If one were to take all the concepts found in Ephesians 1:7-12 and try to translate them all as a single unit there would be too many grammatical and lexical parts to control all at once. To attempt translating all these concepts at once becomes very difficult because of the large number of concepts and relationships that would need to be kept in mind all at the same time. It would be better to take the time to make a componential analysis of verses like these before beginning to translate them.

It may seem that a componential analysis would take a longer amount of time. However, what may appear to be a shortcut by not doing a componential analysis could end up taking far more time and result in a translation that is not as accurate as it could have been. It is often better to take the time necessary to sort out the components of meaning in a passage than it is to go into a translation session with only a vague idea about the meaning of a verse. This can end up taking a lot more time, with less fruitful results.

Helps for Interpreting the Bible

A second way to find out the meaning of a verse is to use the various Bible exegetical helps that are available. These helps will aid the translator as he works at determining the meaning of a given verse or passage. There are many translation aids available, but one must know what they are, where he can get them, and how to use them.

Some Available Helps

Even though one should be cautious about using corrupted Bible versions to get help on how to translate a particular verse, these other so-called "versions" of the Scripture may be of some help to a translator who is wondering about how he can express the meaning of a verse in another language. There are over two hundred "translations" and "versions" of the New Testament in the English language.

I am using the terms "translations" and "versions" loosely. Most of these are not translations at all. They are more like commentaries on the New Testament rather than valid translations. Other "versions" have been translated from corrupted texts and are invalid.

The King James Version is the only genuine version of the English Bible, but these other "versions" may be useful to the translator. It all depends on how well these other translations were done and from what text they were translated. One may at least use them to find out how other translators interpreted certain verses and how they attempted to solve certain translation problems. This can be helpful because it will give the translator some possible solutions to ways of translating a passage of Scripture, but they should be used with caution.

National Language Versions

Other translations are especially helpful if they are in either the national language of the country or in a language that is related to the language into which one is translating. If national translations are available, they may be of help to the translator because these translations are often based on grammatical structures that are common to the entire country. The Pidgin English translation of the New Testament in Papua New Guinea is representative of the general grammatical structures that prevail throughout the country. The Tagalog New Testament in the Philippines is based on a grammatical structure that has many features common to other languages in the country. These national-language versions may be helpful to give the translator possible renderings of a verse in his particular language situation.

However, one should be cautious about using these if they have been translated from the corrupted critical texts.

Eight Translations in One Volume

Some English "versions" are bound in one volume, which makes it unnecessary to carry around eight separate volumes. *The Eight-Translation New Testament* published by Tyndale House is such a volume. It contains the King James Version as the standard. It also has the Living Bible, which is more of a commentary, and Phillips, which is also another commentary. It also has the Revised Standard that follows the critical text, Today's English Version, which is not a version but more of a paraphrase, the New International Version that follows the critical text, the Jerusalem Bible, from Roman Catholics, and the New English Bible that is not used much anymore. All of these and many more are also available as part of the Online Bible computer software.[1]

There are other serious attempts to translate the New Testament into English. Some of these may be helpful but should be used with caution. James Moffat, William Beck, Charles B. Williams, Edgar Goodspeed, Francis Weymouth, and others have translated some of the more helpful "translations."

However, none of these "translations" should be used as the basis for a translation into another language. Some of the translators of these "versions" take too much liberty in expressing what they suppose the meaning of a verse to be. Many of these translations would lead a translator astray from the meaning of verses.

Such "translations" as the Living Bible and the Phillips Modern English

Version are of this character. They are highly untrustworthy. The Today's English Version, The New English Bible, and The Revised Standard Version are all from questionable sources since most of the people on their translation committees seriously questioned the verbal, plenary, infallible inspiration of the Bible. Many of them were modernistic, religious unbelievers. For this reason, these "versions" delete many words, phrases, and entire verses. They do so without even a footnote to let one know that the verses have been deleted.

The Revised Standard Version has a definite slant in the direction of modernistic, liberal leanings. (See Isaiah 7:14 for example) The New International Version is not based on the Textus Receptus and so is faulty because of deletions and the relegating of words of Scripture to footnotes. By so doing, this version creates a lack of confidence in the Word of God. The Jerusalem Bible has a Roman Catholic bias and is slanted toward the theological presuppositions of Catholicism.

One other volume with eight translations is helpful. It is called *The New Testament Octapla*, edited by Luther A. Weigle, and published by Thomas Nelson & Sons. It contains eight English versions of the New Testament in the Tyndale-King James tradition. It is essentially a history of how previous English translations contributed to the translation of the King James Version New Testament. It has verses from eight translations printed on large facing pages. The translations begin on the top left with verses from Tyndale's New Testament and then the Great Bible, the Geneva Bible, the Bishop's Bible, and then on the bottom row there are verses from the Rheims, the King James Version, the Revised Version and finally the Revised Standard Version.

The King James Version is the only translation that can be trusted as a basis for translating the Bible into other languages. It can be used as a reference point to find out what has been deleted in the other versions that follow the modernistic, liberal, critical text.

The Need for a Standard

The nearest formal equivalent of the King James Version may be found in Spanish, French, and other languages if these translations were made using the Textus Receptus as the basis for its translation. Most of the older versions in other languages were based on the Textus Receptus but not all of them. One should be careful to find out what was used as the basis for a translation before he considers it trustworthy. There is a need for a standard translation that can be used as the basis for translating the New Testament into other languages. The King James Version and the Textus Receptus provide that standard. If one goes by the standard set by the King James Version, he knows what the Bible says, but if he has several "versions" as his standard, he is never quite sure what God has said.

The standard for Bible translators is the King James Version. This is especially needful if one is to bolster the confidence of ethnic peoples in the Scriptures. They will eventually compare their New Testaments with the national-language version, which in many older versions was like the King James Version. If they find verses and words missing in their New Testaments, this will have a tendency to undermine confidence in the Bible. In addition, if the translation in the ethnic language is a radical departure from the more literal meaning of the national-language version it will cause a loss of confidence in their ethnic translation. Missing verses and radical interpretations will cause the ethnic peoples to think of their New Testaments as inferior to the national-language translation, and they may put it aside in favor of the national-language version even though they understand their own language best. This is especially true in some countries where the national language is looked upon by the ethnic peoples as being superior to their own language.

The Use of Bible Commentaries

Another helpful tool for the translator is that of reliable Bible commentaries written by doctrinally sound Bible teachers. Good Bible commentaries may be useful in several ways:

1. Commentaries give a summary of the historical context.

Someone has well said, "When the plain sense of Scripture makes common sense, seek no other sense, but take every word at its primary, literal meaning unless the facts of the immediate context clearly indicate otherwise." However, sometimes we do not understand what the "facts of the immediate context" are. Commentaries can help us understand what the immediate context of a book is. This context is crucial to a proper interpretation of the book.

For example, Second Corinthians is one of the most difficult books in the New Testament to interpret. Only a thorough understanding of the historical context in which the book was written will yield a satisfactory understanding of that book. When one realizes that the historical setting of Second Corinthians is that of Paul defending his authority as an apostle of Jesus Christ against the slander and character assassination of the Judaizers, one is helped in his understanding of some of the difficult verses in this book.

2. Commentaries show the majority opinion.

The majority opinion may sometimes be the wrong one. However, if doctrinally sound Bible commentators all interpret a verse in a certain way, it should at least make us cautious to follow our own radically different interpretation. The commentators usually have good reasons for choosing one interpretation above another. If we depart from this majority opinion, we should have some sound exegetical reasons for doing so. The commentaries may help balance us and keep us from radical interpretations that are extremely individualistic and probably wrong. In fact, when one makes a decision about the best interpretation of a verse, he should make such a decision based upon the fact that there are, at least, three reliable commentaries that agree with his interpretation.

3. Commentaries help one understand the meaning of verses.

Commentaries can help clear up some words or phrases that may be puzzling to us. If we have a clear understanding of a passage of Scripture in our own mind, this will make it easier for us to explain the meaning of the passage to our translation helper. The work of reading commentaries should be done before the work with the translation helper begins. This prevents him from sitting idly by while one sits and reads commentaries.

4. Commentaries should be used with caution.

People who are not doctrinally sound in the faith have written commentaries. William Barclay's commentaries are sold in many Christian bookstores, but he is a neo-orthodox modernist.[2]

Some commentators have a denominational bias. Lenski, a Lutheran commentator, is usually helpful in his explanations of the Greek grammar of a verse, but when verses touch on certain subjects, he always follows the Lutheran view. If one can ignore his Lutheranisms, Lenski's commentary on the New Testament can be helpful to translators. This is true also of other denominationally oriented writers. Each will adhere to their particular system of biblical interpretation. As long as one knows this, he may separate the wheat from the chaff in the commentaries. One should first study cross-references to related passages and gather information from these passages. Having studied the meaning in the Bible first, one may usually consult some commentaries with profitable results.

5. Commentaries do not always help with interpretation.

When commentators come to verses that are difficult to interpret, many of them say nothing about such passages. What does one do when he comes to verses that are difficult to understand and the commentaries do not help? He should do what he should have done in the first place. He should first pray for guidance from the Author, and then study other Bible references related to the difficult passage. One should seek the mind of God in prayer and study other related verses of Scripture. After that, he may seek help from commentaries, "versions," dictionaries, lexicons, and Bible encyclopedias.

It is also a good thing to consult other people. The translator should ask his co-workers how they understand the verse. If possible, he should ask his pastor how he understands it. All of these pursuits will help shed some light on the Scripture passage under consideration.

If possible, the translator should work closely with a Bible translation consultant. This is especially helpful for beginning translators. The consultant can help get the translator started on the right track and teach him some principles that will help him do a better job. The translator who translates his first chapter should have it checked by a Bible translation consultant. If there is no consultant available, one can ask his co-workers or other missionary friends to check his work.

Books on Translation Principles

Several books about Bible translating are helpful to translators. Although some of the material in the books is questionable, they may be read with some profit. Such books as Eugene Nida's book *Bible Translating* and *Translating the Word of God* by J. Beekman and J. Callow have some helpful material in them. Nida has also written books entitled *The Theory and Practice of Translation* and *Toward a Science of Translating*. Mildred Larson has also written a book called *Meaning-Based Translation*. However, not all of these authors are Textus Receptus oriented. Some of them advocate the dynamic equivalence view of translation and some are non-sectarian (ecumenical). Their books should be read with discernment. Nevertheless, they have some helpful material.

There are some periodicals on translation. *The Bible Translator* is available free to translators from the United Bible Society. This publication has articles of interest to Bible translators. *Notes on Translation* are available from the Summer Institute of Linguistics. These are a collection of notes on problem areas of Bible translating and may have help on a problem a translator may be facing. The back issues seem to be more helpful than the newer ones.

Some commentaries are available to translators from the United Bible Society. They also have books such as *A Translator's Handbook on Mark*. Handbooks for Luke, Acts, and other books of the New Testament may be loaned to Bible translators who request them. The Summer Institute of Linguistics has some commentary compilations on various books of the New Testament. These compilations use several commentaries on a particular book. The most pertinent material relevant to translation is taken out of each commentary and put in the compilation. These compilations may not be available to non-S.I.L. members.

Some commentaries that are helpful to translators have been written by the following authors: Albert Barnes, A. T. Robertson, Matthew Henry, C. J. Ellicott, Plummer, Alford, Lightfoot, Clark, Lenski, Lange, Jamieson-Fausset & Brown, Conybeare and Howson, Edersheim, and others.

A devotional-type commentary is not much help to translators. Bible translators need to know about the grammatical structure of sentences and the meanings of words used in biblical context. Commentaries that allegorize and spiritualize the text are of very little help to a translator.

Dictionaries and Lexicons

The *Expository Dictionary of New Testament Words* by W. E. Vine is one of the most helpful dictionaries for Bible translators. The *Westminster Bible Dictionary* is thorough and helps when facts need to be known about biblical subjects. *The International Standard Bible Encyclopedia* is also helpful on biblical subjects, but the authors sometimes take a liberal view. This is especially true of the newer edition.

The best lexicon on the meaning of words in the Greek New Testament is that of Joseph Thayer. It is called *A Greek-English Lexicon of the New Testament*. The *Englishman's Greek New Testament* lists every occurrence of every word in the New Testament and lists beside it how it was translated into English in every verse. This is especially helpful for studying the meaning of New Testament words.

The *Analytical Greek New Testament* is also helpful. It lists the grammatical structure of every word of the Greek New Testament as well as the meanings of the words.

Back Translations of Other Languages

For purposes of checking through a translation, a back translation of the ethnic language is often made. These back translations can be a great help. One can read them to see how other translators translated certain verses in other languages. This is especially true if the back translation is from a language that is related to the language in which one is translating. Any such translation will usually be similar to the one needed in a related language. It will let the translator see some possible ways he might translate the verse in the language in which he is translating. However, such back translations should not be followed rigidly, for each language is unique. A solution that was helpful in a related language may not be the right one for a similar language.

Propositional Outlines

Some translators have attempted to outline the components of meaning in verses and state the relationships that exist between them. These are helpful in direct proportion to how well they were done. They can be helpful at times but should not be followed without doing one's own research.

Here is a propositional outline of Colossians 1:1-3:

Verse 1:

Paul = I am Paul

an apostle = who is an apostle

of Jesus Christ = who was sent by Jesus Christ

by the will of God = because God willed it (that I should be an apostle)

and Timotheus = (I, Paul) am accompanied by Timothy

our brother = who is our brother (Christian brother)

Verse 2:

To the saints = (we write) to you saints

and faithful brethren = who are obedient brothers (Christian)

in Christ = who are united to Christ

which are at Colosse = who live in Colosse (city/town)

Grace be unto you = may God give you grace (strength)

and peace = may God give you peace (among yourselves)

from God our Father = God is our Father

and the Lord Jesus Christ = the Lord Jesus Christ is God

Such a propositional outline need only be done when a passage of Scripture is complex and difficult to translate. In this case, it would pay to work through the passage propositionally before trying to translate it. It could save you a lot of wasted time and make your translation a better one. This is similar to componential analysis but is a little different.

Several books of the New Testament have been propositionally outlined by the Summer Institute of Linguistics. Some are more helpful than others, depending on how carefully and accurately they were done.

Some Other Helps

There are some other helps available from the United Bible Society. They are listed on the back inside cover of the periodical *The Bible Translator*. These helps are available free of charge to those engaged in Bible translation. Some of the helps listed there are: *Fauna and Flora of the Bible, Section Headings for the New Testament* and others.

The Trinitarian Bible Society

This Bible society is a strong supporter of the King James Version and the Textus Receptus. The growing disillusionment over the United Bible Societies' ecumenical relationships and rejection of the Textus Receptus has led to the founding of The Trinitarian Bible Society. This group is based in England but has branches in the United States and Canada.[3] They publish Bibles in various languages and have notes on books of the Bible to help Bible translators.

The Trinitarian Bible Society is Textus Receptus oriented and can be relied upon for a consistently sound view of Scripture with no entangling ecumenical alliances. There are other Bible translation groups such as the American Bible Society, the British and Foreign Bible Society and the Summer Institute of Linguistics (known in the USA as Wycliffe Bible Translators and G.I.A.L., Graduate Institute of Applied Linguistics). All of these are either New Evangelical, ecumenical or both. Any Bible translator who undertakes work with these groups should do so with caution. They will influence a translator away from a Textus Receptus orientation and toward an ecumenical Bible.

The Bearing Precious Seed Ministry.

Dr. D. M. Fraser initiated this Scripture distribution agency. Several Independent Baptist churches have continued the work of Bearing Precious Seed. These churches can be relied upon as faithful to the Textus Receptus text and Independent Baptist doctrinal position. Different phases of the Bearing Precious Seed work are carried on in several local Baptist churches across the country. It assists missionaries by raising funds for printing Bibles in various languages of the world. Many of these Baptist churches have printing presses and turn out a great volume of first-class material.

This work is having an impact by distributing the Bible in many of the national languages of the world. B.P.S. also sees the need for Scripture for the thousands of Bibleless ethnic languages. Recently the First Baptist Church of Milford, Ohio, dedicated a million-dollar printing press for the work of B.P.S at this church. They have plans for a printing press in India as well.

The Baptist Bible Translators Institute

Baptist Bible Translators Institute is an Independent Baptist school of missions. The Central Baptist Church of Bowie, Texas sponsors it. Dr. George Anderson founded B.B.T.I. in 1973. The current Executive Director of B.B.T.I. is Dr. Charles V. Turner.

Baptist Bible Translators Institute is a sister organization to the Bearing Precious Seed work, since both works originated out of Independent Baptist churches in the Dallas-Fort Worth area. Each group is a separate organization from the other but cooperates closely because of its common heritage and convictions.

Baptist Bible Translators Institute is a Textus Receptus, King James Version-oriented, Independent Baptist organization. B.B.T.I. is not a mission board but supports the work of Independent Baptist churches and mission boards who send out their own missionaries.

Baptist Bible Translators Institute is primarily a missionary training ministry. B.B.T.I. provides linguistic and cross-cultural missionary training for Independent Baptist missionaries going into any country, any language, and any culture in the world.

No matter where a missionary may be going, he would be well advised to take the linguistic training offered by Baptist Bible Translators Institute. This training will greatly aid missionaries in their language learning, Bible translating, preaching in a foreign language, and understanding the customs and culture of people in any foreign land. No Independent Baptist church should be so cruel as to send out their missionary to a land of a hard language and a strange culture without giving them the opportunity to take the training offered at Baptist Bible Translators Institute. Missionaries trained at B.B.T.I. will be thoroughly equipped to learn languages, reduce them to writing, translate Scriptures, preach and teach in the native language, and establish Independent Baptist churches.

Over 3,000 ethnic languages have no translation of God's Word. If they are to have the Bible in their languages, someone must go to them, learn their languages, and translate the Bible into them. Baptist Bible Translators Institute exists for training Independent Baptist missionaries who will become Baptist church-planting Bible translators. For this reason, Baptist Bible Translators Institute provides training in Linguistics, Language Learning, Ethnology, Literacy Teaching, and Bible Translation principles. B.B.T.I. fills an important gap. If more Bible translators are not trained, Bible distributors will be printing and distributing the Scriptures in only a few languages. This will be of little help to over a billion people in 3,000 Bibleless language groups. If you would like to help Baptist Bible Translators Institute in some way or receive a Catalog of Courses, please write or call us.[4]

These instructions were found on an air conditioner in Japan: Cooles and heats. If you want just condition of warm in your room, please control yourself.

Chapter 17

Problem Areas in Translation

Many translation problems are common to all Bible translators. If one is familiar with these problems and how other translators have solved them, it will help him avoid some mistakes. His work as a translator will be easier, more efficient, and of a better quality.

Literal Translation

It would be a lot simpler if one could always translate literally. However, it is not always possible to translate literally what a Bible verse says and still be faithful to the meaning intended by the author. Most people tend to translate too literally. This comes from a sincere desire to be faithful to what the Scripture says. However, this is a misconception. No faithful translation of Scripture is a completely literal one.

A Bible translator is under a constant tension between translating too literally and translating too freely. If he translates too literally, readers may not understand the meaning as intended. If the translates too freely, the readers may understand the meaning but the meaning may not be the one intended by the author. How are we to solve this problem?

First, one must accept the fact that there is no such thing as a completely literal translation. A completely literal translation would not make sense. For example, if Ephesians 2:8 were translated literally from the Greek New Testament, it would read like this: "The for grace by you are saved through the faith and this not from yourselves. God the gift." On the other hand, here is an example of a too-free translation of Ephesians 2:8: "Because of his kindness you have been saved through trusting Christ. And even trusting is not of yourselves. It too is a gift from God." This translation comes from The Living Bible. At least ten words in this translation were added to the Greek text from which it was "translated." The added words do not convey the intended meaning of the original author. The two extremes of too literal or too free could be illustrated like this:

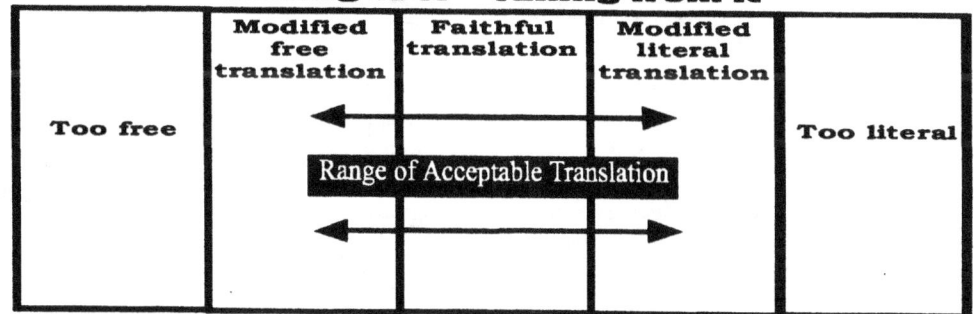

Word Matching Is Not Translating

Most Bible translators have a tendency to simply match a word in the Bible with a word in the target language. In many instances, it is not possible to match word-for-word equivalents between two languages. For example, in English we say, "I am hungry." To say the same thing in the Sinasina language takes only two words, "Kwa golue." The two sentences are not only different in the number of words but are quite different in meaning. The Sinasina word *kwa* means "sweet potato." The other Sinasina word, *golue* means "I am dying." Literally, the Sinasina sentence means, "Sweet potato, I am dying." The number of words in English does not match the number of words in Sinasina. The word meanings in Sinasina are quite different from the word meanings in English but the Sinasina sentence, *Kwa golue* is the nearest formal equivalent of the English sentence, "I am hungry."

Grammatical Matching Is Not Translating

Different languages have different grammatical systems for constructing sentences. For example, the English language has only one word for "my" (first-person possessive). We may say, "It is my shirt" or "It is my apple." However, it is not possible for the people of Woodlark Island to use a single word for "my." A Woodlark Islander must choose one of three different words for "my." One form of "my" means "My (object for eating)"; another form means "My (object intimately related to me)"; and yet another form means "My (object distantly related to me)." The Woodlark language requires one to decide if the object of possession is intimately related, distantly related, or an object for eating.

In addition, one must learn what objects the Woodlark people consider as distantly related, intimately related, or objects for eating. If a Bible translator were not aware of these distinctions, he could unknowingly choose the form of "my" meaning "my object for eating" when he was referring to his shirt. This would probably provoke some laughter from the Woodlark Island people.

In Mark 8:17, we read that Jesus asked His disciples, "Have ye your heart yet hardened?" This phrase was translated into the Pidgin English New Testament as, *Ating bel bilong yupela i pas a*? This translates into English as, "I think that perhaps your stomach is blocked?" The word for *heart* in Pidgin English is *bel*, which means "Stomach." When I asked my translation helper to say this Pidgin sentence in the Sinasina language, he replied, *Den miriye si gii dimio?* When I asked what that meant, he said, "It means that Jesus was asking the disciples if they were constipated." The literal translation was nowhere near the meaning intended by the Lord's words.

A friend of mine was trying to translate Genesis 39:9 where Joseph says to Potiphar's wife, "How then can I do this great wickedness, and sin against God?" His translation helper translated the word "how" literally by matching the English word *how* with the Sinasina word for "how." However, the Sinasina word for "how" means "by what means." The literal meaning of the verse in the Sinasina language meant, "Could you suggest to me a means by which I could do this great wickedness, and sin against God?" This meant that Joseph was asking Potiphar's wife to suggest a way he could commit adultery with her without being caught! Literal translating can mean the opposite of what was intended.

General Motors has always boasted of how their auto bodies are made by Fisher. "Body by Fisher" was their boast in English. However, their sales in Belgium were hindered by the translation of the words: "Body by Fisher." It meant, literally, in Flemish, "Corpse by Fisher."

Chevrolet tried to sell a car in Spanish-speaking countries with the name "Nova." Not many people wanted a car named "Nova," which in Spanish literally means, "It will not go."

The Parker Pen Company advertised in Spanish what they thought meant, "Avoid embarrassment (from ink leaking out of the pen). Use Parker Pens!" However, the Spanish word chosen for "embarrassment" was "embarazar," which literally means, "to become pregnant." The advertisement literally read, "Avoid becoming pregnant. Use Parker Pens!" The public thought that Parker Pens must be a kind of contraceptive.

The order in which events occur can be a problem if translated literally into another language. The Sinasina language usually requires that events be stated in the order in which they occur. A literal translation of Luke 10:34 into Sinasina would give a false impression as to what actually happened. This verse says that the Good Samaritan "bound up his wounds, pouring in oil and wine." If this verse were translated literally into Sinasina, it would mean that the Samaritan first bandaged the wounds and then poured oil and wine onto the bandages.

Figures of Speech Must Not Be Translated Literally

Figures of speech are usually unique to the language using them and cannot, therefore, be matched word for word from language to language. For example, a foreign journalist translated the American expression, "There will be a hot time in the old town tonight" as; "It will be excessively warm tonight in the older section of town." In a similar way a literal translation of Matthew 23:14, "Ye devour widows' houses," would mean in many languages, "You hungrily eat the houses of widows." The reader would think that the houses must have been made of gingerbread or some other edible substance.

Abstract Words

Another problem for the translator is finding the nearest formal equivalent meaning in the ethnic language for such abstract Bible words as *peace*, *hope*, *glory*, *love*, and *repentance*. The English language permits us to change verbs into abstract nouns. Not every language permits this. For example, "He repented" (an English verb phrase) can become the English noun *repentance*. "He forgives" can become *forgiveness*. "He baptized" can become *baptism*.

Many languages have a different structure from that of English. Instead of using abstract nouns, these languages do the opposite. That which is an abstract noun in English must become a verb phrase in these languages. For example, *baptism* must be changed into a verb phrase "He baptized him." The word *repentance* must be expressed by the verb phrase "He turned from sin to God."

In the Sinasina language, many English nouns are expressed by a verb phrase. The English word *friend* becomes "He with whom I share food." The English word *teacher* becomes "The one who strikes learning to them." The word *carpenter* becomes "The man who habitually builds houses."

English grammar allows one to change an event (verb) into a noun (person, place, or thing). In English, "God saves people" can become the noun "salvation." "God declares people to be righteous" can be changed into "justification." "God pays the price and sets people free" can become "redemption."

An abstract English noun that stands for an event (verb phrase) can be seen in 1 Corinthians 13:4, "Charity envieth not." In this verse, the word "charity" is an abstract noun that stands for the event, "Someone loves someone." Neither the one who loves nor the one who is loved is expressed in the word "charity." To translate this word into many languages it is necessary to change "charity" into the event it represents and supply the subject and object of the verb. Therefore, "Charity envieth not" would become "A person who loves people, is not jealous of them."

Another example would be Matthew 26:66, "He is guilty of death." The word "death" is an abstract noun that represents an event that someone does; namely, *they die*. Therefore, "He is guilty of death" becomes "He is guilty and should be killed."

Another example is Acts 4:12, "Neither is there salvation in any other." The word *salvation* is an abstract noun that stands for an event. The event is, "Someone saves someone." Therefore, we may state the event in Acts 4:12 as, "No one else can save people."

Another example is Matthew 5:10, "Blessed are they which are persecuted for righteousness' sake." The word *righteousness* is an abstract noun that stands for an event; namely, "Someone does that which is right." Therefore, we may state the event in Matthew 5:10 as "Blessed are those who are persecuted because they do that which is right."

If one refuses to make necessary grammatical structural changes, he will be guilty of taking away from the meaning of the Bible. Please notice the words *necessary grammatical structural changes*. Such changes are only made when it is necessary to preserve the meaning of the Scripture text. I do not advocate being a "Bible Corrector." Revelation 22:18,19 warns about adding to the text of Scripture, and taking away from it. We must neither add to God's words nor take away from them.

Homework

Find the abstract words in the following phrases and adjust them to the events they represent. Then restate the phrase with your adjustment. For example, James 1:15 says, "Sin bringeth forth death." The abstract words are *Sin* and *death*. *Sin* is a noun that can be changed to the verb phrase "Someone disobeys God's laws." *Death* is a noun that can be changed to the verb phrase "Someone dies." Restate James 1:15 as "Because people disobey God's laws, they must die."

Colossians 1:8, "declared unto us your love in the Spirit."

John 4:10, "If thou knewest the gift of God..."

John 3:19, "because their deeds were evil."

In Japan, "I am sorry" is an expression of good will even when the person offering the apology is not at fault. However, a Japanese tourist in America who says, "I am sorry" when in an auto accident is thought to be admitting guilt and is held liable for the accident.

Chapter 18

Genitive Structures

A genitive structure is a phrase in English made up of two words that are related to each other by the preposition *of*. For example, "the love of God." The preposition "of" tells us that there is a relationship between the two words "love" and "God," but it does not tell us what that relationship is. We do not know if the phrase *the love of God* means God's love for us or our love for God. This grammatical structure, called a genitive construction, is common in the New Testament and has many meanings. It is especially common in Paul's epistles, on the average of one time per verse. In the entire New Testament, it occurs about twice in every three verses.

Acts 21:8 "The house of Philip"

The word *of* indicates a relationship between the word "house" and the word "Philip." The relationship between the two words is that of possession. It is Philip's house. This is the possessive usage of the genitive structure.

Luke 1:27 "The house of David"

The word *of* indicates a relationship between the word *house* and the word *David*, but in this case, the relationship is not that of possession but that of kinship. It means those who are *related* to David by kinship; namely, David's descendants.

Romans 2:4 "The goodness of God"

In this case, the word *goodness* describes the word *God*. It means that God is one who does good things for people.

Matthew 23:28 "Full of hypocrisy"

The word *full* indicates the degree of the second word *hypocrisy*. It means, "very hypocritical."

Matthew 20:30 "Son of David"

The word *of* indicates a kinship relationship between the words *Son* and *David*. When Jesus was called the "Son of David," this was a way of saying that He was a descendant of David.

Matthew 15:31 "God of Israel"

The word *of* is used to indicate that God is Israel's God. Not in the sense of possession but in the sense that God has a unique relationship with the nation of Israel.

Matthew 1:1 "Bethlehem of Judea"

The word *of* relates the word *Bethlehem* to the word *Judea* to mean that Bethlehem is located in Judea province.

Luke 24:49 "The city of Jerusalem"

The word *of* relates the word *city* to the word *Jerusalem* to mean that the name of the city is Jerusalem.

Matthew 10:42 "A cup of cold water"

The word *of* relates the words *a cup* to the words *cold water* to mean that the cup contains cold water.

Luke 13:21 "Three measures of meal"

This means that the amount of the meal was three measures.

Mark 1:1 "Gospel of Jesus Christ"

This means that the Gospel is the history about Jesus Christ.

Revelation 12:1 "A crown of twelve stars"

This means that the crown consisted of twelve stars.

Acts 1:22 "The baptism of John"

The word *of* relates the word *baptism* to the word *John* to mean that John baptized people.

Matthew 12:31 "The blasphemy of the Spirit"

This means that a person slanders the character of the Spirit.

2 Thessalonians 2:10 "The love of the truth"

This means that "the truth" is the receiver of the event word *love*. It means, "They love the truth."

Ephesians 4:30 "Day of redemption"

This means that the word *day* is the time when God will redeem people.

Philippians 4:9 "God of peace"

This means that God causes people to have peace.

John 5:29 "The resurrection of damnation"

The word *of* relates the word *resurrection* to the word *damnation* to mean that there is a chronology of events. First, God will raise certain people from the dead and then He will condemn them to damnation.

1 Thessalonians 1:3 "Work of faith"

This means that because people have believed in Christ, they work for Him.

1 Corinthians 1:12 "I am of Paul"

The word *of* relates the words *I am* to the word *Paul* to mean, "I follow Paul."

Luke 4:34 "Jesus of Nazareth"

The word *of* relates the word *Jesus* to the word *Nazareth* to mean that Jesus was brought up in the city named Nazareth.

Acts 1:22 "A witness of his resurrection"

This means that a person will tell people that Jesus was truly raised from the dead.

Analyzing Genitive Structures

Genitive structures may also be analyzed using the four components of referential meaning; namely, Things, Events, Abstracts, and Relationals. In the same way that we would analyze the referential meaning of any other sentence or phrase, we can also do this with genitive structures.

For example: Galatians 3:2, "This only would I learn of you, Received ye the Spirit by the works of the law, or by the hearing of faith." What does the genitive structure "the hearing of faith" mean?

1. Analyze the components:

the hearing of faith
A   (T) E (T)   R   (T) E (T)

2. State the events:

Someone hears that which someone said.

Someone believes that which someone said.

3. State the relationship of the components to indicate the meaning of the verse:

"This only would I learn from you. Did you receive the Spirit by obeying the law and doing good works or by hearing the Gospel and believing it?

Homework

1. Read in *Bible Translating* by E. Nida, page 64, at 5.2, through page 70.

2. What is meant by "text material" in an ethnic language?

3. How many pages of text material should be gathered before a translator begins translation work?

4. What is the meaning of the genitive constructions in the verses below?

Mark 3:17 "The sons of thunder."

Revelation 1:1 "The revelation of Jesus Christ."

Hebrews 13:15 "The fruit of our lips."

An American missionary was flying on British Airways. As he walked to his seat, he spotted a cute little girl about 3 years old. He remarked to the girl's mother, "She's a cute little bugger." The mother was furious. In British English "little bugger" means, "little prostitute."

Chapter 19

Rhetorical Questions

A characteristic of Eastern Semitic culture is the use of rhetorical questions. An American asked a Jewish friend why it was that when he was asked a question he always replied with a question. His friend replied, "Why not?" Not all cultures use rhetorical questions, but in Bible times, people indicated many kinds of meaning with rhetorical questions. This is quite different from American culture where a question is primarily used to ask for information. An answer to the question is expected.

A rhetorical question is actually not a question at all. The one asking a rhetorical question is not asking for information. Instead, he is using the question to communicate information. By using a rhetorical question, he may want to ridicule, call attention to a point, or emphasize a fact.

When we read questions in the Bible, we do not hear the voice inflections of the speaker, so we do not always know whether the question is a real one or a rhetorical one.

The Sinasina people use rhetorical questions primarily to ridicule. They will say, "Are your ears plugged up?" This means, "You should listen, stupid!" In Genesis 39:9 the question Joseph asked Potiphar's wife is rhetorical, intended to express the horror of sinning against God. Joseph says, "How then can I do this great wickedness, and sin against God?" This is not a question asking for information. Joseph is speaking to Potiphar's wife, who is tempting him to commit adultery with her. He is saying, "I most certainly will not do such a great wickedness and sin against God!" If the translator does not realize this and translates this verse as a real question, it would mean in many languages that Joseph was asking Potiphar's wife for her suggestion on how they could get away with committing adultery together.

Matthew 18:12, which reads, "How think ye? If a man have an hundred sheep, and one of them be gone astray, doth he not leave the ninety and nine and goeth into the mountains, and seeketh that which is gone astray?" If this were translated as a literal question in many languages, it would mean just the opposite of what was intended. It would mean, "A man who had one hundred sheep and one of them got lost, he surely wouldn't leave the ninety-nine while he went to look for a single lost one, would he?" In this case, the question would be taken as ridiculing such a foolish idea. However, the question in the Bible was intended to show the reasonableness of leaving the ninety-nine to go and find the one lost sheep. It may be necessary to remove the rhetorical question and make it a statement of fact: "A man who has an hundred sheep, and one of them is gone astray, he will leave the ninety and nine and go into the mountains to find the one which has gone astray."

A Rhetorical Question or a Real Question?

There are two things we must consider when interpreting a question:

1. Is this a real question asking for information? If not, it may be a rhetorical question.

2. What is the purpose being served by this question? If it is used to indicate the speaker's attitude about certain actions, it may be a rhetorical question.

If someone other than the questioner answers a question, it is most likely a real question. However, if it remains unanswered, or if the questioner answers it himself, it is probably a rhetorical question. The context of each question will have to be carefully considered.

The Meaning of Rhetorical Questions

There are about 1,000 questions in the New Testament. These may be divided into two groups: questions asking for information and rhetorical questions. About 70 percent of the questions in the New Testament are rhetorical and as such are intended to indicate the following kinds of meaning:

1. An emphasis on the negative or positive aspect of a statement.

2. The certainty or uncertainty of a statement.

3. The speaker's evaluation of a situation, whether favorable or unfavorable.

4. A command or exhortation.

5. The introduction of a new subject or some aspect of a subject.

1. Emphasis

Rhetorical questions are used to indicate an emphasis on the negative or positive aspect of a statement. For example, Luke 12:14 reads, "Who made me a judge or divider over you?" By using the rhetorical question an emphasis is placed on the meaning, "No one made me a judge or divider over you!" In John 18:35 we read, "Pilate answered, 'Am I a Jew?'" This rhetorical question emphasizes the fact that Pilate is not a Jew. He used the question to ridicule Jesus, who was a Jew.

2. Certainty

Sometimes rhetorical questions are used to indicate certainty or uncertainty. For example, Luke 11:12 reads, "Or if he shall ask an egg, will he offer him a scorpion?" The rhetorical question here is intended to indicate the certainty of the fact that "He surely will not offer him a scorpion!" A similar example is found in 1 Corinthians 12:17, which says, "If the whole body were an eye, where were the hearing?" This rhetorical question is intended to indicate the certainty that there would be no hearing if the whole body were made up of only an eye. Matthew 6:30 says, "Shall he not much more clothe you?" This rhetorical question is intended to show the certainty that God would surely clothe you.

Matthew 26:55 says, "Are ye come out as against a thief with swords and staves for to take me?" This is a rhetorical question with the meaning of "You have come out to take me as you would a thief!" Mark 3:23 says, "How can Satan cast out Satan?" This is a rhetorical question which means "Satan certainly does not cast his own demons out!" Luke 16:11 says, "If therefore ye have not been faithful...who will commit to your trust the true riches?" This rhetorical question means, "If you have not been faithful, no one will commit the true riches to your trust!" Matthew 13:56 says, "Whence then hath this man all these things?" This rhetorical question means, "We are not sure from whom he learned all these things!" Matthew 6:31 says, "What shall we eat? or What shall we drink? or Wherewithal shall we be clothed?" These are rhetorical questions meaning, "We are uncertain about what we will eat, drink, or wear."

3. Evaluation

Rhetorical questions are often used to express an evaluation of a situation or an opinion about what should be done. Matthew 7:3 reads, "And why beholdest thou the mote that is in thy brother's eye, but considerest not the beam that is in thine own eye?" This is using a rhetorical question to say, "You should judge your own greater faults before you judge your brother's minor faults." Matthew 8:26 says, "Why are ye fearful?" This is a way of saying, "You should not be fearful." Mark 2:7 says, "Why doth this man thus speak blasphemies?" This is an evaluation meaning, "This man should not speak blasphemies!" Mark 14:4 says, "Why was this waste of the ointment made?" This is their evaluation, meaning, "This waste of ointment should not have been made."

4. Exhortation

Some rhetorical questions are used to indicate a command or exhortation. For example, Mark 14:6 says, "Why trouble ye her?" This is a way of saying, "Stop troubling her!" Romans 14:10 says, "Why dost thou set at nought thy brother?" This is a way of using a rhetorical question to say, "You should not set at nought your brother!"

5. Introduce a New Subject

Sometimes rhetorical questions are used to indicate the start of a new subject or to introduce some new aspect about the same subject. For example, Matthew 11:16 says, "But whereunto shall I liken this generation?" This is a way of saying, "I will tell you what this generation is like" (and then going on to say what it is like). Another example is Matthew 12:48 where Jesus says, "Who is my mother? And who are my brethren?" These rhetorical questions mean, "I will tell you who my mother is and who my brethren are." (Then he tells them who they are). John 13:12 reads, "Know ye what I have done to you?" This is a rhetorical question meaning, "I will tell you the meaning of what I have done to you." In Mark 13:2 Jesus says, "Seest thou these great buildings?" Jesus is using a rhetorical question to say, "I will tell you something about the great buildings you are seeing." In Matthew 11:7 Jesus says, "What went ye out into the wilderness to see?" (This was spoken about John the Baptist.) This rhetorical question means, "I will tell you about this person you went into the wilderness to see."

Other Uses of Rhetorical Questions

Rhetorical questions are often used to prohibit an action. We read in 1 Corinthians 6:16, "What? know ye not that he which is joined to an harlot is one body?" In this verse, the rhetorical question is used to condemn an action and prohibit it from taking place. Paul says in 1 Corinthians 3:5, "Who then is Paul, and who is Apollos, but ministers by whom ye believed?" Paul is using a rhetorical question to belittle and prohibit the factious attitude of putting one servant of God above another. In Matthew 3:14 we read, "But John forbade him, saying, I have need to be baptized of thee, and comest thou to me?" John is using a rhetorical question to show a polite disapproval but not an absolute refusal to do what the Lord wanted him to do. Mark 4:41 says "And they feared exceedingly, and said one to another, What manner of man is this, that even the wind and the sea obey him?" Here the rhetorical question is possibly used to show surprise and astonishment, but it could also be a real question.

Adjusting Rhetorical Questions

The translator must find out how rhetorical questions are used in the ethnic language. Some language groups do not use rhetorical questions at all. Others use them in ways different from those used in the New Testament. Rhetorical questions are a reflection of the culture.

Sometimes the speaker wishes to reduce the harshness of an action, as when John registered a polite disapproval of his baptizing Jesus. John said, "I have need to be baptized of thee and comest thou to me?" Because other cultures are different from biblical culture, they may use rhetorical questions in ways that are different from the ways used in the New Testament. We will need to know what the function of a question is in a particular verse, and we will need to know how this meaning can be translated into the ethnic language. If a question in the Bible is consistently misunderstood in an ethnic language where the people use rhetorical questions only to ridicule or emphasize the negative aspects of an action, some adjustment may be necessary.

There are at least three possible ways to adjust rhetorical questions to make them understood in the way intended.

1. Change the question into a statement.

2. Change negative questions to positive ones.

3. Supply an answer to the question.

1. Change the Question into a statement

In John 18:35 Pilate asks Jesus, "Am I a Jew?" If this question is repeatedly taken to mean that Pilate was not sure whether he was a Jew or not and therefore was asking Jesus if He knew, it might be necessary to change this to the statement, "I am not a Jew!" Matthew 5:13 says, "If the salt have lost his savour, wherewith shall it be salted?" This may need to be changed to read, "If salt has lost its savour, the savour cannot be restored." Matthew 5:46 says, "If you love them which love you, what reward have ye?" This may need to be changed to read, "If you love only those who love you, you will not be rewarded for that." Romans 3:9 says, "Are we (Jews) better than they?" This may need to be changed to read; "We (Jews) are no better than they are." Romans 6:15 says, "Shall we sin, because we are not under the law, but under grace?" This may need to be changed to read, "We should not sin just because we are not under the law, but under grace." Hebrews 1:5 says, "For unto which of the angels said he at any time, Thou art my Son?" This may need to be changed to read; "He has never said to any of the angels at any time, you are my Son."

2. Change Negative Questions to Positive

It says in John 7:19, "Did not Moses give you the law?" This question may need to be changed to read, "Moses gave you the law." Matthew 5:46 reads, "Do not even the publicans the same?" This question may need to be changed to read, "Even publicans do that." In Matthew 13:55 it says, "Is not this the carpenter's son?" This may need to be changed to read, "He is only the son of a carpenter."

3. Supply an Answer to the Question

In Romans 8:31 it says, "If God be for us, who can be against us?" We can supply the answer: "No one!"

In 2 Corinthians 6:15 it says, "And what concord hath Christ with Belial?" We can supply the answer: "None at all!"

In Mark 8:37 it says, "Or what shall a man give in exchange for his soul?" Because this verse is often taken to mean that a man can give *something* in exchange for his soul, an answer to the question may be given, "He can't give anything in exchange for his soul!"

Homework

1. Change the question in John 6:70 to its nearest formal equivalent statement.

2. Change the negative questions in Matthew 13:55 into positive statements.

3. Supply the answers to the questions in Romans 8:31.

During the Sunday school service at Easter, a pastor announced, "Mrs. Jones will now come up and lay an egg on the altar."

Chapter 20

Passive Grammatical Constructions

In many languages, there is no equivalent grammatical construction for an English sentence in the passive voice. These languages do not have the passive voice. All passives must be changed to active voice.

When the subject of a sentence is performing the action, as in "John is hitting the dog," the sentence is in the active voice. John, the subject of the sentence, is acting by hitting the dog, the object. There is a subject (John), a verb (is hitting), and a receiver of the action (the dog).

John   is hitting   the dog.

(subject) (verb) (object)

When the subject is the receiver of the action, as in "The dog is being hit by John," the sentence is in the passive voice. The dog, the subject of the sentence, is the receiver of the action of the verb *hit*. There is a subject (the dog), a verb (is being hit), and a receiver of the action (the dog).

The dog is being hit by John.

(subject) (verb) (agent)

Another example: "My father gave a watch to me." The subject is "father," the verb is "gave" and the object is "me." The subject (father) is acting, and the receiver of that action is "me." This sentence is in the active voice. This same sentence may be changed to the passive voice, "I was given a watch by my father." The subject is "I," and the verb is "was given." The receiver of the action of the verb (was given) is the subject (I).

Another Kind of Passive Voice

When there is no subject in a declarative sentence, it may be considered in the passive voice. For example, Mark 6:14 says, "John the Baptist was risen from the dead." At first glance, one would think that "John" is the subject of the sentence, but John did not raise himself from the dead. The One who raised John from the dead was God. Because the subject of the sentence is not stated, the sentence is in the passive voice. To change it to an active voice the sentence would need to have God as the subject of the sentence, as in "God raised John the Baptist from the dead."

Ephesians 1:13 reads "Ye were sealed with that Holy Spirit." This sentence has no subject (the one who did the sealing is not in the subject position). Therefore, the sentence is in the passive voice. To change the sentence to the active voice, the sentence would need a subject so it would read, "God sealed you with the Holy Spirit."

Mark 1:9 reads, "Jesus was baptized of John." Jesus is the subject and the receiver of the action of the verb *was baptized*. Therefore, this sentence is in the passive voice. To change it to the active voice, we must make "John" the subject and "Jesus" the receiver of the action of the verb. We would say, "John baptized Jesus."

Mark 2:5, says, "Thy sins be forgiven thee." This sentence is in the passive voice because there is no subject. We could change it to an active voice by supplying a subject. Jesus was speaking, therefore the sentence would read, "I forgive your sins."

John 19:20 reads, "The place where Jesus was crucified." This is in the passive voice because there is no subject. To change it into a sentence in the active voice we supply the subject by saying, "The place where they crucified Jesus."

In the sentence "I am tempted of God," (James 1:13,) the subject "I" is receiving the action of the verb "tempted." This verse is in the passive voice because the subject is being acted upon. To put it into the active voice we would need to say, "God is tempting me."

Only Passive Voice

On the other hand, some languages have only passive voice sentences and no active voice. In these languages, all active-voice sentences must be changed to passive.

Mark 13:5 says, "Take heed lest any man deceive you." This sentence is in the active voice. The words *any man* are the subject, the word *deceive* is the verb, and the word *you* is the object. In languages that only use the passive voice, this active-voice sentence would have to be changed to read, "Take heed lest you be deceived by some man."

Acts 1:6 says, "Lord, wilt thou at this time restore again the kingdom to Israel?" To change this to the passive voice we would say, "Lord, will the kingdom be restored to Israel at this time by you?"

Homework

1. Recast the following phrases into the active voice:

Mark 2:5, "Thy sins be forgiven thee."

Colossians 1:11, "Strengthened with all might."

Mark 1:14, "Now after that John was put in prison."

2. Study the following terms and concepts.

Translation: This occurs when the meaning of a message, which has been encoded by the words of one language, is communicated by the nearest formal equivalent words of another language. Compare translation to transliteration.

Encode: A message is encoded when a person's thoughts are put into words, either spoken or written. Messages can be encoded in other ways, but the speaking and writing of symbols are the most important to a Bible translator.

Decode: A message is decoded when one understands a message through hearing it, reading it, or in some way comprehending it. Messages can be decoded in other ways, but the hearing and reading of them are the most important to a Bible translator.

Source: The source of a message.

Receiver: The receiver of a message.

Source Language: The language in which the original message was encoded. In the case of Bible translation, this would be Hebrew and Greek.

Receiver Language: The language into which one is translating. (Sometimes called the "Target Language")

Semantics: The study of how word symbols acquire meaning.

Referential Meaning: The meaning of a word when it refers to an object in the physical world, an event that happens, an abstraction which can be seen by the eyes, or a relationship that exists between objects and events.

Connotative Meaning: The meaning of a word that results from the emotional involvement one has with that word.

Literal Translation: The transferring of one word in the source language for one word in the receiver language without regard to context.

Transliteration: When a word is not translated from one language to another but is merely transferred from one language to another letter by letter. For example, the word "baptize" in Romans 6:3 is a transliteration, not a translation. The Greek word *baptizo* in verse three is transferred almost letter by letter into English as *baptize*. No translation has occurred. Only transliteration has occurred.

The Inspiration of Scripture: That extraordinary supernatural control exerted by the Holy Spirit upon the writers of the Bible by which their words were rendered as the words of God, and therefore perfect and without error.

Inerrant: This word, when applied to the Bible, means that there are no errors in it. No words were added to what the original writers wrote, and no words are missing from the text they wrote. God not only inspired His Word but also providentially preserved the inerrancy of it through His churches. This preservation has continued down through the centuries until the present day.

Back Translation: The translator back translates the receiver language text into an English structure that reflects the meaning of the receiver language text. This is done to enable a translation consultant to check the translation for accuracy, deletions, additions, and so on. The consultant checking the translation would not know the receiver language, but from a well-done back translation of it, he can tell what the receiver language text is saying and be able to check it.

Exegesis: The bringing out of the meaning that is inherent in the words and grammar of a Bible verse. Exegesis is the opposite of eisegesis. Eisegesis is the placing of one's own meaning into the words and grammar of a Bible verse regardless of what the words and grammar mean inherently.

An Idiom: An expression consisting of several words, the meaning of which cannot be understood by taking the words literally.

The Majority Text: That Greek text of the New Testament that was derived from adding up the number of manuscripts that agreed on what textual variants were in the majority of the manuscripts. Those variants, which agreed with the most manuscripts, were chosen as the original reading. This is how we got the Textus Receptus, a Latin phrase meaning "Received Text." Christianity accepted this text as the only valid one until 1881, when the first Critical text appeared.

The Critical Text: The Greek text of the New Testament that has been arrived at by applying the rules of textual criticism. This involves judging whether a variant reading of Scripture is the original one or not. This critical decision is based on external evidences, internal probabilities, and the vague and self-opinionated rules of textual criticism.

Componential Analysis: A literary method that uses the four components of referential meaning (Things, Events, Abstracts and Relationals) to analyze the grammar of the source language text to discover its meaning.

Source Text: The text of the Bible that is used as the basis for a translation into another language. The source texts that should be used as the basis for Bible translating are the King James Version, the Masoretic Hebrew text and the Textus Receptus Greek text.

Canon of the Bible: The books of the Bible that have been declared by faithful churches to be part of the true body of Scripture. The word *Canon* is a transliteration of the Greek word κανον. It means a measuring rule or standard. The early churches set up standards by which they decided whether a book or letter should be included in the Bible. In AD 397 at the Council of Carthage, the Canon was decided upon and was closed to any further writings. Although faithful churches had already judged the books of the Bible canonical before the Council of Carthage, this was the time when a formal recognition of the books was made. Faithful churches decided the canonicity of a book or letter based on three criteria:

1. The acceptance of the book or letter among the churches.

2. The obvious marks of inspiration upon the book or letter.

3. The edification churches received from reading the book or letter.

The Canon of Scripture, as authenticated in AD 397, continued until 1545 when a pope, presiding over the Council of Trent, decided that the fourteen books of the Apocrypha should be included in the Canon of Scripture. However, this decision by a pope has never been accepted by faithful New Testament churches or by the Jewish community. For this reason, the pope's decision to include the Apocrypha as part of Scripture is considered invalid.

The name Coca-Cola was first translated into Chinese as Ke-kou-ke-la. Unfortunately, the Coca-Cola Company did not discover until after thousands of signs had been printed that the phrase Ke-kou-ke-la means, "Bite the wax tadpole."

Chapter 21

Indirect Quotations

Many languages do not use indirect quotations. An example of an indirect quotation is Mark 5:20, "And he departed, and began to publish in Decapolis how great things Jesus had done for him: and all men did marvel." In many languages, the grammatical structure of the language would make it necessary to change this indirect quotation to a direct quotation. Mark 5:20 would then read, "And he departed and began to tell them in Decapolis, 'Jesus has done great things for me:' and all men did marvel"

Mark 5:18 is a similar example, "And when he was come into the ship, he that had been possessed with the devil prayed him that he might be with him." In many languages, this indirect quotation must be changed to a direct quotation. It would read, "And when he was come into the ship, he that had been possessed with the devil said to him, 'Let me be with you.'"

Mark 3:9 says, "And he spake to his disciples that a small ship should wait on him because of the multitude, lest they should throng him." In a language which does not use indirect quotations this verse would read, "He said to his disciples, 'The crowd is rioting to touch me. Get a small boat for me to board so they cannot trample me.'"

Mark 9:10 says, "And they kept that saying with themselves, questioning one with another what the rising from the dead should mean." This may need to be changed to a direct quote that would read, "They discussed what He had said saying, 'What did Jesus mean when He said, 'I will die and rise from the dead?''"

Direct Quotations in Other Languages

In many languages, people express thoughts, opinions, and desires by direct quotations. In the Sinasina language, many things are expressed using a quotation. For example, *Prrr dipumue* in Sinasina means, "Saying *prrr* (sound of wings), it went," meaning, "The bird flew away."

The Sinasina people also say, *Kolare beee dimue*. This literally means, "The chicken is saying *beee*," meaning the rooster is crowing. When a Sinasina man goes hunting he will say, "Kabe sinale dipiyue." This literally means, "Saying, 'I shall kill animals' I am going." The phrase in Romans 2:15, "Their conscience also bearing witness," is translated in the Sinasina New Testament with a direct quotation. It reads, "Their innermost thoughts cry out saying, 'You do wrong or you do right.'"

Problems of Direct Quotations

There are some problems with putting what was said indirectly into direct quotations. The first problem is that we may not know the exact words that were spoken. Since it is a direct quote, it is supposed to be exactly what was said. Usually, it is possible to construct from the context exactly what was said, but not always.

Using Quotation Marks

If you are using quotation marks in your translation, keeping track of where all the marks go can become complicated. Leaving the quotation marks out of the translation would be the best answer to the problem if the language structure itself indicates where a quotation begins and ends.

Homework

1. Change the indirect quotation in Mark 9:10 to a direct quotation.

2. Change the indirect quotation in Mark 7:26 to a direct quotation.

A sign in a Tokyo shop said, "Our nylons cost more than common, but you'll find they are best in the long run."

Chapter 22

Implied Information

Implied information is information the original readers of the Bible understood without it being stated in the text. The writer took it for granted that his readers knew the information so there was no need for him to state it.

This is one of the characteristics of Matthew's Gospel. Matthew, writing to Jewish readers, took it for granted that his readers understood Jewish history and culture. Matthew leaves information about Jewish history and culture implied because his readers clearly understood it without it being stated.

The problem arises when the book of Matthew is translated into an ethnic language that does not have Jewish history and culture in its background. These people are not familiar with Jewish history and culture, so they will not be able to fill in the implied information that every Jewish reader took for granted.

In Matthew 16:14 we read, "And they said, Some say that thou art John the Baptist: some, Elias; and others, Jeremias, or one of the prophets." This verse has at least two bits of implied information that ethnic language readers would not know. The first is that the men mentioned here had died. Jesus was thought of as one of these men who had died and had been raised from the dead.

The other bit of implied information is that Elias was thought of as the one who would return in person to prepare the Messianic kingdom for Israel. People thought Jesus was the Elias for whom they had been waiting. They had glorious visions of Elias coming to exalt Israel and deliver them from their humiliating subjugation to the Roman government. None of this information would be know to ethnic readers.

Another example of implied information is found in John 8:32, which says, "That the saying of Jesus might be fulfilled, which he spake, signifying what death he should die." The original readers of the Gospel of John knew this meant that Jesus died by crucifixion. Readers in another culture who are unfamiliar with the Roman law that required crucifixion as the death penalty would not understand this information.

Matthew 8:21-22 says, "And another of his disciples said unto him, Lord, suffer me first to go and bury my father. But Jesus said unto him, Follow me; and let the dead bury their dead." Jesus words sound harsh, for it appears that He is telling the man not even to attend the funeral of his dead father. The implied information that is not stated here is that the man is asking for a postponement of his following of Jesus until after his father dies. His father was still alive and well.

Mark 11:8 says, "And many spread their garments in the way." Implied information: Because they were happy and considered Jesus a very important person, they spread their *outer* garments in the way. (Note: without this implied information, some people have thought that the people had disrobed to the nude. It would also seem a strange custom to spread one's clothing on the road.) Matthew 28:17 says, "And when they saw him, they worshipped him: but some doubted." Implied information: some doubted that it really was Jesus. They thought that perhaps He had come from the grave in the form of a ghost.

Reasons for Including Implied Information

The translator must decide when to include implied information in his translation. Usually, implied information should *not* be put into the translation unless the receiver language makes it *necessary* for understanding the verse correctly. In many cases, the implied information may be left to teaching. One will have to teach the people about the things for which they have little or no background. However, several possible circumstances may make it necessary to include implied information.

1. The Grammar of the Language May Require It.

In a language that has no passive voice, some verses will need to be changed to active voice. Matthew 3:16 "And Jesus when he was baptized." may need to be translated as "And when John had baptized Jesus." Some languages require an object of the verb. One cannot simply say, "They believe." So Acts 4:32 "And the multitude of them believed" must be translated as, "And the multitude of them that believed the Gospel."

2. The Word Structure of the Language May Require It.

Some languages use inclusive and exclusive person indicators. They do not say merely, "We will eat now." They must say, "We will eat now" (including the one spoken to) or "We will eat now" (excluding the one spoken to.) Mark 4:38 says, "Master, carest thou not that we perish?" If this verse were translated into a language using inclusive or exclusive person markers, the translator would have to decide whether the disciples meant, "Carest thou not that we perish" (Us but excluding you) or if they meant, "Carest thou not that we perish" (Us including you). Which one did they mean? One may not know, but because the language word structure dictates that the word *we* must be inclusive or exclusive one will have to decide which one it was whether he wants to or not.

3. A Consistent Misunderstanding of the Text May Require It.

Mark 2:4 says, "And when they could not come nigh unto him for the press, they uncovered the roof where he was." If the implied information that they climbed up on the roof is left out, it could indicate that they were suddenly transferred from the ground to the roof by some miracle of God.

Acts 2:15 says, "For these are not drunken, as ye suppose." In some languages, the use of the word "these" would indicate "these" were exclusive from Peter. This would mean that although Peter was drunk, the others were not. It would be necessary to add a person indicator that would include the speaker with those about whom he spoke.

There are many verses where the King James Version translators added implied information to the text. They indicated that they had added the implied information by printing the implied information in italics. Matthew 1:6 says, "And Jesse begat David the king; and David the king begat Solomon of her *that had been the wife* of Urias;"

Romans 11:4 says, "But what saith the answer of God unto him? I have reserved to myself seven thousand men, who have not bowed the knee to *the image of* Baal."

Ellipsis

Another type of implied information involves words or phrases that are left out of a sentence. This is elliptic information. We use ellipses in English when we reply to the question, "Where are you going?" by saying, "Nowhere." The ellipsis is *I am going nowhere.*"

Another example of ellipsis is Matthew 26:5 that says, "But they said, Not on the feast day, lest there be an uproar among the people." The ellipsis is the words "*Let us not arrest him* on the feast day, lest there be an uproar among the people." Galatians 2:9 says, "That we should go unto the heathen, and they unto the circumcision." The ellipsis is the phrase, "to preach the Gospel." With the ellipsis filled out the verse would read, "That we should go unto the heathen to preach the Gospel to them and they should go to the circumcision to preach the Gospel unto them." John 7:21 says, "Jesus answered and said unto them, I have done one work, and ye all marvel." The words "*on the Sabbath day*" are an ellipsis. With the ellipsis filled out the verse would read "I have done one work *on the Sabbath day* and ye all marvel." Matthew 9:6 says, "But that ye may know that the Son of Man hath power on earth to forgive sins." The words "*I will say, arise and walk*" are an ellipsis. With the ellipsis filled out the verse would read, "But I will say, 'Arise and walk' that ye may know that the Son of Man hath power on earth to forgive sins."

Luke 1:9,10 says, "His lot was to burn incense when he went into the temple of the Lord. (Ellipsis: so he went into the temple) And the whole multitude of the people were praying without."

See also Matthew 6:28 that says, "neither do they spin (ellipsis: neither do they spin *cloth to make their clothing*)."

Single words may imply information that may not be known to readers in another language. For example:

"Centurion" (a commander of 100 soldiers)

"Pharisee" (a strictly orthodox Jewish religious leader)

"Nazareth" (a city called Nazareth)

When to Include Implied Information

The translator should avoid extremes when dealing with implied or elliptic information. He should add implied information when the source language text used statements that left information implied. However, he should avoid adding so much implied information that his translation reads like a commentary. The chart on the following page may be used as a guide to decide when to include or exclude implied information in the text.

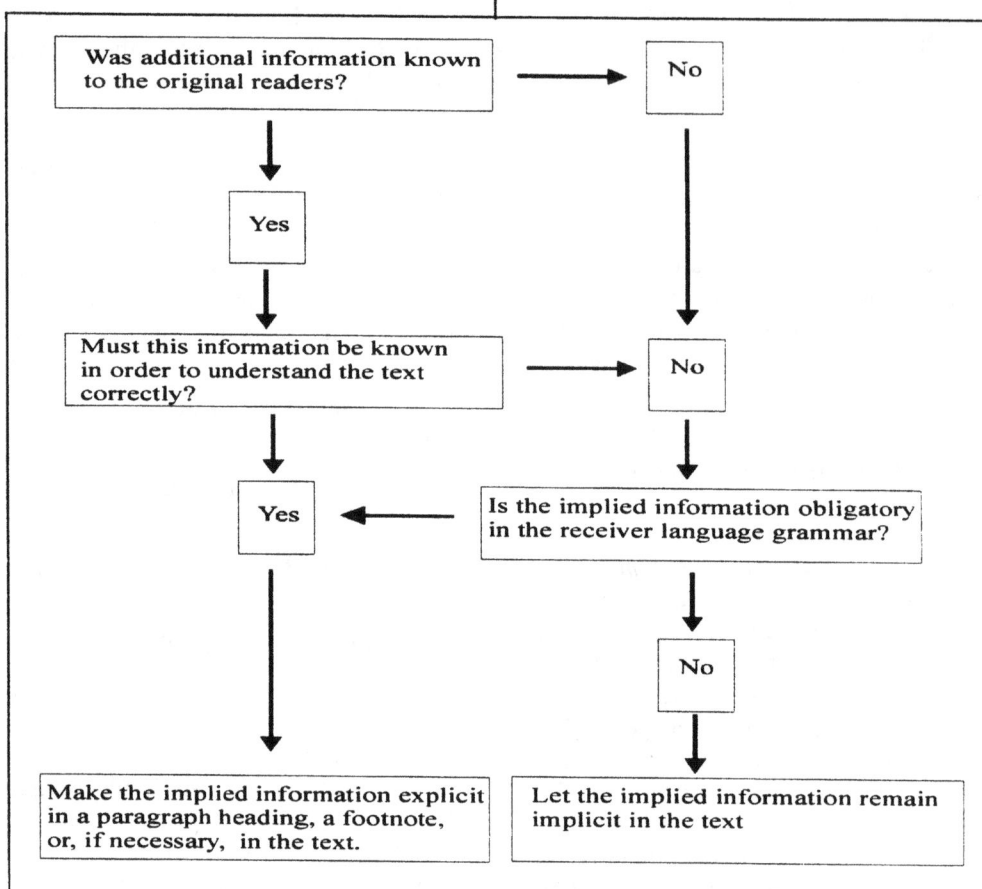

Homework

1. Read *Bible Translating* by Nida, page 243, 14.1 to page 250, 14.2.2.

2. Rewrite the following verses making the implied information explicit.

Luke 12:5

Mark 2:27

Matthew 4:4

A sign in a Hong Kong supermarket said, "For your convenience, we recommend courteous, efficient self-service."

Chapter 23

Figures of Speech

Words that are used in a nonliteral sense or an unusual sense are called figures of speech. The figurative sense of a word is based on an association that exists between the referential meaning of that word and the extended figurative meaning of it.

For example, in Luke 13:32 Jesus says, "and tell that fox" (referring to Herod). A fox is an animal belonging to the canine family, but Jesus is using the word *fox* in a figurative sense. He does so by associating some characteristic of the fox with Herod.

The referential meaning of a word is the literal meaning of that word when read in a list without any context. The word *fox* usually means a dog-like animal. However there is a figurative meaning of the word. The figurative sense shares some characteristic of the referential meaning. This sharing of characteristics often causes translators problems.

First, one needs to know what the shared characteristic between the referential meaning and the figurative meaning is. Next, one will need to know what that shared characteristic implies. For example, we may know that *fox* means a canine animal and that its extended meaning is based on the characteristic of the cunning ways of a fox. However, other cultures do not use the same animal to carry the figurative meaning of *cunning*. In some languages, the rabbit is the cunning animal.

The word *flesh* as used in the New Testament has the referential meaning of "the soft substance surrounding the skeletal structure of the body." However, several extended figurative meanings exist.

For example, Romans 11:14 says, "them which are my flesh" meaning "those who are of my same ancestry, or fellow Jews." Here the word *flesh* has been extended by Paul to mean "Jewish ethnicity." The association between "flesh" and "ethnicity" results from the fact that Paul received his flesh (body) by being born into an ethnic group. The relationship of "flesh" to "body" and to "ethnicity" looks like this:

Referential	Extended	Extended
"Flesh"	"Body"	"Ethnicity"
The soft substance that covers the bones.	The whole physical part of a person.	People who are descended from a common ancestry.

There are other extended meanings of the word *flesh* used in verses like Acts 2:17, which says, "I will pour out my Spirit upon all flesh." Here the word *flesh* is being extended in meaning by the fact that the body is the essential part of a person. This results in the figurative meaning of *flesh* being "people." The meaning of the verse is "I will pour out my Spirit upon all people."

Again, the word *flesh* is used in John 8:15, which says, "Ye judge after the flesh." Here the word *flesh* has the meaning of "human." Jesus is saying that their judgment is based on merely human understanding as opposed to divine understanding. This is based on an association of the word *flesh* to the word *body,* which is the place where one makes judgments; namely, in the mind, which is a part of the human body. John 8:15, therefore, has the meaning of "You are judging on the basis of human logic."

Romans 7:5 says, "For when we were in the flesh." Here the word *flesh* has the meaning, "under the control of the sinful desires of body." The word *flesh* in this verse is the place where these sinful desires exert themselves.

When Paul writes in Galatians 6:14, "I...glory...in the cross of our Lord Jesus Christ," he is using the word *cross* in its extended figurative meaning. This results from an association between the referential meaning of two pieces of wood made into a cross and the extended meaning of the Person who accomplished the work of atonement by dying on that cross. Paul is not exalting the cross as a wooden object but rather the Person of Christ who achieved the atonement for sins on that cross.

In Galatians 2:9, the words *circumcision,* and *uncircumcision* represent a physical act. The association between the physical act of circumcision and the people who perform this act extends the referential meaning to mean "Jews." Therefore, the word *circumcision* means Jews and the word *uncircumcision* means Gentiles. This association of figurative meaning results from the fact that the Jews perform circumcision, and the Gentiles do not.

Simile and Metaphor

The figures of speech that compare two things as being alike in some way are called similes or metaphors. The difference between a simile and a metaphor is that a simile actually states what is being compared to what and a metaphor does not. In 1 Peter 1:24 the phrase, "All flesh is as grass." states what the comparison is in the phrase itself. Flesh is being compared to grass. In a metaphor, the comparison is made but not actually stated. A metaphor only *implies* the comparison, as in "All flesh is grass." The two mean the same, but one makes the comparison explicit, and the other only implies it. It is not always critical to remember the names of the various figures of speech, but one should be able to recognize a figure of speech when it occurs in the Bible.

Similes and metaphors usually involve three parts. These three parts are diagrammed in the following chart as A, B, and C.

When A is compared to B, the resulting meaning is C. This can be seen in the following chart:

When A is	compared to B	it results in C
All we	like sheep	have gone astray Isaiah 53:6
All flesh	is as grass	perishable 1 Peter 1:24
Faith	as a grain of mustard seed	small amount Matthew 17:20

Identifying Similes and Metaphors

The Bible translator should first identify all three parts of the comparison being made and then translate the simile as the author intended.

The referential meaning should be stated. That which the referential meaning is being compared to should also be stated, and the extended figurative meaning that results from the association should be clearly stated as well. If "human beings" are being compared to "sheep," the meaning should be "Human beings go astray like sheep go astray."

Translating Similes and Metaphors

Similes and metaphors can be adequately translated in the following ways:

1. Teach the people what the metaphor means. The simile or metaphor may be translated literally and later explained by teaching and preaching.

2. Use a similar type of comparison, which the people already understand. In some instances in the New Testament, the basis of comparison was not immediately apparent. However, those hearing the comparison were able to understand it because of similar types of comparisons with which they were already familiar. For example Mark 8:15 and the verses following, says, "Beware of the leaven of the Pharisees." The disciples, at first, did not know what the basis of comparison was between leaven and the Pharisees. Later when Jesus taught them the basis of comparison, they understood that the effect of leaven was similar to the effect of the teaching of the Pharisees. Yeast spreads through dough affecting the whole lump like the teaching of the Pharisees adversely affected the spiritual welfare of the people who followed their teaching. We may translate the simile or metaphor literally, and explain the meaning during teaching sessions. This is what the Lord did in Mark 8:15.

A metaphor that Jesus used in John 6:53 has been greatly abused. Jesus said, "Except ye eat the flesh of the Son of man, and drink his blood, ye have no life in you." Jesus did not mean that we should literally eat his flesh and drink his blood. We know this because in verse 63 He said, "It is the spirit that quickeneth (gives life); the flesh profiteth nothing." Jesus was using food as a simile. What Jesus said is similar to what we would say about a football fanatic. We would say that he "eats and sleeps" football. We mean that his time and energies are given over to that sport. When Jesus said, "eateth my flesh, and drinketh my blood," He meant those whose time and energies are given over to intimate fellowship and service to Him. Such people truly have God's eternal life in them.

3. Change a metaphor to a simile by adding the word *like*. The metaphor "I am the door" (John 10:9) may be translated as "I am like the sheepfold door." The word *like* gives a clue to the reader that a comparison is being made. The way in which Jesus is like a sheepfold door is not explicitly stated. However, the context of the shepherd who puts his sheep into the sheepfold through the sheepfold door may give the readers some idea of what is meant. If not, the meaning of the comparison will have to be stated or taught.

4. Spell out the comparison to show exactly what is being compared to what, and what the resulting meaning is.

For example, "Like sheep enter into the sheepfold by going in the door, so you must believe in me to enter into heaven." This may become more of a commentary than a translation and should be avoided. However, this may need to be done if the comparison is consistently and badly misunderstood.

5. Remove the figure of speech altogether and state the meaning of the comparison. This should only be done in extreme circumstances when misunderstanding the figure of speech could result in severe doctrinal problems. In this case one would translate "I am the door" as "If you believe in me you will enter into heaven just like the sheep enter into the sheepfold."

6. Substitute a cultural equivalent. This may be used if it does not violate the historical context. For example, "I am the door mouth (entrance of the house)." The Sinasina people distinguish the door part that fills the doorway from the doorway opening. They call the opening the "door mouth." This is an acceptable cultural substitution since it does not violate anything in the historical context.

7. Translate the simile or metaphor literally, but use a paragraph heading to indicate what is being compared to what. For example, just before the passage of Scripture about Jesus being the door, a paragraph heading can be put in like this: "Jesus compares Himself to the door of the sheepfold." The reader is told that the paragraph headings are not a part of Scripture. Such a solution should only be used when necessary.

Homework

State the referential meaning of the words, the topics of comparison, and the resulting figurative meanings that are found in 1 Corinthians 3:1-8. (For example, "brethren" compared to "babes" equals "spiritually immature Christians.")

A sign in a Belgrade hotel elevator said, "To move the cabin, push button for wishing floor. If the cabin should enter more persons, each one should press a number of wishing floor. Driving is then going alphabetically by national order."

Chapter 24

Euphemisms

A euphemism is the substituting of an agreeable or inoffensive expression for one that may offend or suggest something embarrassing. For example, Mark 5:25 says, "And a certain woman, which had an issue of blood twelve years." The term "an issue of blood" is used to remove some of the harshness of saying the woman had a menstrual disorder. This kind of sensitivity should be carried over into the receiver language. The translator will have to translate this verse with the same meaning, "a menstrual disorder," but he will have to find a way to say it in the receiver language that is not vulgar, overly explicit, or offensive to the people's sensitivity.

In translating the word *circumcision*, one would have to do the same thing. It should be translated in such a way that it can be read publicly without embarrassing the listeners.

Acts 13:36 says, "David...fell on sleep (died), and was laid unto his fathers (was buried), and saw corruption (rotted)." The translator should check each word with his translation helper to see which ones have a special sensitivity and which do not.

Other Possible Euphemisms

Some of the more sensitive areas of language deal with death, pregnancy, and bodily functions. Some examples of euphemisms are found in Luke 2:5, "Mary...being great with child" (pregnant), Luke 7:37, "A woman in the city, which was a sinner" (prostitute), Matthew 22:13, "and cast him into outer darkness" (hell), Acts 1:25, "Judas by transgression fell, that he might go to his own place" (hell), and Acts 22:22, "Away with such a fellow from the earth" (Kill him!).

Although there is general agreement about sensitive topics, what may be a euphemism in one language may not be in another. Different cultures consider different things sensitive and express euphemisms in different ways. For example, Genesis 4:1 says, "And Adam knew Eve his wife." This verse is translated rather insensitively as "had intercourse with" in the Today's English Version.

Hyperbole

Hyperbole is an exaggeration for emphasizing a point. It is not meant to be taken literally.

For example, Matthew 11:18 says, "For John came neither eating nor drinking." This does not mean that he did not eat or drink at all but that he ate and drank sparingly.

Paul says in 1 Corinthians 1:17, "For Christ sent me not to baptize." This statement is a hyperbole to emphasize how much more important it is to preach the Gospel than it is to worry about who baptized you, whether Paul, Apollos, or Cephas.

Luke 15:24 says, "For this my son was dead, and is alive again." The son was not actually dead, although he was in a sense as good as dead because he was estranged from his father.

Other examples are; John 21:25, "The world itself could not contain the books." (It would take a great number of books to record all that Jesus did and said.)

Acts 17:6 "These that have turned the world upside down." (Those who have caused uproar wherever they have gone.)

John 12:19, "The world has gone after him" (Large crowds were following him.)

Some languages do not use hyperboles to exaggerate, emphasize, or make a dramatic effect. In such languages, the hyperbole might be taken literally with the resulting meaning being not the one intended. In such a case, the translator must determine the meaning of the hyperbole and translate the meaning of it rather than preserving the hyperbole itself. For example, Mark 1:5 says, "And there went out unto him *all* the land of Judea." We know this verse does not mean that every single person from Judea went out to John because the same verse adds, "and were *all* baptized of him in the river of Jordan, confessing their sins." John did not baptize every person in Judea. He had refused to baptize those who were unrepentant. The phrase, "And there went out unto him all the land of Judea" could be translated as "Large crowds of people from Judea went out unto him."

Litotes

Litotes is a literary device that lowers one thing in order to magnify another thing by way of contrasting the two. It is used not to call attention to the smallness of the thing lessened, but to the importance of that which is put in contrast with it.

For example, Acts 20:12 says. "And they brought the young man alive, and were not a little comforted." This means, "They were very much comforted." Acts 21:39 says, "A citizen of no mean city." This means that he was "a citizen of an important city." Luke 17:9 says, "Doth he thank that servant because he did the things that were commanded him? I trow not (i.e., I think not.)" This means, "I know very well he does not thank him."

Metonymy

A metonymy is a literary device whereby one word is used to stand in the place of another that is closely associated with it.

For example, James 3:6 says, "and it (the tongue) is set on fire of hell." Here the word hell is used in place of the one who is associated with hell; namely, Satan. He tempts people to use their tongues in a way that destroys people. Mark 8:34 says, "Let him deny himself, and take up his cross, and follow me." The word *cross* is used in the place of what happened on the cross; namely, Jesus died on it. Jesus means that if one would be a disciple of His, he should be ready to die, as He is about to die. Acts 4:30 says, "By stretching forth thine hand to heal." The word *hand* is used in the place of the power of God that causes healing. Galatians 3:8 says, "And the Scripture...preached before the gospel." Here the word *Scripture* stands for the writer who preached the Gospel by writing it in Scripture. Acts 21:21 says, Thou teachest all the Jews...to forsake Moses." The word *Moses* stands for that which is closely associated with

Moses, namely, the law that was given to Moses. Acts 7:18 says, "Till another king arose, which knew not Joseph." This means another king arose who did not know the history about Joseph. Mark 3:23 says, "How can Satan cast out Satan?" The second word *Satan* in this question stands for those who serve Satan, namely, his demons. This verse has the meaning of, "Certainly Satan would not cast out the demons who serve him."

Synecdoche

A synecdoche uses a part to stand for a whole. Luke 1:66 says, "The hand of the Lord was with him." The phrase *hand of the Lord* stands for the Person who was with him, namely, God. Matthew 15:37 says, "They took up of the broken meat that was left seven baskets full." Here the word *meat* stands for food, or bread. Romans 3:15 says, "Their feet are swift to shed blood." The word *feet* means the persons who were swift to shed blood, and *shed blood* stands for the people who are killed by such persons. Mark 1:11 says, "And there came a voice from heaven." The word *voice* is a part of the whole Person who spoke, namely, God. Matthew 8:8 says, "The centurion answered and said, Lord, I am not worthy that thou shouldest come under my roof." The word *roof* is the principal part of the house and so stands for the house itself.

Irony

Irony involves the use of words to say one thing but mean the opposite of what is said. It gives a powerful effect to words that are intended to show the foolishness of such a thought or action.

In Mark 7:9, Jesus says, "Full well ye reject the commandment of God, that ye may keep your own tradition." The words, *Full well,* normally mean "You do very well," but here the words mean just the opposite. "Full well" means "You do very wrong." Irony is used to show the utter folly of placing human tradition above God's Word.

Irony is often used to show the attitude of the speaker, who is usually signaling a sense of ridicule of the idea expressed. It is using irony to say, "You think you have done such a fine thing by rejecting the commandment of God so you can keep your own tradition, do you?"

In 2 Corinthians 12:13, Paul tells the Corinthians that he had served them without demanding payment for his services. Then he says, "Forgive me this wrong." He is not saying he did something wrong. He is using irony to show how foolish it was of the Corinthians to reject him as an apostle simply because he refused to demand payment from them. He says in effect, "I served you freely and did not demand to be paid. I'm sorry I did such a wicked thing!"

Again in 2 Corinthians 11:4, Paul says, concerning the false apostle who came to the Corinthians, "Ye might well bear with him." Paul is not saying that they should be tolerant of him and bear with him. Paul is using irony to say how foolish the Corinthians were to tolerate this false apostle who came to them and preached a different Jesus than the one Paul had preached to them. It is a forceful way of saying, "When that false apostle came and preached heresy to you, you swallowed it hook, line, and sinker!"

Apostrophe

An apostrophe is used to address something that is not alive as if it were a living person. For example, 1 Corinthians 15:55, "O death, where is thy sting?" has the meaning of "Because the guilt of his sins has been forgiven, dying is not a spiritually painful experience for the Christian." Matthew 2:6 says, "And thou Bethlehem, in the land of Judah..." Here Bethlehem stands for the people in Bethlehem. Luke 13:34 says, "O Jerusalem, Jerusalem, which killest the prophets...that are sent unto thee." Jerusalem represents the people who make up the nation of Israel.

Personification

Personification attributes human qualities to nonhuman things.

For example, Revelation 11:8 says, "And the nations were angry." This means the people in the nations were angry." Revelation 16:20 says, "And every island fled away." This means the islands were destroyed. Romans 8:22 says, "The whole creation groaneth and travaileth in pain." This means the world is being dissipated by corruption just like we humans are. Revelation 20:14 says, "And death and hell were cast into the lake of fire." This means the people who had died, and who were in hell, were cast into the lake of fire. Acts 20:32 says, "The word of his grace, which is able to build you up." This means the teaching about being saved by the grace of God is the teaching that builds you up. Hebrews 4:12 says, "For the word of God is a discerner of the thoughts and intents of the heart." This means that when people understand the word of God that is preached to them, the Holy Spirit uses it to reveal the thoughts and intents of their hearts to them.

The translator will not need to remember the name of every figure of speech that is used in the Bible. However, he needs to be aware of when a figure of speech is being used and how it is being used to represent the meaning intended. Once the translator is clear in his own mind about the function and meaning of a figure of speech, he is in a position to translate that figure of speech accurately. It is important to recognize a figure of speech. If one fails to recognize it and translates it literally, the meaning is likely to be something other than what was intended.

Homework

Write a statement that reflects the nonliteral meaning of the following figures of speech.

Colossians 1:18, "He is the head of the body."

Mark 1:17, "I will make you fishers of men."

Matthew 5:6, "Blessed are those who hunger and thirst after righteousness."

Matthew 27:25, "His blood be on us, and on our children."

Luke 16:29, "They have Moses and the prophets; let them hear them."

1 Corinthians 2:9, "Eye hath not seen, nor ear heard."

The back translation of a careless Spanish translation of "Out of sight, out of mind" is: "Invisible, imbecile."

Chapter 25

Idioms

An idiomatic expression consists of several words whose meaning cannot be understood by taking the words literally.

1 John 3:17 says, "And shutteth up his bowels *of compassion* from him." The phrase "shutteth up his bowels" is an idiom from the Greek language that has the means *compassion*. To the person speaking Greek, the bowels are the place where the emotion of compassion occurs. Therefore, the Greek New Testament uses the phrase, "shutteth up his bowels." The translators of this idiom knew that by translating the word *splankna*, (bowels) without some explanation, it would not make much sense in English, so they added the phrase, "of compassion." By so doing, they kept the Greek idiom (bowels) and explained what the idiom means. The phrase *of compassion* is put in italic type to show that the translators added the phrase.

Another idiom is found in John 8:52, which says, "He shall never taste of death." The Greek language can speak of "tasting" death, but some languages would not use this idiom. They would say; "He will never die." If we force this idiom into their language without some information in the text that explains it, we may cause them to create some weird doctrines based on a misunderstanding of this idiomatic phrase. Some ethnic groups have customs where they eat parts of the person who has died. They could easily think the idiom *taste death* means *taste the dead*.

An idiom is used in an extended figurative sense. It is not possible to add up the meaning of each word and determine the meaning of the expression. It should not be taken literally. In Acts 2:30 the expression "the fruit of his loins" has the meaning of "his descendants." In Mark 2:19 the phrase "the children of the bridechamber" has the meaning of "wedding guests of the bridegroom, his friends." It is unlikely that an idiom from the Jewish culture will carry over into another culture with exactly the same meaning. Romans 12:20 says, "For in so doing thou shalt heap coals of fire on his head." If this verse were translated literally into some languages, it would imply a kind of Christian torture. The phrase, "heap coals of fire on his head" has the meaning: "By so doing you will *cause them to be ashamed of the bad things they did to you.*"

Mark 10:5 says, "For the hardness of your heart he wrote you this precept." In Papua New Guinea Pidgin, "hardness of your heart" has a near equivalent: "blocked up your intestines," which means, "You are constipated." The verse would read, "*Because you are constipated* he wrote you this precept." The meaning intended was, "Because of *your resistance* to God, he wrote you this precept." This same "hardness of heart," if translated literally into the Shipibo language of Peru, would mean "brave." To say that a person is not "submissive" in Shipibo, one must use the idiom "He has holes in his ears." We use a similar idiomatic expression: "It went in one ear and out the other," meaning he paid no attention to what was said. Luke 9:51 says, "He set his face to go to Jerusalem." This is an idiomatic way of saying, "He was determined that nothing would stop him from going to Jerusalem." In Romans 10:9, the idiom "Believe in thine heart" is used. It does not mean one believes in the muscle in his chest that pumps the blood around in his veins. It has the meaning, "to believe in one's innermost being where the seat of the decision making process takes place." The Sinasina people do not believe in their hearts. They believe in their "inside thoughts." Other languages speak about believing in one's liver, spleen, or stomach.

How to Translate Idioms

In dealing with idioms in the New Testament, it is important that the translator first be able to recognize idioms as such. If he fails to recognize nonliteral speech and translates it literally, he will most likely distort the intended meaning. After a translator recognizes that a part of a verse is an idiom or some other figure of speech, he must then determine what the intended meaning of that idiom or figure of speech is. After that, he will have to decide what is the best way to say the nearest formal equivalent meaning in the receiver language. The translator may choose to carry the idiom over into the other language with an explanation of it in the text, as did the translators of the King James Version. This is one way to take care of the problem of idioms. Another way is to remove the figure of speech altogether and translate the meaning of the idiom. This was done by the King James Version translators in Matthew 1:23. There the phrase "shall be with child" is a translation of the Greek idiom "shall be with stomach."

Translating idioms and figures of speech is difficult to do properly. It should be done with caution and sensitivity to the intended meaning of the original writer of Scripture. Equally so, it should take into consideration what the idiom or figure of speech will mean to the person who reads it in the receiver language. The original author may have intended to emphasize a point, indicate an attitude in the speaker, or arouse a certain emotional response in the hearer. The translator must try to achieve the nearest formal equivalent effect in his translation. The study of text material in the receiver language will help the translator find out if figures of speech are used, how they are used, and with what frequency they occur.

Historical Context

Certain figures of speech are so deeply imbedded in the historical context of biblical history that they cannot be changed at all lest the historical facts be distorted.

For example, John 1:29 uses the term "the Lamb of God." This figure of speech could be spelled out by giving some clue to the reader in a paragraph heading that "the Lamb of God" means "One who is like a lamb that is sacrificed to make atonement for sins." This may become too bulky in the number of words involved. However, the figure of speech "the Lamb of God" must be preserved. It is so deeply a part of biblical history that to change it to some other animal or figure of speech would be a falsification of the facts. This is similarly true of the word *blood* as used in Ephesians 1:7, which says, "In whom we have redemption through his blood." The biblical theme of redemption by blood is woven right through the warp and woof of Scripture. The entire

Levitical system involves the shedding of the blood of the sacrificial lamb. This theme permeates the Old Testament and is fulfilled in the New Testament. Blood cannot be substituted by any other word lest the historical context of Scripture be violated. Paul's use of the word *blood* in Ephesians 1:7 is without doubt based on the Levitical system where the sacrificial lamb was slain. The blood of the slain lamb was the symbol of a life given to make atonement for sins. It is wrong to use the word *death* here in the place of blood even if it could be argued that blood is a figure of speech standing for the shedding of blood that causes death.

Homework

1. Read pages 274 to 279 in *Bible Translating* by Nida.

2. Each of the following verses contains a figure of speech. Restate the verse to show the meaning of the figure of speech. By restating the meaning of the verse in writing, this will help to clarify the meaning of the verse in your own mind.

Luke 1:12, "and fear fell upon him."

Matthew 8:8, "come under my roof."

Acts 5:28, "to bring this man's blood upon us."

Acts 8:30, "heard him read the prophet Esaias."

Luke 1:42, "Blessed is the fruit of thy womb."

A sign in a Copenhagen airline ticket office said, "We take your bags and send them in all directions."

Chapter 26

Doublets

A doublet involves using two words to say nearly the same thing.

John 3:5 says, "Jesus answered, Verily, verily, I say unto thee." The duplicating of the word *verily* is probably a doublet. The duplication of the word *verily* has the meaning of emphasizing the truth of the statement that is about to follow. The meaning of the doublet is, "I tell you truthfully." Unless your language uses duplication in the same way, you may have to reduce the two "verilys" to the intended meaning, "I tell you truthfully."

John 2:19 says, "Jesus answered and said unto them." The words *answered and said* are probably a doublet. To use the same kind of duplication in some languages would violate the normal usage of words and sound very strange. In some languages, it would sound like this: "Jesus answered and then he said something else." The reader would be left wondering what Jesus had answered before He said what He said. This would be confusing. It would be sufficient to translate a doublet in other languages that do not use them as simply, "Jesus answered" or "Jesus answered saying."

Focus

Adjustment may have to be made in the receiver text when the focus of a verse is distorted. Matthew 19:24 says, "It is easier for a camel to go through the eye of a needle, than for a rich man to enter into the kingdom of God." The focus of meaning in this verse is on the *impossibility* of such a large object going through the eye of a needle. This focus may be lost if the translator uses a long phrase explaining what a camel is. The reader's focus would be on what a camel is like. The intended meaning of the above verse is to show the impossibility of a person going to heaven as long as his heart is given over to material things, just as it is impossible for a camel to go through the eye of a needle. This focus must be kept in the verse without distortion.

Matthew 8:4 says, "Shew thyself to the priest." The translator may distort the focus of the verse by a long translation of the word *priest*. The reader would be left with the impression that this verse is an explanation of what a priest is. The translator must find a way to maintain the center of attention in a verse or passage of Scripture. This can often be done with a concise phrase that does not explain everything about a camel or a priest, but does serve as the person or thing being spoken about. Fuller explanations about these persons or things can be left to teaching later.

1 Corinthians 5:6 says, "A little leaven leaveneth the whole lump." A long explanation of what yeast is and how it spreads throughout the dough could distort the focus of the verse to mean, "This is an explanation of what yeast is and how it works," rather than meaning, "A little evil spreads rapidly." Acts 15:4 says, "And when they were come to Jerusalem, they were received of the church, and of the apostles and elders, and they declared all things that God had done with them." The focus in this verse is on "all things that God had done with them." However, this focus can be lost in the translation of the words for church, apostles, and elders. These

three words must be translated in such a way that they do not distort the main intention of the verse which is, "all things that God had done with them."

Matthew 2:11 says, "They saw the young child (main focus) with Mary his mother (not in focus), and fell down, and worshipped him (main focus)." The focus in Matthew 2:11 is on the fact that they saw the young child (Jesus), and fell down to worship Him. The focus is not on His mother Mary.

Flashback

John 18:14 says, "Now Caiaphas was he, which gave counsel to the Jews, that it was expedient that one man should die for the people." This verse in John 18:14 is a flashback to what had happened in John 11:50. If translated without some indication that this is something that has already taken place, it could indicate to the reader that it is a repeat of what had happened before. Some clue may be needed to let the reader know that this is a flashback to a previous event, not the event happening over again. By adding a time word, such as, "Caiaphas was he, which *before* had given counsel..." the problem is solved.

John 4:39 is a flashback to verse John 4:29. Verse 39 says, "And many of the Samaritans of that city believed on him for the saying of the woman, which testified, He told me all that ever I did." Adding the word *before* can indicate the flashback here. The verse would then read, "And many of the Samaritans of that city believed on him because of what the woman had testified before, when she had said..." It will be important for the translator to study enough native-language text material to find out how the receiver language handles flashbacks. If the readers recognize verse 39 as a flashback, then no adjustment in the receiver language is necessary.

Mark 6:16-17 reads, "But when Herod heard thereof, he said, It is John, whom I beheaded: he is risen from the dead. For Herod himself had sent forth and laid hold upon John, and bound him in prison for Herodias' sake, his brother Philip's wife: for he had married her." Verse 17 is a flashback to a time in the past when Herod killed John the Baptist. Therefore, this verse may be better understood by adding a time word or a time affix to show that this is a flashback to events already transpired. One possible way to translate it would be to begin verse 17 with, "The meaning of what King Herod said is this: Before (time word) when John was still alive, Herod..."

Flashforward

Flashforward also occurs but less frequently than flashback.

Mark 3:19 says, "And Judas Iscariot, which also betrayed him." This verse occurs many verses before the account of the actual betrayal of Judas. This is a flashforward to what would take place later in Mark 14:43. If the readers do not have another one of the gospels to read, they could misconstrue this when they read about it in Mark 14:43. They may think it is happening a second time. This would distort the facts.

Matthew 27:53 says, "And came out of the graves after his resurrection." (His resurrection had not yet taken place in the narrative). Mark 14:24 says, "This is my blood of the new testament, which is shed for many." Here Jesus speaks of His blood being shed as if it had already taken place.

Homework

Choose one of the verses below and read at least three reputable commentaries on it to find out the meaning of the verse. Decide what you think the meaning is and make a statement of it in writing. Make a list of the names of at least three reputable commentaries that agree with your interpretation of the verse. Wives must choose a verse other than the one chosen by their husbands. The verses to choose from are:

1 Peter 3:21, "baptism which saves us."

1 Corinthians 15:29, "baptized for the dead."

1 Timothy 2:15, "saved in childbearing."

Mark 9:48 "where their worm dieth not."

Mark 9:49, "every one shall be salted with fire."

A sign in a Pennsylvania cemetery said, "Persons are prohibited from picking flowers from any but their own graves."

Chapter 27

Collocational Clash

Another problem area for a translator is the translating of phrases that may put words together that should not be. For example, English allows us to say, "a flock of geese," but requires us to say, "a herd of cows." One cannot say, "a flock of cows." The words clash and do not belong together. This kind of problem is called collocational clash.

Romans 9:17 says, "For the scripture saith unto Pharaoh." In this verse, the words *scripture saith* are placed side by side. This has been found to be a collocational clash in many languages. In these languages, only people talk; inanimate books do not. This may have to be adjusted to read, "It is written in the scripture that God said to Pharaoh." Another possible way to adjust this verse would be, "They wrote in Scripture that God said to Pharaoh."

Matthew 6:10 reads, "Thy kingdom come." It is often not possible to speak of kingdoms *coming* in other languages. Some require the translation to say, "May the time for you to rule as king happen." Kingdoms do not come in these languages. Only people go and come.

John 4:1 says, "The Pharisees had heard that Jesus made and baptized more disciples than John." In many languages, the word *made* is limited to the meaning of "manufactured." If one uses the word *made* in his translation, it could mean that Jesus manufactured disciples out of clay or some other material.

John 12:30 says, "This voice came..." The translator must find out if it is proper in the ethnic language to say whether voices come or not. Usually voices are heard. It should not be taken for granted that voices come. Do sounds come? Are they heard? The Sinasina people speak about hearing the neck (voice) of a person. They do not speak about a voice coming.

John 16:6 says, "Sorrow hath filled your heart." Does the language permit one to say that sorrow filled your heart like water filled a container? Some languages limit the word *filling* to water containers. It cannot be used to speak of filling a heart. Shipibos say, "in your heart you are very sad" as the equivalent for "Sorrow hath filled your heart." Sinasina people say the equivalent of "sorrow filled your heart" as, "You feel your liver very much." John 8:51 says, "He shall never see death." In many languages, it is not possible to say one sees death; one simply dies.

John 16:22 says, "and your joy no man taketh from you." The verb *take* is limited to concrete objects in many languages. One may take a person's coat or pig, but one does not take abstract qualities such as *joy* from another person.

John 10:17 says, "I lay down my life, that I might take it again." Does the receiver language use the word *lay* in conjunction with the word *life*? Can one speak of "laying down life" and "taking life again?" This should not be taken for granted. If there is a collocational clash, one may have to use something like "If I want to die and be raised by God to life again, I can do that."

Other languages also speak about the planting and harvesting of crops in a different way than we do in English. To the Sinasina people corn "hits" when it is ripe and is "folded over" when it is picked. Sweet potatoes "go big" when they are ready for harvest and are "pulled out" when harvested.

The translator must not assume that the language into which he is translating will use the same kind of word groupings as that of his own language.

Cultural Substitutes

Substituting an item in one culture for another item in another culture should be done with great care and usually only as a last resort.

Luke 11:11 says, "If a son shall ask bread of any of you that is a father, will he give him a stone? or if he ask a fish, will he for a fish give him a serpent?" First, this is probably a rhetorical question, but even so, it would be answered in many cultures with the answer, "Certainly he would give him a serpent for everyone knows how much more delicious snake meat is than fish meat!" If the translator translates this verse literally, the point of the verse could be lost. He may say, "If he ask a fish, will he for a fish give him a poisonous serpent (one that would bite him)?" The answer would then be, "Certainly not."

Luke 18:13 says, "And the publican...smote upon his breast, saying, God be merciful to me a sinner." The intended meaning of *beating upon his breast* was to show remorse and repentance for sins. However, in other cultures, beating the breast can indicate anger or a show of one's strength. A possible solution might be to say, "Because he was sorry for his sins, he beat his breast."

Acts 14:14 says, "Which when the apostles, Barnabas and Paul, heard of, they rent their clothes." This can be adjusted to another culture by saying, "They, being distressed, ripped their clothes." This explains what would be very strange behavior in many cultures where clothing is considered too valuable to be torn needlessly.

Luke 12:3 says, "That which ye have spoken in the ear in closets shall be proclaimed upon the housetops." To proclaim something on the housetops is probably equivalent in many cultures to proclaiming it in the village square or some other public place. It would be very strange behavior for someone to climb up on a grass-roofed hut to proclaim something.

When to Use Cultural Substitutes

1. When the cultural form being used in Scripture is not deeply imbedded in the historical context, and it would not matter if it were one item or another similar to it, then a cultural substitution may be made.

For example, in Matthew 6:26, Jesus says of the birds, "They sow not." The particular way the seed is sown, whether scattered or put in the ground one at a time, is not at issue. Therefore, a cultural substitute like "they don't plant seeds" may be acceptable. However, in the parable of the sower, this is not the case in Matthew 13:18. In this verse, the particular kind of sowing is crucial to the meaning of the parable. Here the sowing must be some type of scattering. Therefore, the translator will have to use words that indicate sowing by scattering, even if in the local culture seed scattering is not done.

2. When a cultural item in the Bible is deeply embedded in the historical context of Judeo-Christianity, no cultural substitute is acceptable.

However, when a cultural item is not crucial to the point of the narrative or a part of the overall context of biblical history, a cultural substitute may be possible. For example, John 1:29 reads, "Behold the Lamb of God." No cultural substitute for the word *Lamb* is acceptable here. However, in Matthew 5:40 Jesus says, "Let him have thy cloak also." Here the possibility of a cultural substitute for *cloak* may exist, because the word *cloak* means clothing in general.

3. One should not substitute a cultural item that would introduce something into the biblical context that did not exist at the time when the original author wrote the book.

For example, Luke 12:3 says, "shall be proclaimed upon the housetops." This cannot be substituted for the cultural equivalent "shall be announced on the radio" because radios did not exist when Luke wrote this verse.

Cultural substitutes should be made only as a last resort, when necessary to keep the readers from needless misunderstanding.

Homework

Read pages 201-211 in *Translating the Word of God*, Beekman-Callow.

A notice in a Tokyo Hotel said, "Is forbitten to steal hotel towels please. If you are not person to do such thing is please not to read notis."

Chapter 28

Chiasmus

Chiasmus involves words that are not in their usual logical or chronological sequence.

For example, Matthew 7:6 says, "Give not that which is holy unto the dogs, neither cast ye your pearls before swine, lest they trample them under their feet, and turn again and rend you." In this verse, the order of the words in the first two phrases is dogs and then swine, but in the second two phrases, the order of the words is swine and then dogs. If left in this order it results in the swine doing both the trampling and rending (biting). To remove the chiasmus the order should be "Do not give dogs what is holy, lest they turn to bite you, and do not throw your pearls before swine, lest they trample them under foot."

In Matthew 13:15 we read "For this people's heart is waxed gross, and their ears are dull of hearing, and their eyes they have closed; lest at any time they should see with their eyes, and hear with their ears, and should understand with their heart, and should be converted, and I should heal them." In this verse, the order of words is heart-ears-eyes in the first three phrases, and eyes-ears-heart in the second three phrases. If one removes the chiasmus, and the verse is put in sequence, it would read, "For this people's heart is waxed gross, lest at any time they should understand with their heart, and their ears are dull of hearing, lest at any time they should hear with their ears, and their eyes they have closed, lest at any time they should see with their eyes and should be converted and I should heal them."

Philemon 5 reads like this, "Hearing of thy love and faith, which thou hast toward the Lord Jesus, and toward all saints." The order of words is love and faith in the first clause, but it is the Lord Jesus and all saints in the second. Love should be matched with all saints, and faith should be matched with the Lord Jesus. Removing the chiasmus, the verse would read, "Hearing of your faith in the Lord Jesus and of your love for all the saints."

Order of Elements

The order of elements involves the chronological ordering of events as they actually happened. For example, Luke 8:26-30 has this order of events: first, they arrived; second, Jesus got out of the boat; third, a demon-possessed man met him; fourth, the demon-possessed man cried out; fifth, Jesus commands the evil spirit to leave the man.

However, the actual chronology of the events happened in this order: first, they arrived; second, Jesus got out of the boat; third, a demon-possessed man met him; fourth, Jesus commanded the evil spirit to leave the man; fifth, the demon-possessed man cried out. Most ethnic languages prefer a story to happen in actual chronological order of the events. Otherwise, they will take it that the events happened as stated. This would be a distortion of the facts. The demon-possessed man did not cry out first and then Jesus commanded the evil spirit to leave him. Jesus first commanded the evil spirit to leave the demon-possessed man and then he cried out.

Acts 8:1-2 has a similar order of events. In verse one, Stephen has just died, with Paul consenting to his death. Next, the verse speaks about a great persecution at that time. Then, verse 2 says that devout men carried Stephen to his burial. The order of events as they are stated in the verses makes it seem as if Stephen is killed, a great persecution occurs, and then devout men bury Stephen after the persecution breaks out. The actual chronological order was first, Stephen is killed; second, devout men bury Stephen; and third, a great persecution breaks out.

In Mark 16:3-4 the order of events is stated in this order: first, they talked among themselves, wondering who would roll the stone away from the sepulchre; second, they looked and saw that the stone had been rolled away; and third, the stone is said to be very great. Some languages may require the events to be reordered in their logical sequence, "Because the stone at the door of the sepulchre was very great, they talked among themselves wondering, who would roll the stone away from the sepulchre. Then they looked and saw that the stone had already been rolled away."

2 Thessalonians 2:8-9 says, "And then shall that Wicked be revealed, whom the Lord shall consume with the spirit of his mouth, and shall destroy with the brightness of his coming: even him, whose coming is after the working of Satan with all power and signs and lying wonders." The order of elements as stated in the verse is: first, that Wicked is revealed; second, the Lord consumes that Wicked; and third, that Wicked comes. The actual order is: first, that Wicked (one) is revealed; second, that Wicked (one) comes; and third, the Lord consumes that Wicked (one). If the order is not changed it sounds like the Wicked (one) is revealed, the Lord consumes the Wicked one, but the Wicked (one) comes even after being consumed by the Lord.

Pronominal Reference

Sometimes it is not immediately apparent to whom the pronominal referent refers.

For example, Matthew 10:28 says, "And fear not them which kill the body, but are not able to kill the soul: but rather fear him which is able to destroy both soul and body in hell." This verse has often been misunderstood because the pronominal reference is given to the wrong person. Some have thought that "*him*" means Satan. The pronominal reference "him" is to God, not Satan. To avoid this misunderstanding the pronominal reference could be supplied, so that the verse would read, "Fear God who is able to destroy both soul and body in hell."

2 Corinthians 5:21 says, "For he hath made him to be sin for us, who knew no sin; that we might be made the righteousness of God in him." There are six pronouns in this verse and one could easily miss the point of who is doing what to whom.

John 19:30 says, "When Jesus therefore had received the vinegar, he said, It is finished." The last antecedent to the pronoun *it* was vinegar. However, the word *it* does not refer to Jesus finishing (drinking) all the vinegar. The word *it* refers to the finished work of Jesus who completely paid the price for the sins of all humanity. We know this, but will those ethnic peoples of limited Bible background understand it? It may be that one will have to translate this verse as "My work is finished."

John 5:38 says, "And ye have not his word abiding in you: for whom he hath sent, him ye believe not." If the phrase *him ye believe not* is to be understood correctly, it may be necessary to change it to "I, the one whom God sent, ye do not believe me." If the phrase is left in the third person "him," it could mean that Jesus was talking about someone other than Himself.

Matthew 3:16 says, "Jesus, when he was baptized, went up straightway out of the water: and, lo, the heavens were opened unto him, and he saw the Spirit of God descending like a dove, and lighting upon him." The antecedent to "he saw" is Jesus, but in fact, the "he saw" refers to John the Baptist, not Jesus. John was told how he would know who the Son of God was in John 1:33-34: "Upon whom thou shalt see the Spirit descending, and remaining on him, the same is he which baptizeth with the Holy Ghost. And I saw, and bare record that this is the Son of God."

Homework:

1. Reorder the elements in Luke 2:7.

2. Adjust the pronouns in Mark 8:8.

A sign in the Budapest zoo said, "Please do not feed the animals. If you have any suitable food, give it to the guard on duty."

Chapter 29

Sentence Length

In Colossians chapter 1, a sentence begins at verse 9 and ends at verse 17, nine verses without a full stop. Many languages do not have sentences this long. The sentence length may have to be adjusted.

The languages of Papua New Guinea have the potential for making very long sentences because of a grammatical preference for participles and medial verbs that tie clauses together to make long and involved sentences that, though possible, are not practical because the information load in such long involved sentences makes them very difficult to read much like the sentence you are reading now which is why long sentences sometimes need to be shortened so the person reading them will not grow weary of them just like you probably are growing weary of this long sentence because I purposely wrote it lengthy so you would get the point, I hope.

When people are newly literate, long sentences are difficult for them to read. On the other hand, sentences should not be so short as to seem like baby talk. The ideal is a translation that is easily read aloud in public while the people who listen comprehend most of the meaning from the oral reading.

Spoken Style or Written Style?

The spoken style of people's languages will not totally serve as a good model for a written style of their language. A written style is developed over time through an interaction between the translator and the people for whom he translates. This written style must be true to the genuine native speakers' oral style, but it must be adapted to practicality in the written form of the language.

Sometimes the communication load in a group of verses will have to be shortened to units that are more manageable. For example, 1 John 1:1-3 is one sentence in English. These three verses are eleven sentences in the Sinasina New Testament.

One of the best ways to develop a written style of a language is to study text material to find the significant units of the spoken style. After this, the translator can encourage the people who become literate to write letters and stories for him. By observing the way native speakers of the language write, one may gain a good approximation of what the written styles should be. The translation should be written in a style that would be similar to the way a native speaker would have written it. The translator may not always be able to reach this ideal, but he should do his best to work toward it.

Ambiguity

A verse of Scripture is sometimes ambiguous; that is, it could be interpreted correctly in one of two different ways. For example, the phrase in Matthew 9:13, "I will have mercy, and not sacrifice," can be taken to mean either "I (God) would rather you show mercy to people than have you offer sacrifice to me" or "I (God) would rather deal with you in mercy than for you to approach me on the basis of sacrifice."

This ambiguity would need to be reproduced in the ethnic translation. If it makes better sense to remove the ambiguity, then a choice of which meaning will be used will have to be made by the translator.

Romans 6:3 says, "Know ye not, that so many of us as were baptized into Jesus Christ were baptized into his death?" Many people have tried to say that there is not a drop of baptismal water in Romans chapter 6. This is not true. Paul deliberately used the Greek word *baptizo* so that the passage could refer both to our Spirit baptism into Christ and our water baptism into His church. Both meanings are in this verse and both are important to a person's Christian experience. We need to know that the Spirit of God joins us to Christ so that we understand our union with the death, burial, and resurrection of Christ. This sets us free from the bondage of sin. We also need to know that we should become a part of Christ's body, the local church, because this is also vital for our spiritual growth and maturity.

Another example of ambiguity is 2 Corinthians 5:14, "For the love of Christ constraineth us; because we thus judge, that if one died for all, then were all dead." Does this mean that Christ's love for us constrains us, or does it mean our love for Christ constrains us? It is ambiguous. It could mean either one.

Ephesians 5:25 reads, "Even as Christ also loved the church, and gave himself for it." Does this mean Christ loved the local church, or does it mean He loved the church as an institution? In fact, it means both. The word *church* in this verse is the generic use of the word that includes within it the specific sense as well.

A good translation should make good sense. A verse that is so ambiguous that it does not make sense in any way it is read should be removed and a verse that does make sense should replace it. People have a way of making sense out of nonsense and coming up with all kinds of strange doctrines. However, if the ambiguity can be preserved so that it makes sense in one of two ways to the readers, then it may be preserved in the receiver text.

Anachronism

Anachronisms happen when things that did not exist at the time of the writing of the New Testament are introduced into the New Testament text in the receiver language. We have already seen that Luke 12:3, "proclaimed upon the housetops," should not be translated as "announced over the radio."

This also applies to introducing the name of Jesus into Old Testament quotes found in the New Testament. Although it is true that Jesus existed at the time the Old Testament was written, His name was not known at that time as Jesus. For example, Acts 2:25 says, "I foresaw the Lord always before my face." It would not be correct to translate this as "I foresaw the Lord *Jesus* always before my face." Although Jesus is the one being referred to by David, it would violate the chronology of biblical events and would be an anachronism.

A possible anachronism occurs in Acts 12:4. In this verse "Easter" is a translation of the Greek word πασχα (*paska*) from which we get the English words *paschal* lamb, the Passover meal, or the Passover as a whole. When Luke wrote the book of Acts in 34 A.D., there was no holiday that was referred to as "Easter." The word *paska* refers to the Passover feast when the paschal lamb was slain, roasted, and eaten with unleavened bread. The word *paska* is translated "Passover" twenty eight times in every other place it occurs in the New Testament. Most likely, it could have been translated as Passover in this verse as well.

The Passover meal and the feast of unleavened bread are two parts of the one event; namely, the Passover. Luke 22:1 reads, "Now the feast of unleavened bread drew nigh, *which is called the Passover*." This verse shows that the feast of unleavened bread is part of the Passover. The context of Acts 12:4 is given in verse 3. There it says, "Then were the days of unleavened bread." The mention of "the days of unleavened bread" makes it clear that the context of Acts 12:4 is the Jewish Passover, not the holiday of Easter.

However, it should be noted that at the time of the translation of the King James Version, the translators considered the word *Easter* as interchangeable with the word *Passover*.[1] They thought of Christ as the Passover lamb who died for our sins. Even though the word *Easter* was interchangeable with the word *Passover* in 1611, it is no longer interchangeable with *Passover* in the 21st Century. This fact causes the problem of a possible anachronism.

Concordance

Concordance means that a word must be translated the same way in every verse. However, if the same Greek word is translated the same way throughout the New Testament, regardless of the context, the meaning of the word will be distorted.

For example, the Greek word *pneuma*, meaning "spirit," can either refer to the wind, the spirit of a man, the Spirit of God, a disembodied spirit of the dead, a demon, or the attitude of a person. The context in which the word occurs will decide which of these meanings should be used.

The phrase *Kingdom of God* is a phrase that is used in at least five different ways in the New Testament. The context determines which way is meant. Some verses speak about entering the kingdom of God, some about preaching the kingdom of God; some say that it is at hand; some say it is like something, and other verses speak about not being worthy of it. "To enter the kingdom of God" can be translated as going into the kingdom of God, meaning a place (heaven), or becoming a member of the group over which Jesus is King. To preach the kingdom of God is to preach and urge people to submit to the King of the kingdom of God. To say the kingdom of God is at hand is to say that the King (Jesus) has come and it is time for people to submit to His reign. To say the kingdom is like something is to say what it is like when people are under the rule of the King. To speak of not being worthy of the kingdom of God is to say one is not worthy to be among the people whom the King rules. Each of these five contexts will make it necessary to translate "the kingdom of God" in a different way. Concordance does, however, mean that in parallel passages the word used to translate a certain word in one verse should be the same one used in another parallel verse.

For example, if a verse in Mark uses the same word as a parallel verse in Luke, then the same word in Mark should be used in Luke as well. The search-and-replace feature of a computer word processing program is ideal for this.

Comparatives

Comparatives are phrases where one thing is said to be greater than another thing.

For example, Matthew 18:6 says, "It were better for him that a millstone were hanged about his neck, and that he were drowned in the depth of the sea." A comparison is being made: it would be better for one thing to happen than the other thing to happen. The first half of the comparison is stated; namely, "It were better for him..." However, it does not say what it would be better than. Verse 8 tells us it would be better to have a millstone hanged about his neck and drowned in the depth of the sea than for him to be cast into everlasting fire. In many languages, a comparison must have both the thing being compared and what it is being compared to.

In other languages, there are other ways of making comparisons. They may say, "It goes up and puts the other one down." This means that one is greater than the other. They may say, "One is big, the other is not big." This means one is more important than the other." They may say, "One is big. One is small." This means one is larger than the other.

Homework

Rewrite the words in John 15:16 and John 20:19 using at least three or more sentences.

A sign in an Austrian hotel catering to skiers said, "Not to perambulate the corridors in the hours of repose in the boots of ascension."

Chapter 30

Kinship Terms

Many kinship terms in the New Testament are used in a nonliteral sense. For example, Paul often speaks of "the brethren." This is a figurative use of the primary meaning of "brother," a male child born of the same mother. However, the extended meaning of *the brethren* is, those who by believing in Christ have become members of the same household of God.

John 8:39 says, "If ye were Abraham's children," meaning, "If you were Abraham's (spiritual) descendants." Mark 2:5 says, "When Jesus saw their faith, he said unto the sick of the palsy, Son, thy sins be forgiven thee." In this verse, the term *son* does not mean the offspring of Jesus. The word *son* is a term of endearment used by the Lord to indicate the compassion He feels for this man. John 13:33 says, "Little children, yet a little while I am with you." "Little children" is a term of endearment used by the Lord to speak to His disciples. This may be difficult to translate into another language unless the word *children* is used in a figurative way in the other language as well.

John 8:44 says, "For he is a liar, and the father of it." In Sinasina culture, the equivalent of *father* in this verse is "mother." The Sinasina people speak of the "father of the land" meaning the owner of it, but they speak of Satan as the "mother" who gives existence to lies, meaning he is the source of lies. Acts 3:25 says, "Ye are the children of the prophets." This means, "You are the ones who follow the teaching of the prophets." In Matthew 9:15 Jesus speaks of "the children of the bridechamber." These are not children. They are the friends of the bridegroom. John 17:12 says, "the son of perdition," meaning, "a person who will suffer perdition." All these kinship terms are used in a figurative sense and may need to be translated in a way that indicates their nonliteral meaning.

If kinship terms are not used in a figurative sense in the ethnic language, it is possible to translate the meaning of such terms directly. For example, "Son of David" may be expressed as "a descendant of David." "Son of perdition" may be expressed as "One who will suffer perdition." For "He is a liar, and the father of it," one might say, "He is a liar, and the source of lies."

Loan Words

Loan words are those words adopted by a language from other languages such as Spanish, English, German, etc.

Luke 15:22 says, "And put a ring on his hand, and shoes on his feet." Sometimes the receiver language may have words for "rings" and "shoes," but very often, these words will be adopted from the national language of the country or from the language in which the people first heard them spoken.

If such loan words are understood by most of the people, these soon become their own words, and people forget that they were taken from another language. The Sinasina people use a term that is part English and part

Sinasina to express the meaning of a car stuck in the mud. They say, *Stak elmue*. This means: "Stuck it does" (It is stuck). *Stak* is a valid Sinasina word now. It has been adopted from English. Other loan words are often used along with Sinasina words. For example, *kame-kilwa bret* means "banana-mush bread."

In Matthew 26:2 the word *Passover* may become "the holiday to remember the Jewish people's deliverance from Egypt," or "the holiday to remember how the angel spared the first-born sons of the Jews." This can get long and involved, so it may be better to simply say, "A Jewish holiday called Passover." It would be necessary to explain in teaching sessions what *Passover* means.

The translator should be careful to check out any new transliterated words. When Danny Leahy, the first white man to walk through the Sinasina valley, met the first Sinasina people, they greeted him with "Denie! Denie!" Because his name was Danny, he thought they were saying his name but he knew this was impossible. What the people were saying was "Den (your excrement) nie (I eat)." This is a term used by the Sinasina people to say, "My friend! My friend!"

This also works the other way. Sometimes an English word, when pronounced by a Sinasina person, sounds like a word in his or her own language. If we were to say the word *Passover* it would sound like the Sinasina word "Ba suwa," which means, "She kills the moon," meaning she has a menstruation period. The two words could be mistaken for one another with very unwanted results.

The word *Jehovah* was transliterated into the Simbari language in Papua New Guinea and was pronounced in that language as *Tsihowa*. This pronunciation was very similar to the Simbari word meaning "cucumber." For a time, the people thought the missionaries were talking about a cucumber when they spoke about Jehovah. (For more information on loan words, see Nida, *Bible Translating*, pages 139-146.)

Obligatory Grammatical Meanings

Some languages have meanings for words that must be expressed whether one wants to express them or not.

For example, some languages make a distinction between older or younger brother when the speaker is referring to his male siblings. Therefore, verses like Acts 12:2, which says, "James the brother of John," will have to tell the reader whether James was the older or younger brother of John.

Other languages have an obligatory distinction of inclusive or exclusive in the first-person plural. The translator must decide, whenever the word *we* occurs, whether to translate it by using the word "we" that means *the speaker including those addressed* or to translate it by using the other word "we" that means *the speaker but not including those addressed.*

Some languages have two obligatory suffixes that must go on all verb endings to indicate the involvement of the speaker. The one obligatory suffix must be used to indicate that the speaker actually saw what he is recounting. The other obligatory suffix must be used to indicate that the speaker is recounting something that was told to him by someone else.

Other languages have obligatory verbal forms that indicate the speaker's spatial relationship to the person or things being spoken about. In the Yagaria language of Papua New Guinea, there are three obligatory verb forms for going. One does not simply go if he speaks Yagaria. One "goes" in relation to the amount of elevation involved, whether going-on-the-level, going-up, or going-down. To the Yagaria, who live in mountainous terrain, this kind of information is important. When such grammatical affixes are obligatory to the verb structure, they cannot be left out of the translation.

Verb Tense

It may be necessary to reflect the tense and aspect (kind of action) signaled by the verbs in the Bible. The Old Testament was originally written in Hebrew and the New Testament in Koine Greek. Hebrews 10:26 says, "If we sin wilfully after we have received the knowledge of the truth, there remaineth no more sacrifice for sins." This verse appears to indicate that if we willfully sin one time we are lost. However, the word *sin* in the Greek New Testament is a present active participle and has the meaning, "If we are habitually continuing to sin."

1 John 3:8 says, "He that committeth sin is of the devil." This verse also seems to say that if you sin one time you are unsaved. The English translation does indicate the meaning of the present active participle in Greek. The *-eth* in committeth is the old English way of saying "continued action in present time." The Greek participle has a similar meaning, "He that continually practices sinning is of the devil."

Such expansions on the verbs in the Greek New Testament can be overdone and become cumbersome. This should usually be avoided. However, if the readers, without the expansion, continually misunderstand the intended meaning, a translation of the grammatical information in the verb may be warranted.

Transitions Between Sentences

The way in which one verse leads into another verse is often very important. For example, Mark 1:4 says, "John did baptize in the wilderness, and preach the baptism of repentance for the remission of sins." This verse is a transition from the previous two verses. Mark 1:2-3 quotes two Old Testament prophesies. Verse 4 begins in fulfillment of the Old Testament prophecies mentioned in verses 2 and 3. To indicate that verse 4 is a transition from verses 2 and 3, it may be necessary to show this by saying, "In fulfillment of these prophecies, John came baptizing in the wilderness."

1 John 3:12-13 says, "Not as Cain, who was of that wicked one, and slew his brother. And wherefore slew he him? Because his own works were evil, and his brother's righteous. Marvel not, my brethren, if the world hate you." It appears that there is no relation between verse 12 and verse 13. However, verse 12 is the example of Cain who killed his brother. Verse 13 is an application of the example given in verse 12. This transition from example to application should be indicated something like this: "Since Cain did like that, don't be surprised if the world hates you, too."

Names of People and Places

The name "Decapolis" in the New Testament may be translated as "a place named *Decapolis*, which means Ten Cities." "My name is Legion" may become "My name is Very Many." Simon the Zealot may become "Simon who fought the Roman government." The name Jesus, as used in Matthew 1:21, may become "Call His name Jesus because the meaning of the name Jesus is 'He shall save His people from their sins.'"

Numbers in the Bible

Sometimes numbers will need to be adjusted. For example, Matthew 14:21 says, "And they that had eaten were about five thousand men, beside women and children." This could be stated as, "Jesus fed very many men—five thousand and many women and children also" Because many ethnic groups are not technologically oriented, they may not comprehend what the number five thousand means.

The results of the parable of the sowing of seed in Matthew 13:8 may read, "and brought forth fruit, some very much—one hundred, some much—sixty, some a smaller amount--thirty." It could also read, "Some bore fruit bountifully--one hundred, some bore fruit much--sixty, and some bore fruit a lot--thirty."

Record Adjustments

Many of the above-mentioned problems may need adjusting in some way or other. They may not. The translator will have to decide if an adjustment is necessary or not. If he decides certain adjustments are necessary, he should keep a record of any adjustments he found it necessary to make. The record should indicate what the particular adjustment was, the verse in which it occurred, and what the problem was that made the adjustment necessary. This will be of help later when explaining to a Bible translation consultant why one made each adjustment. It will also create a file of problem areas and the solutions chosen to solve the problem. Such information can be of help to other translators who very likely will face the same translation problems.

A sign in the offices of a loan company said, "Ask about our plans for owning your home."

Chapter 31

Word Hunting, Part 1

There are many words in the Bible for which a formal equivalent meaning in the receiver language will be difficult to find. In fact, some of the vocabulary used in the Bible will have no equivalents in the receiver language. However, this does not mean that the speakers of that language cannot find ways to express equivalents of these words. Such words will have to be developed. The contextual conditioning of receiver-language words over time can develop words that are the nearest formal equivalent to Bible words.

Language Focus

This lack of words in a language is due to language focus. All people have cultural situations that are important to them. Therefore, people will have a wealth of words in that area of meaning that is important to their survival, but they will be poor in expressions about matters that do not directly relate to the most pressing needs they have.

For example, some Arabic-speaking groups have 600 terms to do with camels and the equipment involved in using the camel as a beast of burden. South Pacific islanders, in contrast, have no vocabulary to do with camels, but they have hundreds of words pertaining to the coconut palm tree. This tree is practically a supermarket and hardware store for them. Therefore, they have a well-developed vocabulary relating to all the parts of the coconut palm tree and all its uses in daily life.

People in the western world have thousands of words for the automobile. A car is important to them, so they have an extensive vocabulary in this area.

Cultures that have never focused on Christian beliefs will not have a well-developed vocabulary dealing with that area. They have not experienced Christian beliefs, so they will not be able to express something they have not experienced. Their focus in this area of vocabulary is lacking and is in need of development. God has given all people the ability to adapt to other people's way of life. In fact, English has borrowed many words from other languages, and other languages have borrowed words from English.

However, not only are words borrowed from one language to another; concepts are borrowed as well. Usually the meaning of an experience learned in a foreign culture can be expressed by words in one's own language. All people have the ability to express, in their own language, the meaning of an experience that was not originally a part of their culture.

For example, a person who has never seen or heard about an airplane has the ability to speak about that experience as soon as he sees one for the first time. He immediately coins words or phrases that will signal to him the meaning of the experience. The Sinasina people's reaction to seeing seashell beads for the first time was to say, *Silatalwe*, which means, "What is it?" Thereafter, the word *Silatalwe* became the name for seashell beads.

All people have the ability to express new experiences in their language. By doing so, they widen the focus of their language. This expanding of the focus of language makes it possible for the missionary to develop the vocabulary he needs to express New Testament concepts.

Vocabulary Development

The process of developing vocabulary to translate a New Testament should begin the first day one arrives among the ethnic people. In fact, the process is impossible to delay to a more convenient time. There is no choice but to begin communicating a message of some kind. People do not have experiences with other people that they hold over until they can make a better judgment about them. People place a meaning on everything they experience, and they place this meaning on that experience almost simultaneously with its occurrence.

The missionary who moves into an ethnic group cannot take a neutral position and wait until later, when he is fluent in the language, to begin communicating his message. All that he is, does, and has will be communicating messages to the people. They will be giving an interpretation to the missionary's presence that they believe to be the right one no matter what the missionary says or does not say. All that he is, does, and brings with him will be communicating volumes of information about him to the people. However, this does not mean that the people's understanding of one's entrance among them will be understood correctly. Most likely, it will not be understood in the way intended by the missionary. For this reason the missionary must, from the first day, begin trying to relate to the people who he is, and what he intends to do. Moving in to live among an ethnic group is like being thrown into a river before one has learned to swim. One has no choice but to begin struggling to "stay above water." He really has no choice but to begin the struggle to be understood. Since he is communicating some kind of message whether he wants to or not, one may as well begin trying to make himself understood. The process of development may as well begin early rather than later because it cannot be avoided in any case.

It could be argued that if one begins trying to be understood from the beginning, he will make many mistakes and do irreparable damage to his relationship with the people. It is true that he will make mistakes. It is not true that these mistakes are permanent. Most people accept others from the outside into their culture. They realize the newcomer does not know their language and cultural cues. They expect him to blunder, and they make allowances for such mistakes. They are very forgiving of mistakes when they know they are due to ignorance.

However, this will change with time. After one has lived among the people for any length of time, they expect him to have learned their ways and will hold him responsible for his communications. Certainly, the missionary will make mistakes, but it is much better to make them early when the people are much more indulgent of mistakes than to make them later when the people are not as tolerant of cultural and linguistic blunders.

Mistakes cannot be avoided in the process of developing the vocabulary needed to communicate. In fact, there is no choice but to learn by one's mistakes, for the most basic method of learning is through trial and error. A baby only learns the meaning of "hot" by making the mistake of touching something that mother said was *hot*. In a similar way, if one wants to develop Christian words for the vocabulary of the New Testament but does not want to make mistakes in doing so, that is a very noble aim, but it is unrealistic. It is denying the most basic principle of all learning, namely, trial and error. One must be willing to make mistakes and be misunderstood. This does not mean that one is careless and does not make every effort to avoid mistakes. However, after taking every precaution, he still jumps into the river of culture and flounders around until he learns to "swim" in the turbulent waters of communication.

Beginning Early

The advantages of beginning early are several. For one thing, people expect cultural and linguistic blunders from others who are learning. If one waits until later, the people are much less forgiving because they expect you to know your way around. They are also less likely to correct you after you have been there for a length of time.

Another advantage of beginning early is the matter of bonding. It has been shown that the early stage of life is the most productive for learning. A baby begins learning behavioral patterns immediately after birth and begins bonding to the behavioral patterns to which he or she is exposed. New things are most easily learned when one is first exposed to them. After a while, the impact of their presence becomes so usual that the power to learn them has almost completely dissipated.

I have personally observed that missionaries who do not take full advantage of language and culture learning experiences during the first two years of their life among the ethnic people will not learn the language and culture of the people well enough to be effective missionaries. They either become mediocre communicators or leave the field discouraged. The first two years are critical. To fail to learn language and culture during that time when one is most impressionable is to fail altogether.

Another reason for beginning early is this: A vocabulary that is in accord with the concepts of the New Testament will have to be developed over an extended period of time. This process of development is necessary because of language focus. None of the languages in the world will have a "tailor made" vocabulary just waiting to be discovered. While it is true that a great deal of vocabulary can be discovered in the text material of the ethnic language, there will still be words that will have to be developed over time.

For example, the Hebrew word *qadosh*, meaning "holy," was originally a heathen word that meant "prostitute." How is it possible that a word meaning "prostitute" could develop to the point that it means "holy"? This is how the process developed. In the Canaanite culture, a *qedeshah* was a woman "set apart" from the normal duties of life to be used exclusively in the sexual fertility rites of the god Baal. The essential meaning of the word *holy* is "to be set apart from ordinary use for a special purpose." The *qedeshah* was set apart especially for the sexual rites performed in the temple of Baal. It is a matter of to whom one is set apart. One may be set apart to Baal, as a prostitute or one may be set apart to the holy and pure God to do His will. By associating the word *qedeshah*, with the holy God, the word that originally meant, "prostitute" came to mean "holy."

Likewise, this is true of the New Testament word that means, "to appease by sacrifice." Originally, this word was a Greek word that referred to the sacrifices that were made to heathen gods. This term was adapted to explain the fact of Christ's death on the cross as being that which appeased the holiness of God, who must demand perfect moral justice for every offence of His laws.

The Greek word *kurios* (lord) was originally used to refer only to Caesar. He was considered a god and called lord (Kurios). In the process of time, this word came to be used by Christians, who could rightly call Jesus "Kurios."

Another example of early Christian vocabulary development is the word *sunagogen,* which means "synagogue" or "to gather together." This word is used in James 2:2 to describe the meeting of early Christians whose most common experience of worship had been in the synagogue. It was only natural that they should refer to their meeting as a *sunagogen* meaning, "synagogue." However, they stopped using this word because of its close association with Judaism, from which they had come out. Gradually, the Christians began to refer to their meeting as the *ekklesia* (church), which meant "those called out from the world to gather together to serve God." This meaning of the word *ekklesia* can be understood by the way it is used in Acts 19:32. There we read, "Some therefore cried one thing, and some another: for the assembly (*ekklesia*) was confused; and the more part knew not wherefore they were come together." In this verse the word *ekklesia* is used of those who had been "called out from their daily life to gather together for preserving the worship of the goddess Diana. This is the secular meaning of the word *ekklesia*. It was only natural for the Christians to begin using the word *ekklesia* in reference to their being called out from their daily life to meet together to serve Christ.

The vocabulary of the New Testament did not develop instantly. It came into existence through a process of development. One can imagine that some of the Jewish Christians would particularly object to such a heathen term as *Kurios* (lord) being applied to the Messiah. However, in the process of developing New Testament vocabulary, this word became accepted as rightfully belonging to the Lord Jesus Christ alone.

Homework

1. Why is it important to begin learning to communicate the Gospel to the ethnic people from the first day one takes up residence among them?

2. What does the term *bonding* mean, and what application does it have to language learning?

A sign in a clothing store said, "Wonderful bargains for men with 16 and 17 necks."

Chapter 32

Word Hunting, Part 2

Words are pliable. Contextual conditioning can modify the meaning of a word. If I were to arbitrarily make up a word and give it the word symbol *Ku*, what would this symbol mean to you? You would not know. If I say, "He has a broken Ku," you would still not know what is meant, but you now have some idea about the meaning. Upon further observation, you see that the broken "Ku" referred to is a bone protruding through the skin. You guess that *Ku* means "bone." After that, you might hear me say, "He hits big *Ku*." You think I mean that someone is hitting a big bone. It does not make sense to you. Suppose you hear me say this in the Sinasina area after some men come back from a fight. Someone says, "We were almost overrun by the enemy, but our leader hit big *Ku*, and we rallied to defeat them." Now you begin to think that *Ku* means, "bravery." Later when we are at church, an old woman walks laboriously up the hill toward the church. Someone observing her says, "She bakes *Ku* and comes to church every Sunday." At first, you wonder what the baking of bone has to do with coming to church. You soon realize that the phrase "She bakes *Ku* has the meaning, "She *faithfully* comes to church." You realize that the word *Ku* can mean "bone," "bravery" and "faithful." The context around the word conditions it. Even an arbitrary symbol can be given a meaning just by surrounding it with context.

Choosing a Word for God

This same kind of contextual conditioning can be done with a word that one intends to use for *God*. In the Yagaria language of Papua New Guinea, the word *God* was transliterated as "Got." Yagaria phonemic structure does not allow this word to end in a consonant, so an "i" was added, and the name for God became *Goti*.

Naturally, this word did not mean much the first time the Yagaria people heard it. Through the translation of the New Testament and many years of teaching, the word *Goti* has come to mean the God of the Bible.

The word *Goti*, became the nearest formal equivalent of the word *God* by the contextual conditioning of the word in many experiences; some of which were real life experiences and others were those recorded in Scripture. New Testament vocabulary can be developed primarily in this way. One can make up a word like *Goti* and condition it to mean *God* by surrounding it with sufficient contexts that cause it to mean exactly that.

Limiting Meaning by Context

Suppose the Yagaria missionaries had chosen to use some other name for God. Suppose they chose the name of a tribal god. For the sake of illustration, let us say they chose a god whose name was "Bo." The missionaries realize that *Bo* is in some ways like God, but in other ways, he is not. Nevertheless, by means of careful contextual conditioning the missionaries delimit the wrong meanings about "Bo" and gradually build into the word all the attributes of the God of the Bible.

Admittedly, this is somewhat risky, but it can be done with care and sensitivity to both the biblical attributes of God and the feelings of the people. If the ethnic people mostly ignored "Bo" and in general thought of him as a creator of the world, the delimiting of wrong meanings about "Bo" would be minimal. However, if "Bo" is an important part of tribal fertility rites and has many characteristics of evil spirits, then it may be more difficult to delimit these meanings but it can be done. As Bible truth is taught, the wrong meanings can be delimited in the minds of the people and the right meanings restored.

Such contextual conditioning may come about like this. The missionary may say to the people, "You thought Bo was not interested in anything but the fertility of gardens and pigs. The Bible says that Bo is not like that. The Bible says He is like this." From that point on the contextual conditioning (teaching) begins to delimit wrong meanings and expand right ones.

Conditioning of Bible Words

This same process can be done with any word of the New Testament.

For example, the word *holy* may have as its nearest equivalent in the ethnic language a concept that means "forbidden." This is a possible starting point and may be used to expand the meaning of the word to include God's holiness, His aversion to sin, His purity, and His righteousness.

One may begin using this word *forbidden* for the concept of "holy," but as the language helper begins to understand the concept, he may volunteer a word in his language that comes closer to the desired meaning. In this case, the translator may abandon the old word and use the new one.

Coining New Words

Another possibility for developing New Testament vocabulary is to make up a word or phrase that carries at least some of the intended meaning.

After making up the new word, one can elaborate on what is meant. The people may suggest a way to modify the term to make it more like what the translator wants, or they may suggest a new term altogether. They may just accept the newly coined word and learn the meaning of it through teaching.

For example, it is possible to say "born again" in any language if one knows how to say, "to be born" and "again." After coining the word, one should find out what meaning it signals to the people. At first, the term may not mean very much to them. It might mean something strange, the way it did to Nicodemus in John 3:3. The translator must find some point of reference in the people's own experience that is similar to the concept of "born again."

Of course, all people know what birth is, and they know how to say, "to be born again." Their knowledge of physical birth can be a point of reference to begin talking about what they know, and then proceed to explain what is meant by a spiritual birth. This explanation should proceed by single, easy, and logical steps, using what the people already know to explain the new concept. After the people realize what is meant, they may suggest adding a word or two to modify the newly coined term, or they may begin to use the term but understand it in a new way.

This approach to developing New Testament vocabulary must involve the missionary in a ministry of teaching, for it is impossible to give words new contexts without explanations of how those words are being used in new contexts. The developing of vocabulary goes on simultaneously with language learning, teaching the Bible, and learning the culture of the people. If one is to go from what the people know as a basis of explaining what they do not know, one must first find out what the people know and how they express it in their language. After that, one can use what they know as a basis for making up new words that will explain new concepts to them.

Summarizing the Process

Translating the New Testament is usually the result of about ten to twenty years of work. During that time, the translator learns native-language words that may be the nearest formal equivalent to New Testament words. The people also offer possible equivalents. After they understand what the translator means, they will volunteer a word or phrase to suit that meaning. Once they have experienced salvation, they quite naturally begin to express themselves in terms of that experience.

However, you may ask, how could they express a meaning for something they have not experienced? There are ways to take people from what they know to what they do not know. At first, the points of contact may be vague and remote from each other. However, all people have the ability to adjust. This makes it possible to find a way to communicate even when words are at first inadequate.

The new words will at least express a concept that is close to the New Testament meaning. These "close" concepts must be developed until the new words used by the missionary have been comprehended by the people in the way intended.

For this to happen, it is necessary that both the missionary and the people adjust the words used. When new combinations of words have been adjusted by the contributions of both the missionary and the people, then both the missionary and the people can share the same meaning for the words chosen. Words can be developed until the new combinations of words, and the specialization of their usage has resulted in the missionary adjusting meaning on his part and the people adjusting the meaning of their words to the meaning used by the missionary. The interaction between the missionary and the people will lead to the people experiencing salvation and expressing it in their own words. The missionary must also experience the people's language and culture so that he can adjust the words he finds there to New Testament meanings.

Homework

1. Explain in your own words what the concept of teaching from the known to the unknown means.

2. What is the meaning of the term *contextual conditioning*? Write an example to illustrate "contextual conditioning."

A sign in a Tacoma, Washington men's clothing store said, "15 men's wool suits-$100-They won't last an hour!"

Chapter 33

Word Hunting, Part 3

There are several ways to employ the words already in use in a language and give them new meanings.

Widen the Focus of Words

One can give old words new meanings. The focus of a language can be widened to express concepts that were not originally a part of the local cultural setting. For example, the Sinasina people were originally not acquainted with things like airplanes and cars, but today they have a vocabulary they use to talk about such things. For the *carburetor* of a car they say, "Where it eats the benzene (gasoline)." For the *headlights* they say, "Where the fire burns." These are all fitting expressions of concepts that were not originally a part of their culture.

We can do the same thing in expressing biblical concepts. We can explain a concept to the language helper, and as soon as he understands the concept, he will be able to verbalize it even if the concept is completely new to him.

Using Old Words in New Ways

Much of the vocabulary in the Old Testament developed in a similar way. After Abraham came to the land of the Canaanites, he began to use the words of the Canaanite language in new ways. For example, Genesis 38:22 uses the phrase; *There was a harlot in this place.* The word *harlot* is the Hebrew word "qedeshah." In Exodus 22:31 the phrase *Ye shall be holy men unto me* occurs. The word "holy" in this phrase comes from the Hebrew word "qadosh" meaning "to be set apart from ordinary use for a special use." Thus, a harlot "qedeshah" was one who had been set apart from ordinary use for participating in the sexual rites used in the Canaanite worship of the fertility god Baal. When Moses wrote Genesis, he chose this same root word to express the concept of "holiness." Moses took what had been an old heathen word and used it to express new meaning.

The New Testament writers did the same thing. For example, Paul uses the phrase *our Lord Jesus*. The word *Lord* is the Greek word "kurios." Originally, the Roman people reserved the word "kurios" for Caesar. The early Christians were called atheists because they did not accept Caesar as a god. Paul, in essence, said that the real and only true "Kurios" (Lord) is the Lord Jesus. He took what was a heathen word and widened its focus to express new meaning.

This is not an isolated case. Less than fifty words are unique to the New Testament. Even these words may someday prove to be everyday language words that were used at the time of the writing of the New Testament. Even if we allow fifty words that are unique to the New Testament, these words make up less than one percent of the total vocabulary used. This should indicate to us that the vocabulary used in the New Testament was not some "heavenly" language. It was derived from words already in use among the common people. For more information on this subject, see page xv in the General Introduction of the book *Vocabulary of the Greek New Testament* by Moulton and Milligan.

Missionaries in Africa

One of the most unusual examples of vocabulary development has been the use of the word *Ndjambie* for the name of God among the Kaka people of Africa. They considered *Ndjambie* to be a venerated spider that, having spun the web that supports the universe, became submerged in the universe and lost all interest in it. He was not immoral but amoral. He did not care about whether people did right or wrong and was the epitome of unpredictable fate. How is it possible that such a word as *Ndjambie* could ever be used to represent the God of the Bible? The process of development went like this:

(1) The missionaries learned the Kaka culture in order to understand what *Ndjambie* meant to the people. This gave them a basis for making changes in the people's concept of God.

(2) The missionaries used the word *Ndjambie* in many biblical contexts. The things said about *Ndjambie* in these new contexts caused this word to take on new meanings. By teaching history as recorded in Scripture, but using the word *Ndjambie* in the places where God is mentioned, the people began to realize that he was not a cosmic spider who had spun the universe, but a loving person who had created the world and mankind.

Several Kinds of Contexts

To contextually condition a word in order to give it new meaning involves the use of several kinds of contexts.

Written Context

A word occurring in the written context of Scripture will have the meaning of that word determined by the context surrounding it. When the Kaka people read about *Ndjambie* in the context of the Bible, they realized that He is quite different from the god mentioned in their mythology. The biblical contexts divested *Ndjambie* of certain characteristics attributed to him in tribal lore and reinterpreted him in terms of what the Bible says.

See for yourself how context determines the meaning of words. Read the paragraph below and try to understand the meaning for the words *smoogle* and *comcom*.

"All smoogles have comcom. In the spring, when the smoogle emerges from hibernation, his comcom is quite inferior in quantity and quality, and not much use to man. If smoogles are given a high-protein diet during the spring months, the comcom can be sheared by late May or early June. After shearing, the smoogle can be turned loose until the next Spring. The comcom of about fifty smoogles is needed to make a lady's sweater."

Having read the written context surrounding the words *smoogle* and *comcom*, you now have a nearly complete concept of what the meaning is for these two words. You know that a *smoogle* is some kind of animal that has fur called *comcom*. (This illustration comes from David Berlo's book *The Process of Communication*, page 207.)

Verbal Context

What about people who have no Scriptures? It would be impossible to contextually condition words by a written context. In this case, verbal contextual conditioning can be used. This involves hearing a word in several spoken contexts and thus arriving at its meaning. This happens when we learn the meaning of a word. For example, among the Sinasina people I heard the word *yobilage* used when they were pointing to a bone. Therefore, I concluded that *yobilage* meant bone. Then I heard them ask God to give them "bone" to endure trials. This added a second meaning for the word to my vocabulary. In this context, it meant "strength."

Living Context

The living context is the way in which words are used in the day-to-day life of people. For example, how can people who have known only hatred and deceit learn the meaning of the word *love*? The only way they can learn it is by seeing it demonstrated in real-life situations. This is related to the old adage that says, "What you do speaks so loud that I can't hear what your saying." If we are selfish individuals, it is unlikely people of another culture will learn the meaning of the word *love* from us. It is not enough to merely tell them the meaning of biblical terms. They are not just "souls with ears." They are people who must be loved if they are to learn what love means.

One Papua New Guinean told me about another missionary saying, "He loves our people." He concluded this when he saw this missionary cry at the funeral of one of the deceased Christians. In this manner, people will learn who God is in terms of what they see Him to be in the daily life of the missionary. Much as a child develops his concept of what God is like by observing his parents, so ethnic people learn who God is from the way missionaries act towards Him in real-life situations.

Local Church Context

One of the most important ways to give a word a new context is to do so in a local New Testament church. As ethnic people become Christians and are joined together in a body of baptized believers, they will begin using words to express their common experience. In this way, old words are given new contexts. For example, the Sinasina people, at first, found it difficult to sing songs to certain tunes in their church services. This was because these melodies were sung at the annual pig-killing ceremony where immoral practices occur. However, in the early days when the churches began, there were no other tunes. So, of necessity, these old melodies were used. Now, many years later, these tunes have been "converted." The tunes have lost their old meanings and they are now considered "church" songs.

I first heard the Sinasina word for God when a Christian referred to God as *Abo Kun*, meaning, "Father the powerful one." I had heard this word used about men who were respected leaders who were rich, powerful, important men. When I heard this Christian refer to God by using the same word, I thought this was inappropriate. However, this word "Kun" has become the standard word used of God the Father (Abo Kun), God the Son (Kun Wam), and God the Holy Spirit (Kun Sugugilamie). This word developed out of the experience of Christians much like the word Lord has developed in British English. A "lord" among English gentry was a rich and important leader among the people. As English-speaking people, we now use this same word Lord as a title for God.

This is also the case in Spanish. It is rather shocking to hear Spanish speakers refer to you as Señor (Mr.) and then use the same term, Señor, to refer to God. However, this is how people develop words in local situations. Words that usually have a limited meaning are used in special senses to communicate adequately what the people want to say.

Combine Old Words into New Combinations

When words are put together in combinations, these combinations are a form of immediate context that can qualify and make a distinction in the meaning. For example, the New Testament Greek word *krino* means "I decide," but when the preposition *epi* meaning *upon* occurs with the word, as in *epikrino*, the word means "I judge." *Epi* makes the word *krino* much stronger. It no longer means just to decide. It means to judge the matter decisively with conclusive judgment."

Similarly, the German people who saw the first potatoes imported from Bolivia did not know what to call them. The potato was similar to their apple, but they knew it grew in the ground so they called it an *erdapfel* (earth-apple). Similarly, the French gave the potato the name *pomme de terre*, meaning "apple of the earth."

In the Sinasina language, it was easy to combine the word "to be born" with the word "again" to form a possible equivalent for the term "born again" as in John 3:3. This combination was, at first, rather meaningless. After a week of teaching on the subject of what Jesus meant by the term "to be born again," those who understood the concept suggested that two more words be added to the original combination. They suggested, that the word *inner person* be added to the words *born again*. The phrase means, *a rebirth of the inner person.*

A word such as *Jerusalem* can be the name of a person or just a funny-sounding word to people who have never heard of the place. However, if the word "Jerusalem" is combined with the word *city*, it is given explicit meaning. A word like *Jordan* can be put in combination with the word *river* to indicate that Jordan is a river, not a town, or a person.

The Sinasina people had no word for ships at sea, but they make a large wooden bowl that is carved out like a dugout canoe. They call the bowl a *bale*. To say *canoe* in Sinasina they use the word "water" together with "bowl" to mean canoe (a water-bowl). To say ship in Sinasina they combine the words "water," "bowl" and "sipi" (literally a water-bowl-ship). A word for *tent* did not exist in the Sinasina language, but by combining the words "cloth" and "house" it was constructed. The word "tent" literally means, *a house made of cloth.*

Listen for Words Used by Christians.

A translator should be listening closely to Christians when they pray, preach, teach, witness, or give testimonies. The vocabulary used by Christians is a source of words the missionary can use in his preaching and translation of Scripture. I first heard the word for *prayer* as I listened to them pray. I used a large picture to teach Bible stories to people. Then I would ask someone from the group to tell the same story in their own words using the same picture. As I listened to them retell the story, they used words that helped bring new vocabulary to light.

Marianna Slocum wrote an article in *The Bible Translator* about how the Tzeltal New Testament developed. She says, "The fact that the Tzeltal New Testament came into being concomitantly with the Tzeltal Church means that the vocabulary of the Tzeltal New Testament was forged in the living context of Christian experience. Terms growing out of the convert's Christian experience went into the pages of the New Testament translation, and, in turn New Testament terminology became integrated into the Christian vocabulary by a constant interplay of language and experience." She also said, "A number of terms which went into the New Testament translation came directly out of the native Christian's mouth, as they experienced the power of God in their lives and then expressed their experience in language. One such term, which the translator first heard used by one of the native Christians in prayer, was the very productive idiom *ta stojol Dios*, designating any relationship to God, such as is expressed in the New Testament. This phrase has been combined with a variety of expressions to render such concepts as *to be born of God*, *to turn one's heart to God* (converted), etc. The phrase first came from a native Christian, and has since been adapted by the native Christians in combinations which the translator would never have been capable of devising. Before the native Christians had the experience of being related to God, their language did not possess these expressions; but after having had the experience, they found ways of communicating it in words of new but meaningful combinations."[1]

A sign on a Tennessee highway said, "Take notice: when this sign is under water, this road is impassable."

Chapter 34

Word Hunting, Part 4

The method that follows is one of the most productive ways to find potential New Testament words. It results in a written record that can be studied repeatedly.

Study Native Text Material

The translator should write down native text material such as stories, myths, legends, songs, and proverbs. He should search these texts thoroughly to find useful vocabulary. Text material is anything a native speaker says freely without being told how to say it.

No translator should attempt to do Bible translating until he has analyzed at least 200 pages of text material. Analyzing text material will not only help the missionary understand the linguistic structure of the language, and find new vocabulary, but will also turn up valuable material about the culture of the ethnic people.

The mythology of ethnic peoples is their form of literature. People who do not have written literature will have an oral literature. This *literature* is memorized and passed down from generation to generation. Mythology is usually the best explanation they have for such things as disease, death, and sickness. These stories reinforce the reasons for the control of society. They explain why incest is bad, why a man should work, and why things that are forbidden should not be done. All people have stories explaining the origins of the world, the universe, and humankind. The stories are told to the young to teach them why they should conform to culturally accepted norms.

Recording Text Material

The best way to begin recording the oral literature of a people is to begin with a semi-controlled text. In the beginning, if a native speaker is asked to tell a story into the microphone of a tape recorder, he will talk too long, and the text will be too difficult for the missionary to write down and analyze. The translator should begin with a few semi-controlled texts. In a semi-controlled text, the missionary tells the language helper what the content of the story should be. The story should consist of only two or three simple facts. Let the language helper tell these facts in his own words without interruption. Record it on a tape recorder. This will result in a short text with which to work. The missionary should listen to the tape, and with the help of his language helper, write down the text leaving five or six spaces between lines. In the spaces, he can go back through the text and try to discover the morpheme-by-morpheme, word-by-word, sentence-by-sentence meaning. He should first write the text and then under the text write a word-by-word, translation of the text. Finally, he should write a loose translation of what each sentence means. He may not be able to account for everything in the text. One should leave what cannot be understood and keep looking for the meaning of it in other texts until one discovers the meaning of the entire text. Try to "milk" the text dry; that is, gain from it every scrap of information you can about the phonological structure, the morphological structure, the syntactical structure, and the word meanings.

After analyzing the linguistic structure, one should look for idiomatic expressions. One should look for ways to connect units of thought. Later, as you take down stories about the people's way of life, you will have questions to ask your language helper. The questions should be carefully thought out after the text is recorded. Ask them in such a way that your helper realizes you are simply trying to learn and not criticizing his way of life. You also will need to gain his confidence to the point that he realizes you will not be publicly criticizing the things he has told to you in confidence. If you keep that confidence, your language helper will feel free to tell you most anything you want to know.

By recording native language texts, you will begin to notice major cultural themes. You will begin to see what is important to the people. You will also find hundreds of new words and idiomatic expressions. These should be carefully filed in a dictionary file with cross-referencing to show who told the story and what text the words came from. Cultural data should be filed in your culture file.

One of the most helpful sources of vocabulary for translating God's Word comes from text material. Maxine Morarie, a translator for the Ayore Indians in Bolivia, says, "I truly feel that the work I did on texts made the difference between a technically correct document and a living, communicating translation that sounded like Ayore."[1]

Wayne Gill explains what a text is, how to get one on tape, how to transcribe it, and how to use it. "When I have a situation in the Bible to translate, I try to remember a similar situation, and look it up in text material to see how it was stated. Myths are extremely valuable for getting spiritual vocabulary and seeing how they think. You can't see the value of stories about monkeys and foxes? I found the word for contract (or covenant) in a story about a man selling his son to the devil."[2]

Letters that a native speaker writes to you in his own language are a good source of text material. The recording of sermons by native speakers can also be written down as a rich source of information. Wayne Gill often found vocabulary for translating the New Testament by recording sermons by a native speaker on a certain topic. When looking for a word like *prayer*, he would help someone study the subject of prayer and then record that person's teaching and listen to the tape for the vocabulary he needed to teach on that topic.

Here is a sample text I recorded after I asked my language helper to tell me about a funeral we had observed together. The text tells a great deal about some of the beliefs of the Sinasina people. It can be used as a springboard into other areas of the people's way of life. There are three lines in each section. On the first line are the words as they were recorded on the tape recorder. The next line is a word-for-word translation of each word including the morphology of the word. The last line is a loose translation of the sentence. Read it and see if you can find out anything about the language and culture of the Sinasina people from the text that follows.

The Funeral of Kua

(1) *Ena   yalta   kam   Kua.*
So then, man-a name-his Kua.
So then, (there was) a man named Kua.

(2) Yali yobal si-si ewa.
    Man-he people hit-hit did-he.
He hit [killed] many people.

(3) Yali are igene teran yobal milege suwa.
    Man-he sun time one people many hit-he.
In one day, he killed many people.

(4) Kamin kware yal, golmue.
    Sky long ago man die-he
Because he was very old, he died.

(5) Gongoro bol balere,
    Die-after-he, box carving
After he died, they carving a coffin,

(6) gal ire, yobilere,
    cloth taking, wrapping,
taking cloth, wrapping him,

(7) bol igal domue.
    box inside put they.
they put him in a coffin.

(8) Erekilage balere kamamene ige pire
    tree-crossed carving, religious house going,
Carving a cross and going to the church,

(9) kamamene ditomue.   Ditere
    religious-talk say-give to him. Saying it,
They preached to him.   After saying it,

(10) gilpenel maul sire yalta kam Sa,
     graveyard hole hitting, man-a name-his Sa
they buried him at the graveyard, and a man named Sa,

(11) erekilage tere el ditomue, "Kua,
     tree-crossed giving, like say-to him, "Kua.
gave a cross to him and said to him, "Kua.

(12) Koginan enga, bawa dimue.
     Work-your you did, done is it.
Your work is done."

(13) En erekilage ire Kun molawal po."
     You tree-cross taking, God be-at   go!
You take (this) cross and go to God!"

(14). El dire tomue.
      Like saying, gave-he to him
Saying like that, he gave it to him.

(That is, he stuck the cross in the ground at the head of Kua's gravesite.)

There is a wealth of information in this text about the Sinasina language and culture.

Use Generic Words to Find Specific Words

The translator can use generic words to help him find specific words, or he can use specific words to help him find generic words. Words such as *furniture* and *vegetable* are generic words, whereas such words as *rocking chair* and *carrot* are specific words. The word *rocking chair* is included within the generic word *furniture*. The word *carrot* is included within the word *vegetable*. Therefore, one can find a specific word by first finding a generic word and asking for the specific things that are included in the generic word. The words *tal nige dongwa* in Sinasina mean "something no good." It is a generic word and covers a wide range of bad things. If you ask a Sinasina what things are considered *tal nige dongwa*, meaning *something no good*, he will say, "Killing people, stealing, adultery and other bad things." From the general word "something no good" we can quickly learn specific words for murder, stealing, and adultery. On the other hand, if we knew the specific words for stealing, murder, and adultery, we could ask, "What is the term which covers all these bad things?" The Sinasina people would reply, "All those things are *tal nige dongwa*," which means, "something no good."

If a missionary were not careful to find out if a word has a generic meaning or a specific meaning, he may use words in his translation that mean something like this: "For all have stolen and come short of the glory of God." (Romans 3:23) "Stolen" is too specific a word for this verse because it limits sin to stealing. This verse needs a more generic word that would cover all the areas defined as sin by the moral law of God.

John Beekman says, "The translator who worked with the Manobo language in the Philippines was searching for a term to translate the concept 'to blaspheme.' He started with the generic term to criticize, modified this with a manner component, and arrived at the generic expression, 'to criticize by speech.' With this generic expression, he asked his language helper for different kinds of verbal activity whereby one could criticize another. This produced a set of eight words, some of which had not before been encountered. Comparing and contrasting the meaning of each of these words revealed significant components which were essential in choosing an accurate equivalent for the biblical term 'to blaspheme.'"[3]

Use Hypothetical Situations

This method for discovering potential New Testament formal equivalent words involves some understanding of the language and culture of the ethnic people. The missionary must be able to describe culturally appropriate situations. After explaining these situations to the language helper, he can ask for words that describe the situations mentioned. From the responses of the language helper, he may find new words to use.

For example, a missionary found the term *salvation* by telling the language helper about four situations that could happen in the local culture. The first one was of a boy cutting a tree that fell on him, leaving him pinned under a heavy branch. A man named Roberto came and cut the branch to free the boy. The second was a story about a man capsized in a canoe, who could not swim. Roberto pulled him out of the water. The third story was of a man who shot a wild pig, only wounding it. The pig was attacking the man when Roberto happened along and killed the pig. The final story was of a burning house in which a child was trapped. Roberto went into the blazing house, and brought the child out safely. This question was asked of the translation helper: "What did Roberto do for these people?" The answer to the question would be something about delivering them, saving them from harm, or helping them. The reply of the language helper produced a word that was a possible term for *salvation*.

Similarly, one can find out how a Greek word was used in everyday life. The contexts in which the word was used will indicate its meaning. Trench did this when he tried to find the meaning of the Greek word *repentance*. He found in Plutarch's writings an example of two murderers who, having spared a child, afterward *repented* and slew him. By finding several examples of how a word is used in context, we can tell what that word means.

Borrow Words

All languages borrow words from other languages. The English word "chocolate" is actually an Aztec Indian word from Mexico.

One may borrow words from the national language for use in translation, but should do so only when one knows what that national language word means in the ethnic language. In Spanish the word *santo* is used by Roman Catholics to mean "holy," but to many Indians in Latin America the word *santo* means the images of the saints who are referred to as "santo."

Three Ways a National Word Can Be Used

(1) We can use a national word that is not understood by the ethnic people and contextually condition it to fit the desired meaning. This was done in the Yagaria language of Papua New Guinea. The missionaries began talking about "Goti" (God). At first, they knew nothing about who Goti was. Thirty years later, this word is the nearest formal equivalent to the God of the Bible.

(2) One can use a national word that is only partially understood by the ethnic people. Eventually, through teaching, their partial understanding of the word can be expanded to include all that the word means.

(3) A national word may be used in the ethnic translation because the ethnic people understand it correctly. The Hamtai people in Papua New Guinea use a transliteration of the English word *elder*. The Hamtai Christians use the word "Elda" to describe the men who are the pastors of their churches.

We should not be overly protective of the ethnic language by trying to keep it pure from foreign words. Words will be borrowed from the national language no matter how much it may be discouraged. Such words, when properly understood, become part of the vocabulary of that language. However, excessive borrowing of words from the national language should be avoided.

Ask Questions

This is probably the most difficult way to find words needed for translating. It is difficult to ask the right questions in the right way that will yield the desired results. Many ethnic societies are sensitive to direct questions. They will often give the reply that they think the person asking the question wants. We can still ask questions if we take the answer "with a grain of salt." One should not consider them valid until proven true in other ways.

Questions should go from what the language helper knows well, to that with which he may be less familiar. The questions should be specific and concrete. If one wanted to know about marriage in the United States, it would be too general to ask someone, "What is marriage like in the United States?" It would be better to ask, "John, how did you get your wife?" After asking several people this question, one should have a good understanding of marriage in the United States. Questions that ask *why* are usually not the most productive for getting reliable answers. It is possible for a person to be so involved with his culture that he does not know why he does the things he does. You may ask someone in the United States "Why do you wear a necktie to church?" It would be difficult for them to give a logical reason for such neck-strangling behavior. "Why do Americans drink iced tea with their meals?" This would also be hard to explain. Sometimes a "why" question will produce good information, but one should realize that his language helper cannot always tell him why certain things are done. They just are.

Questioning can be especially useful in finding out about spirit beings. One can ask, "Who is this spirit? What does this spirit do? Can he do other things? Where does this spirit live? What is this spirit like? What power does he have? Does he help people?" To find a word for God, We can ask, "Who made the earth? Did someone make the first man and woman? Who has more power than anyone else?"

Sometimes the way we ask a question will result in wrong information. Unless questions are asked with care and sensitivity, the information gathered may be worthless or misleading.

Find Words through Teaching

By teaching the meaning of a word until it is understood clearly, the translator may find many productive expressions. If a language helper comes to a clear understanding of the meaning of a word, he will be able to express the meaning of that word in his language. A phrase like *born again* can be taught. By using what people know about physical birth, one can explain spiritual rebirth. Once the people understand the concept, they can give you ways to say it in their language.

Even the word *sin* can be explained from what the people themselves consider wrong. All people consider certain acts as socially unacceptable. There are also government laws that must be obeyed. All the concepts, which they already understand, can be used to explain what they do not yet understand.

One of the basic ways new things are learned is by comparison. My mathematics teacher explained division by drawing a pie on the board. She said, "If I cut this pie down the middle we call this side one half. If I cut it across again from side to side we have four pieces, and we call each of them one fourth." I was able to understand this immediately because she had taken me from what I already knew (cutting a pie) to what I did not know (the meaning of division). We can do the same thing with ethnic people. The problem, of course, is for us to learn what they know. Once we understand something about their culture, we can use this as a basis to explain new concepts and ask what they call them. Once they understand the concept, they have no problem telling us how they say it in their language.

Testing a Word

The translator should test words to see if they are being understood correctly. Even when a word is inadequate, it is better to work with inadequate words than none at all. One cannot correct misunderstandings by silence. Inadequate words can lead to adequate words and finally to the nearest formal equivalents of New Testament words. Silence has its own meaning and cannot be improved upon, since a silent communication has no verbal feedback to use for the improvement of communication. We assume wrongly that to say nothing is better than saying something wrong. Silence on the part of the missionary merely allows the ethnic people to put their *own* meaning on everything the missionary says.

We should use a given word even though it may not have all the meaning we desire. By using it, we make a beginning that allows for a process of development. One should consider any new word as a *potential* formal equivalent of a New Testament term, not as an proven equivalent. Only follow-up checking and continued use of feedback will finally confirm if a word is the nearest formal equivalent to a New Testament word. This checking of a potential term should be done by finding out how the term is used in various contexts. For this, it may be helpful to use a different language helper other than the one who originally gave you the word. You may have overly influenced the original person who gave you the word. Ask the second language helper how the word would be used in situations in village life. Once we know several contexts in which the word is used, we are nearer to a reliable understanding of that word.

The English poet Coleridge summed up the potential for vocabulary development when he said, **"Language is the armory of the human mind, and at once contains the trophies of its past, and the weapons of its future conquests."**[4]

A sign in a New York restaurant said, "Customers who find our waitresses rude ought to see the manager."

Chapter 35

Checking the Translation

After a translator has translated a few chapters of a book of the Bible, a translation consultant should check them. This is not just to find all the mistakes of the translator, but also to get him started on the right track. A large part of translation checking involves the consultant helping the translator learn some "tricks of the trade." The things he learns from the checking sessions will help him do a better job in less time.

The checking session should be far more than just bringing mistakes to light. It should be a time of learning from someone who has already done translation. If a translator is willing to accept help, he will be a better translator. His translation will be better than if he had not submitted it to the unbiased scrutiny of others. The book of Proverbs says, "He that is first in his own cause seemeth just; but his neighbor cometh and searcheth him." We all have blind spots. We may think our translation is the greatest thing since the King James Version, but when someone else looks at it, it most likely will need some help.

Proverbs 11:14 says, "Where no counsel is, the people fall: but in the multitude of counsellors there is safety." A translation that is made without the counsel of others will be the poorer for it. Wise is the translator who submits his work to someone who has already walked the translation road and knows how to avoid some of the pitfalls and dead-end streets.

The goal of a good translation consultant is not to find everything that is wrong with the translation and point this out to the translator. The goal of a good translation consultant is to help the translator learn to do a better job of translating by becoming his own critic and finding his own mistakes.

2 Corinthians 13:1 says, "In the mouth of two or three witnesses shall every word be established." There is a need for multiple witnesses to the validity of your translation. If someone else has an objective look at it, this lends credence to the validity of your work. There have been translations done that were translated from the wrong text, done without adequate knowledge of the language, done without the help of a native language speaker, done without checking with sound biblical exegetes, and so on. All of the heartache of these kinds of situations can be avoided simply by making use of a good translation consultant.

Translators have translated the entire New Testament without consulting anyone else. Then they wanted it printed immediately and became very defensive if anyone even dared to ask what text was used as the basis of the translation.

It takes an average of three weeks per major book of the New Testament to do an adequate job of checking it. It should never happen (but it does) that a translator has finished several major books of the New Testament or the entire New Testament before having any of it checked by a Bible translation consultant. It is unreasonable to bring an entire New Testament to a consultant and ask him to check it. It can be done this way, but it is a very painful way to do it. The checking of a translation must be done in small, manageable units to be the most helpful.

Making a Back Translation

To check a book properly, it should be back translated into a form of English that reflects the meaning of the ethnic language text. However, the back translation should not be so literal as to make no sense in English. The idioms in the ethnic text should be translated into an English form that the consultant can understand. The translator also must back translate honestly. If he says the ethnic text says such-and-such when it does not, his translation suffers for it. If he wants his translation to benefit from the checking sessions, he should honestly say what his translation says in the ethnic text and not what he *hopes* it says or what he *wants* it to say.

The consultant should receive your back translation at least two weeks in advance. This will give the consultant time to study it.

The following pages include an example of a back translation of the Gospel of Mark in the Yagaria language of Papua New Guinea. It will give you some idea as to how one should do a back translation of the ethnic text.

Yagaria Mark 2:1-7

(1.) All right, later Jesus came again to Kapaneamu (Capernaum) town, and the talk, "He came and is (here)" went-came-did (spread around) and the men-women (people) heard it.

(2.) They having heard, a lot of people came and meeting, they gathering, they filled up inside the house and because it was not open (there was no way) for some other people to come and be (there inside) they crowded together at the doorway also. They did and Jesus proclaiming said to them the gospel talk.

(3.) As he was speaking (thus) to them, some other people came, with-two with-two (four) men came carrying-as-they-came an always not moving-man on a stretcher.

(4.) They came but all the men and women were crowded (packed closely) and (as a result) there was no road way open for them to come to the place of Jesus' skin (near Jesus). Because it wasn't open, they went up on the housetop and opened the roof and as the previously-mentioned man was lying on the stretcher on which they brought him, they released him, and he went down.

(5.) He went down and Jesus saw-perceived their trust (they) saying (or thinking) about him, "He is able to help-him-heal-him, this man" and he (Jesus) said to that previously mentioned man, "My son, I throw-away-remove (forgive) all of the bad actions which you have (more than once) done."

(6.) He said that and some of the teaching-law-talk-men, (being there) heard a lot of ears (thought much) in their stomachs (insides), like this: What's this man up to, they said (thought).

(7.) He is speaking truly bad words, doing-ruin towards God's name (extreme disrespect, blasphemy) they said thought. He said, "I throw-away-remove (forgive) your bad actions," but "the work of removing bad actions is the work of God only," they said.

Why Make a Back Translation?

Why go to all the work of making a back translation?

(1) The first use of a back translation is to check your work. You can do this before the consultant comes. It will help you find any deletions of words, or verses. You can check for over-translating where extraneous information may have crept into the translation. If sections of the back translation seem confusing, you can check to see how a native speaker comprehends them. This should be done with a language helper other than the one who originally did the translation. This will ensure an unbiased reading and verbal translation of the text.

(2) You can pass copies of your back translation to coworkers, who can also do a check and raise any questions they might have. If they follow verse by verse through the back translation, while reading in the English text of the King James Version, they may detect an omission, an over-translation, or a wrong interpretation of a verse.

(3) The back translation will be useful to others who will be translating in related languages or even in distantly related ones. They can consult your back translation for ideas about how to translate a verse or help them solve the problem of interpreting a particular verse.

A Checking Procedure

At the checking session, a translation helper other than the one who translated the book should be used. This will help to ensure objectivity and not put the translation helper in a place where he may become overly defensive. The translator should read the book aloud from the ethnic text one unit of thought at a time. This may be a sentence, a verse, or a paragraph. After the translator reads it aloud, the translation helper should be asked to give a verbal explanation of what the text means to him.

It is best for him to tell what the verse means in a language the consultant understands. If not, the translator must explain what the language helper said. Any dishonesty by the translator about what the language helper said will mean that the translation will be poorer. At this point, some friction could result. Be very careful not to argue with the language helper. He is the final authority on what his language means. If you come to a place that is controversial, consider what the language helper has said, make a note of it, and come back to it later when tempers have cooled down and you can look at it more objectively.

A translator should be willing to change a rendering of a verse, or change his interpretation of a verse, but should not change either unless there is good reason to do so. The translator should try to be balanced in this. Do not be overly defensive of your translation but do not change things that you are not convinced should be changed. One of the main purposes of meeting with a translation consultant is that you may learn how to do a better job. Therefore, listen carefully and consider what he says. Do not follow a consultant blindly, but try to understand why he wants you to change something. Be willing to learn. "Hear counsel, and receive instruction, that thou mayest be wise." (Proverbs 19:20)

Discourse Structure

The translator must become familiar with the way the ethnic language ties small units of thought together into a larger whole. No translation should be done one verse at a time. Regard must be given to how the verses fit together and how this linking structure should be translated in the ethnic language. The translator should analyze enough ethnic text material to become familiar with the way this is done in the language into which he is translating.

Every language has a way of tying units of meaning together. For example, "He is big and tall." The word *and* links the words *big* and *tall*. Links also occur between sentences. For example, "He is big, but I am not afraid." Either phrase can stand by itself. The word *but* links them together to show that a relationship exists between the two. Links also occur between paragraphs. For example, there may be a paragraph explaining how a certain course of action is better than another one. The paragraph following it would begin with the word *therefore*. This word would link the two paragraphs together into a unit of statement and conclusion. The translator must be careful not to translate only verse by verse, but in larger units of thought. These should be translated in such a way that they link together using the ethnic language discourse structure. All languages have a discourse structure as well as a phoneme structure, morpheme structure, word structure, sentence structure and paragraph structure. The translator must find out, from text material, how paragraphs are linked together to form a unit of discourse. The translator should use these same methods to link his translation into a whole discourse.

Some languages have special kinds of discourse usage. One type is used when speaking about things the speaker considers factual. Another type is used when speaking about things considered fiction. It would be tragic not to know the difference and in ignorance translate the Bible using the fictional mode of discourse. It would sound like an English fairy tale beginning with, "Once upon a time, God created the heavens and the earth."

Checking Your Own Translation

One should check his translation before a consultant sees it. This can take care of some of the corrections that would come up in the consulting session. The thing to aim for is accurate feedback from native speakers. Read a complete thought from your translation and ask them what it means. Carefully consider the feedback they are giving you.

Feedback will tell you whether you are achieving your goal of an accurate translation of the Word of God. During World War II, gunners on ships firing at airplanes used tracer bullets to tell them how close their shots were coming to their targets. Because they could see the feedback from the tracer bullets, they were able to correct their errors and bring the stream of bullets to bear directly on the target. Similarly, accurate feedback from native speakers can tell us whether we are "on target." It will also help us to find deletions and wrong meanings.

Eight Ways to Check Your Translation

After the initial translation sessions are over and a first draft has been written, it should be allowed to "cool" for a while. Put it aside and go on to other passages. After a week or so come back to the earlier material and use some of the following ways of checking the translation:

(1) Read it aloud to a group and then ask a volunteer to repeat what he heard in his own words. If the text is narrative, this works quite well. It is harder if the text is from one of the epistles of Paul. When the native speaker attempts to repeat what he heard, it will become obvious what he understood. Often new vocabulary comes out of such sessions as an additional benefit for checking it.

(2) Have a native speaker read aloud while you listen. Mark the places where he stumbles, pauses, or seems confused. Have others read the same text and mark the places where each one has trouble. If three or more marks occur in the same place, this could indicate a lack of clarity.

(3) Read the text one unit of meaning at a time, and have a native speaker tell you what he thinks the text said. This should be done with someone other than the person who originally translated it. If the native speaker is puzzled or misunderstands, make a note of where this misunderstanding occurred and, if possible, indicate what caused the misunderstanding.

(4) Read the text to a native speaker and ask questions to test his comprehension. This is easy to do with narrative. It is harder to do with Paul's letters. However, in either case it can be done with some profit if one asks questions skillfully. Ask who did what to whom. Ask where the events took place and why.

(5) Read the passage but stop at places asking the native speaker to fill in the missing word or words. If he has comprehended up to that point, he should be able to do this.

(6) Give a copy of the passage to some native speakers and tell them to take it home and read it. Have them write down any mistakes they find or comments they have about a passage.

(7) Read the translation to yourself. This will help you find places where some polishing would make it sound better. You may notice some places where you do not understand the meaning yourself. Note this and check it with a native speaker.

(8) Produce a trial edition for use in teaching and for a few people to read. This trial edition should be known as such, and the people's comments encouraged.

During this process, develop a method of recording the first-draft reading and the suggested changes. Lightly cross out the original text but leave enough space to put in the suggested readings. Occasionally, the original reading will end up as the preferred one. So, find a way to keep all the feedback and use it to make your translation a better one.

Finally, decide which reading is the best and put it into print. Revisions and improvements could go on forever, but it must stop sometime.

If you would like to read more about checking a translation, see Katharine Barnwell's book, *Bible Translation*, pages 186-194.

A Tanzanian newspaper advertisement said, "Mt Kilimanjaro, the breathtaking backdrop for Serena Lodge. Swim in the lovely pool as you drink it all in."

Chapter 36

Faithfulness in Translation

What conditions must a translation meet to be considered a faithful one? It is often assumed that any translation of the Scriptures into an ethnic language will have to be a paraphrase and thus not a faithful one. This is not true. Any language will be able to say anything any other language can say. The conditions a faithful translation must meet are as follows:

(1) The Textus Receptus Greek text and the King James Version must be used as the basis of the translation of the New Testament, and the Masoretic Hebrew Text and the King James Version must be used as the basis of the Old Testament translation. If another text is used, it will lack many verses that have been deleted in the critical texts.

(2) The meaning of the Bible text must be transferred into the nearest formal equivalent meaning in the ethnic language text.

(3) The ethnic language reader must be able to read the translation with nearly the same degree of ease, as did the readers of the original book in the first century. If the translation is difficult to read because a phonemic analysis of the language was not done, or because the translation has long sentences that overload the reader, the translation is not communicating what the original author intended and is therefore not a faithful translation.

Five Barriers to Faithful Translation

(1) Incorrectly interpreting the meaning of the Bible text.

If one does not know the meaning of the biblical text or refuses to decide what the meaning is, he cannot translate that text. Transliteration is the only form of translating that can take place without regard to interpretation. Translation can only occur when the nearest formal equivalent meaning is transferred from one language to another. The translator must know what the meaning of the Bible text is before he can begin to transfer it into another language. If the translator misunderstands a Bible text, he produces a meaning in the ethnic translation that was not intended by the original author.

There is a common misconception abroad that a Bible translator should not interpret the Bible. However, a translator must translate what the text means, nothing more, and nothing less. To do this, a translator must be a faithful exegete of the Bible before he can be a faithful translator of it. He must understand what the original author intended by the words he wrote. If he does not know this, or assumes he knows it without careful study, it is most unlikely that he will translate the meaning faithfully. He will introduce into the text a meaning different from the one intended by the original author.

Hebrews 12:17 says, "For ye know how that afterward, when he would have inherited the blessing, he was rejected: for he found no place of repentance, though he sought it carefully with tears." This verse is often interpreted to mean that Esau was unable to repent although he sought it carefully with tears. However, this was not the intended meaning. Esau found no place of repentance in his father Isaac who refused to change his mind about the blessing he had given Jacob even though Esau cried and begged him to do so.

Too often, a translator jumps to a conclusion about what a text means without carefully studying to find out what the author meant. For example, what does the word *so* mean in John 3:16? "For God *so* loved the world..." Everyone knows that this verse means that God loved the world *so much* that He gave his only begotten Son, right? In fact, it does *not* say that. The word *so* in verse 16 is the same word found in verse 14, where it is translated "even so." Verse 14 says, "As Moses lifted up the serpent in the wilderness, *even so* must the Son of man be lifted up." In verse 14, the Greek word 'ουτωσ is translated, "even so," meaning that in the same way Moses lifted up the serpent on the pole, *in this way* must the Son of Man be lifted up on the cross. The word *so* in verse 14 means "in this way." Why would it not mean the same thing in verse 16? In fact it does.

The Lexicon of Liddell and Scott defines the meaning of 'ουτωσ (*so*) as "in this manner." Thayer says in his Lexicon that 'ουτωσ (*so*) means "in this manner." Moulton and Milligan, in their book on the vocabulary of the New Testament, list a quote from a piece of secular literature where the word 'ουτωσ (*so*) is used in this sentence: "As the gods have not spared me, *in the same manner* 'ουτωσ (*sò*) I also will not spare the gods." The word 'ουτωσ (*so*) that is translated "in the same manner" in this secular piece of literature is the same word that is translated as "so" ('ουτωσ) in John 3:16. This verse does not mean that God love the world so much, but that God love the world *in this manner*; that is, He loved the world by giving His only begotten Son. This is *how* God loved people not the *degree* that God loved the world. The author of the book, John, intends to show that God loved people by the self-sacrificing manner in which He gave of Himself for them in the Person of His Son, Jesus.

John says this same thing in 1 John 4:9: "In this was manifested the love of God toward us, because that God sent his only begotten Son into the world, that we might live through him." John says that the love of God was revealed toward us by His sending of His Son into the world. We know the love of God not by the degree of his emotion, but by the depth of his self-sacrificial *action*. We must become accurate exegetes of the Bible. If we do not interpret it correctly, we will make the Scripture say something that God did not say.

(2) Losing some of the meaning in the text.

A loss of information can occur when the translator fails to include in his translation the meaning of all the words in the text. The translator may simply forget to translate words that were in the text and so are omitted in his translation. A loss of words can also occur when the nearest formal equivalent meaning of a word in the source text is not achieved in the ethnic text. The word in the ethnic text is not the nearest formal equivalent of the word in the Scripture.

(3) Failing to keep extraneous information out of the text.

An example of this is Acts 12:4 where the King James translators used the word *Easter* to translate the Greek word *paska*, meaning Passover. They could have translated the Greek word *paska* as Passover. This would have avoided introducing the problem of the word *Easter* into the text.

Another example of introducing extraneous material into the text would be to always translate the Greek present tense as a continuous action verb in the ethnic text even when such information would not be important to understanding the verse correctly.

(4) Failing to produce an accurate phonemic analysis of the ethnic language.

If the alphabet used to represent the ethnic language is not based on a phonemic analysis, it will be difficult for the ethnic people to read the translation. There is also the under-phonemicised alphabet where all the phonemes of the language are not accounted for in the alphabet. The opposite of the under-phonemicised alphabet is the over-phonemicised alphabet where an excessive number of diacritics and unusual symbols are used to represent the phonemes of the language. This also makes it difficult for the people to read the translation.

(5) Failing to keep the translation from being so culturally relevant that it sounds like the biblical events took place just last week in an ethnic village.

A translation must not be so culturally "hip" that it sounds like the "Cotton Patch Version" by C. L. Jordan, who translates as if the historical context of the book was in the state of Georgia. For example, in this version the phrase "Now as touching things offered to idols" becomes "Now about working on Sunday." The phrase "Give none offense neither to the Jews, nor to the Gentiles." becomes "Set a good example for both whites and Negroes." This kind of translating violates the historical context of the Bible.

The translator must also not violate metaphors and similes for the sake of being relevant. Captain Rodgers of the Merchant Marine translates the twenty-third Psalm as if it were in a marine setting. His translation reads, "The Lord is my pilot; I shall not drift." This kind of translation may sound clever, but it is a violation of both the historical context and the metaphor used about sheep in this Psalm.

A Suggested Translation Procedure

First, one must master the ethnic language to the extent that he can discuss translation issues with a native speaker. He must accurately describe the phonological and grammatical systems of the language. He must also write down and analyze several hundred pages of native language text material. Now he is ready to begin some practice translating. The practice translating should be of some rather simple material, probably beginning with either Bill Young's "God's Message for you" (see Chapter 38) or a story form of Old Testament history. The missionary can use this practice translation as a means to learn how to improve his translation skills. After a pre-translation stage, the translator may begin a more formal type of translation. There are two basic ways to approach this.

(1) The translator can do some studying beforehand and be clear about the meaning of what he wants to translate. After that, he can sit down with his translation helper and begin explaining in the language some idea of what he wants the native speaker to say.

If the translator cannot explain the meaning of a verse to the language helper in his native language, he is not ready to begin translating. When you are ready to begin, explain to the language helper the word, sentence, verse, or paragraph you want to translate and have him express it in his own words. Write this down and check it to see if it is what is desired. Ask how the words would be used in the every day life of the ethnic people. After you write a verse that you think is a satisfactory translation, read it back to your helper. See if he likes it that way or wants to make changes.

The pre-translation stage is intended to be a stage of development when you can learn how to translate. Naturally, your translation is suspect, probably stilted, and may even have some wrong meanings. However, you should use what you have as a basis for learning to do better translation work. Encourage the language helper to correct you. Learn how to say things better and how to connect sentences into a free flowing whole. Put what you complete aside for a few days and then come back to it.

Establish confidence and empathy with your language helper. Develop your ability to communicate with him. Be careful about unduly influencing your language helper to say things the way you want them to be said. He knows his language. Heed his advice if he tells you to express the meaning in a certain way.

Most likely, he will tend toward being very literal and may give you things that mean nonsense. Because you asked for them that way, he will give it to you the way he thinks you want it. After a pre-translation stage, the next stage may be translation of Old Testament Bible stories beginning with Genesis: the creation of the world, the fall of humankind into a sinful state, the universal flood, etc. This kind of translating should be done in story form and should not be thought of as strict translation in a verse-by-verse format.

(2) The second way translation can be done is to write out a suggested form of the translation before the session with the language translation helper, then work with him in the session to revise it into a form that he approves.

In either case, the translator must do his study preparation before the session with the translation helper. After that, the translator can either form the translation during the session with the helper, or he can do it before the session and bring it to the native speaker for his corrections. Develop a routine that is the most productive one for you.

(Further help on translating sessions can be found in *Bible Translating* by E. Nida, pages 81-87.)

Homework

Review the following concepts for the final examination:
    Componential analysis
    Figures of speech
    Abstract nouns
    Rhetorical questions
    Genitive constructions
    Passive constructions
    Implied information
    Indirect quotes
    Hyperbole
    Synecdoche
    Personification
    Doublet
    Collocational clash
    Cultural substitutes
    Order of elements
    Ellipsis
    Pronominal reference
    Comparatives
    Transitions

When the Pope visited Miami an Anglo tried to sell T-shirts with the logo, "I saw the Pope" in Spanish. However, he did not know that Spanish has two genders. Instead of printing, "El Papa" (the Pope), he printed, "La Papa" (the potato). No one wanted shirts that said, "I saw the potato."

Chapter 37

Translation Development

The progression through which a Bible translation develops can be divided into three stages:

Stage One: Pre-translation

1. Learning the language and culture.

2. Phonological and Grammatical analysis of the language and reducing the language to writing by producing a phonemic alphabet.

3. Exegetical preparation for understanding the biblical text.

4. Learning to discuss translation problems with the translation helper in the ethnic language.

5. Doing some practice translation to developing translation skills, develop vocabulary and teach Bible truth.

Stage Two: Translation Proper

1. Learning to use translation principles more effectively.

2. Learning to use a native speaker as co-translator.

3. Selection of the nearest formal equivalent meanings by developing vocabulary needed to translate the New Testament.

Stage Three: Post-Translation

1. Checking the translation with a consultant.

2. Improving the translation by revision and reader reaction.

3. Checking the translation for ease of reading by ethnic speakers.

4. Checking the translation for cohesion of the discourse as a whole.

5. Intuitive polishing of the translation for a smoother flow for oral reading in public.

Pre-translation Stage

Because ethnic people do not have an understanding of the chronological order in which biblical events occurred, it is necessary for them to learn some Bible background if they are to fit events into proper perspective. You soon realize the importance of this when one of the ethnic people asks, in all seriousness, if Jesus lived in your town and if you knew Him personally.

This came as quite a shock to the missionaries to the Baruya people in Papua New Guinea. When they first taught them about the Genesis account of the Flood, the Baruya people began to make preparations for the flood that they understood to be coming immediately. The people had no context to put the biblical events, so the only thing they could conclude was that the event was to take place in the present time.

When I spoke to the Sinasina people about Christ, they assumed that I had known Him personally during my lifetime. They had no concept of events that took place two thousand years before. To a people who are accustomed to thinking in terms of three or four generations, the concept of thousands of years is, at first, beyond their ability to comprehend.

Teach the Bible Chronologically

There is a need to teach the people the chronology of biblical events so they can understand Bible truth in biblical context. We must do this for at least two reasons:

(1) The Bible is written with its own context. God did not begin the Bible with the story of the life of Christ. He began at the beginning, in Genesis, to show the need for the coming of His Son into the world. Without an understanding of the events that happened before the New Testament, the life of Christ would not be correctly understood.

We need to give the people the same context that the Bible itself does. We need to teach the events of the Bible chronologically and explain the meaning of them as they happened in the unfolding of the plan of God to redeem mankind. It is presumptuous to expect people with little or no biblical background to understand New Testament concepts unless they understand the Old Testament history that has established the basis for those concepts.

If we do not translate the Old Testament directly, we should have the equivalent in some kind of story form. This will give the people a context into which they can place all the events of biblical history.

(2) Since the Bible begins at the beginning of time, so should we. The translator should begin by making a simple translation of the Genesis creation story. It should be done in story form because a strict verse-by-verse translation may be too difficult to do in the early stage of translation. The translator should make clear to the people that it is story form and not a strict translation of Scripture.

The Genesis account will begin laying down foundational truths about who God is, what He has done, and what He is like. It will also explain who man is and how he became sinful. The most important point of the history of redemption is the need of people to be forgiven of sins. The basis for understanding this need is given in the Genesis account. This will help people understand why it was necessary for the Lord Jesus to come to earth to die for their sins and why they need to repent and receive Him as their Savior.

It is important not to have material in the translation that is not found in the Bible. It should be accurate even though it may leave out many of the details. A verse-by-verse translation can be done later. In the pre-translation stage, a translator's work is mainly for his own learning experience. It will also provide him with material for teaching the people. This teaching will give the people an understanding of the chronological order in which biblical events occurred. This order is listed below:

(Eternity: before time began)

The Creation Story (when time began)

How God Created the World

How God Created Mankind

How God Created Animals

Who God Is

Who Mankind Is

Who Adam and Eve Were

The Fall into a Sinful Condition

Who Satan Is (the originator of evil)

What Sin Is

The Origin of Sin

The Provision for Sin (death of animal, the shedding of blood, coats of skins provided by God)

The Prophecy in Genesis 3:15 of a Coming Sin-Bearer

The Flood of the Earth

The Sinful State of Mankind at the Time of the Flood

Who Noah Was

God's Judgment of the World by the Flood

The Repopulating of Earth, Who Ham, Shem, and Japheth Were

The Pride of Mankind at Babel

The Confusion of Languages

God's Judgment of the Sin of Pride

The Beginning of the Nation of Israel

The Calling of Abram from Babylon

The Covenant of God with Abraham, Isaac, and Jacob

The Twelve Sons of Jacob

The Story of Joseph

The Enslavement of the Jewish People

Who Moses Was

The Exodus from Egypt

The Red Sea Crossing

The Wilderness Life of the Jewish People

The Giving of the Ten Commandments

The Law as a Revealer of Sin

The Jewish People Becoming the Nation of Israel

The Entrance into Their Own Land

The Cycle of Sinning and Restoration

The Nation of Israel Choosing a King

Who Saul, David, and Solomon Were

The Prophets Whom God Sent to Israel

Who Joel, Amos, Isaiah, and Jeremiah Were

The Nation of Israel's Punishment for Idolatry

Captivity in Babylon and Persia

Israel Conquered by Greece and Rome

God Sending of His Son to Earth in Fulfillment of Prophecies

From this point the New Testament narrative continues:

The Christ's Birth, Life, Teaching, Death, Burial, Resurrection, Commissioning, Ascension, and Intercession

The Holy Spirit Coming To Take the Place of Christ

The Church Age

The Story of the Early Churches

The Salvation and Ministry of Paul

The Explanation of the Redemptive Work of Christ in The Epistles

How the Epistles were written.

Christians Going to Preach the Gospel in the entire World

The Church's Completion

The Rapture of the Church

The Judgment Seat of Christ

The Tribulation Period

The Second Coming of Christ to Earth

The Millennial Reign of Christ on Earth

Satan Being Cast into the Lake of Fire

The Judgment of the Unsaved

The New Heaven and New Earth

(Eternity: after time has ended)

A chart of Biblical events in chronological order can be used to teach Bible background information.

The charts on the next pages, when placed end to end, will provide a quick overview of the chronological events of the Bible.

From Creation to the Flood

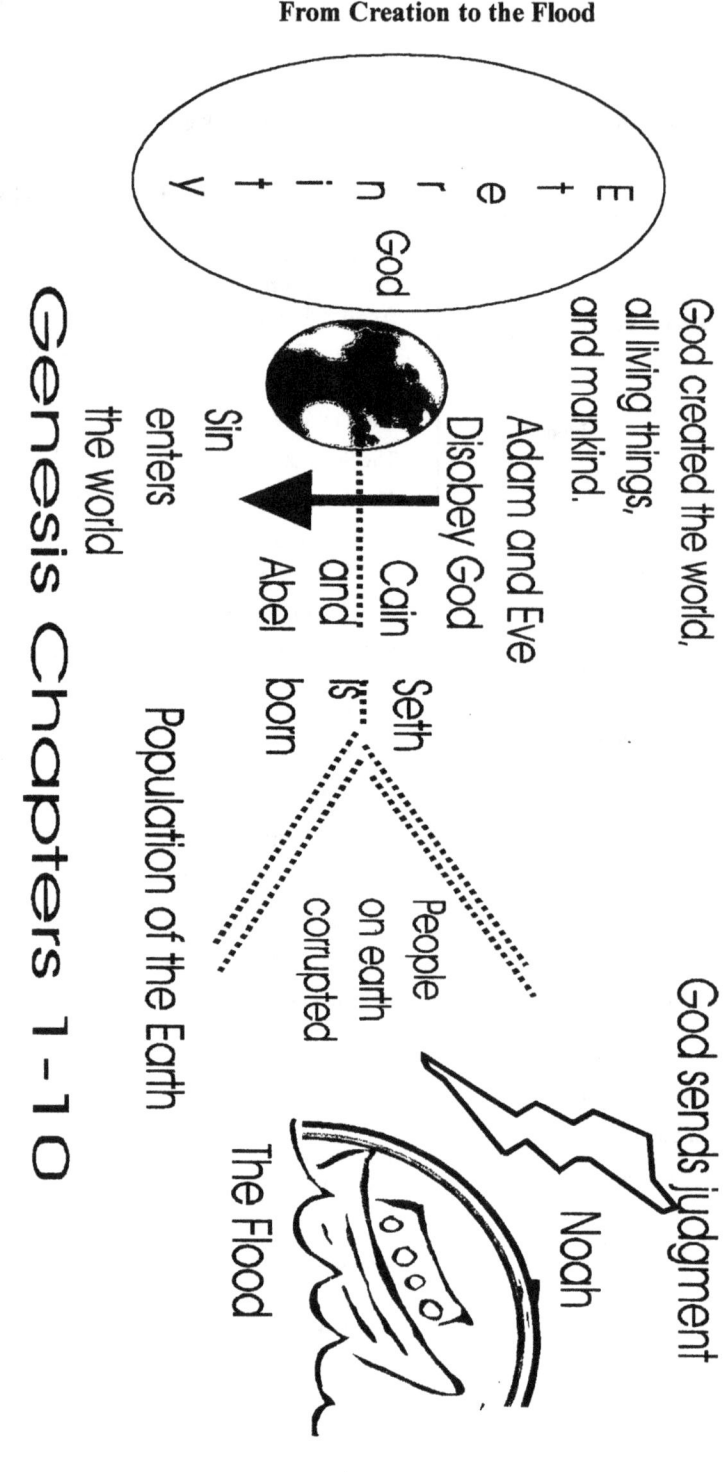

Genesis Chapters 1-10

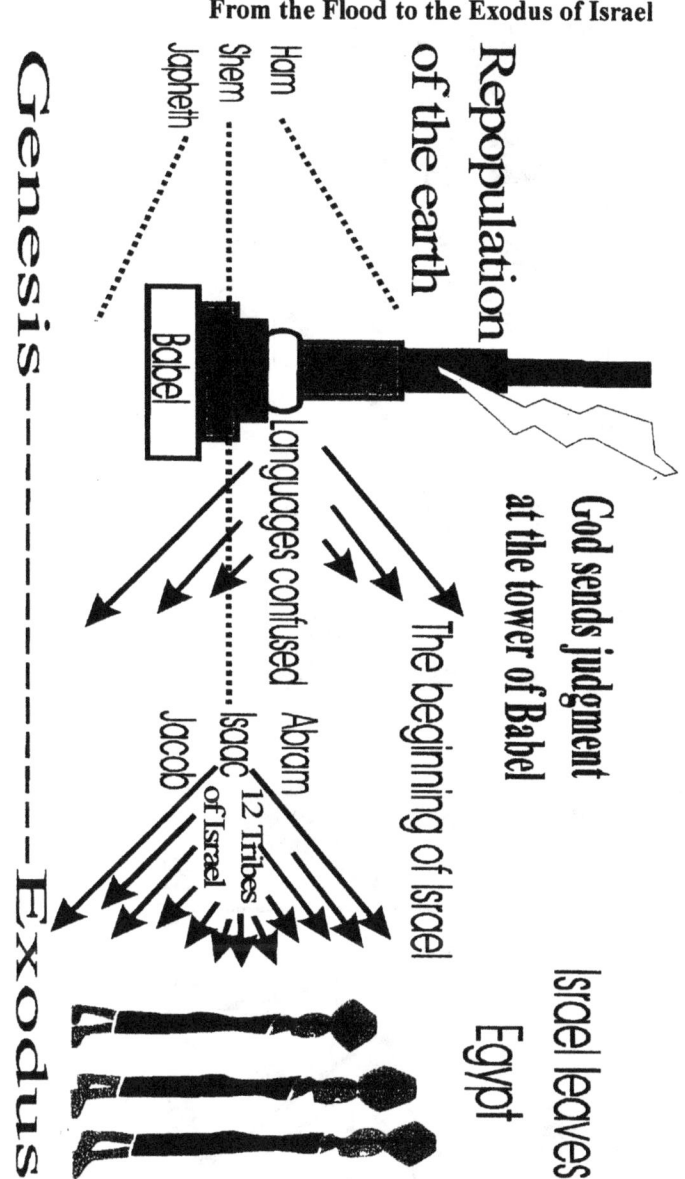

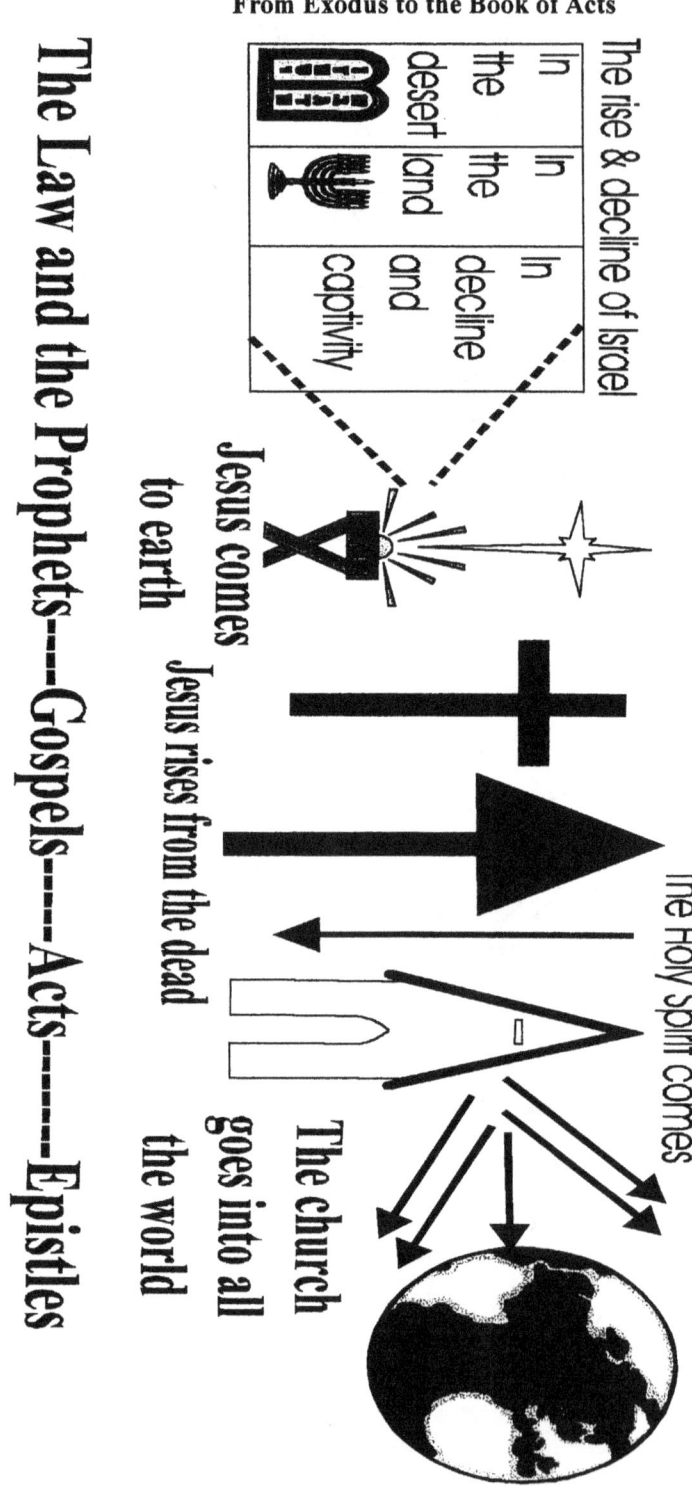

The Book of Revelation

From the Completion of the Church to the Tribulation

The church is completed

The rapture of the church

The saints are judged at the judgment seat of Christ

The Great Tribulation

| 1 | 2 | 3 | 4 | 5 | 6 | 7 |

From the Return of Christ to the Judgment Day

Priorities in Translation

Several considerations should be given priority in translation. Among these are:

(1) The meaning of the translation should take priority over grammatical structure. When it is not possible to translate both the meaning and the grammatical structure of the biblical text, the meaning should be given priority.

(2) Contextual meaning should take priority over verbal consistency. The meaning of a word and its resulting translation should be in terms of the context in which it occurs, not in some effort to translate a word the same way in every verse.

(3) The oral reading of Scripture should take priority over the written form. The translator should be more concerned about how well his translation is comprehended when read in public than about how well it is comprehended when studied privately.

(4) Future needs should have priority over past or present needs. The translation should be made with a view to meeting the needs of Christians during the next twenty years, not the past twenty. Antiquated forms of vocabulary, which are understood only by the older people, should be avoided in preference for vocabulary that is understood by both the old and the young.

Principles for Successful Bible Translating

(1) The most basic principle for success is this: How well have you learned the reality of abiding in Christ? To the degree that you put your personal relationship with Christ first, you will bear fruit and succeed as a Bible translator. It is more important what we are in our character and integrity, than it is in the things that we do for the Lord. Character and integrity come from a close relationship to Christ. This must be our first priority because the only absolute principle necessary for success as a translator and church planter is to abide in Christ. If we fail to abide in Christ, we will fail in all areas of life.

The married missionary must also take care of his family. If he fails to meet their spiritual and physical needs, the Bible says he is worse than an infidel. The missionary who would succeed must have his personal relationship with God in order and he must have his family life in order. The needs of his wife and children must take priority over other things. To fail one's mate will eventually lead to failure altogether.

The real problems of translation and church planting are not technical ones. The critical problems involve one's personal relationship to the Lord Jesus and one's integrity with family and fellow workers. The ultimate success or failure of our work will depend on how well we abide in Christ, so that He causes our lives to bear fruit. The fruit of the Spirit results in a life that bears the marks of humility, and openness to the suggestions of others. The Spirit produces an abiding conviction of the truth of God's Word, a longing to help others come to know Jesus and organize them into a New Testament Baptist church. Nothing else is sufficient to see one through all the heartaches and disappointments involved in the life of a New Testament Baptist church planter.

(2) A second important principle is this: Set a goal for what you want to

accomplish with your life. Everything else should fit into compatibility with this goal. To establish a New Testament church on the written Word of God among an ethnic people who do not know Christ, is a goal worthy of any person's life.

(3) One should set specific, attainable, short-range goals that can be reached by following a definite time schedule. It is still true that if you aim at nothing you will most likely hit it. It has also been said, "If you fail to plan, you plan to fail."

(4) Once priorities are set, do not allow other matters to divert you from them. Many things cry out for the missionary's attention. He can only do so many things.

(5) A daily work schedule should be decided upon. The great Baptist Bible translator William Carey was not brilliant, but he said, "I can plod." He stayed on the job day after day, year in and year out, until it was finished. We need to learn that same kind of tenacity.

(6) Train others to do time-consuming jobs that do not relate directly to your priorities. This will give you the time you need to accomplish your goals. Delegate responsibility to others who can do jobs that would take you away from your main priority of teaching and translating. Be willing to let others do things, even if you know they will make mistakes. After, all, you would probably make some mistakes yourself.

The final word:

"Abide in me, and I in you. As the branch cannot bear fruit of itself, except it abide in the vine; no more can ye, except ye abide in me." John 15:4

A sign outside a Hong Kong tailor shop: "Ladies may have a fit upstairs."

Chapter 38

God's Message to You

-William B. Young

This chapter is for practice translating. This "Gospel Presentation" should be easier to translate than actual verse-by-verse translating. Use it to begin developing the skill of translating from the source language to the receiver language. Simple sentences are easier to translate than Bible verses.

It may not be possible to translate this Gospel Presentation using the exact wording found in this text. It does not have to be followed word for word. It is not the Bible, and this fact should be explained to the readers. It can become a source for developing vocabulary needed later in translating the Bible. It can also become a source for teaching basic truths about God, creation, mankind, sin, and salvation. One may want to adjust it so that it agrees more with the biblical chronology of events. One should put this text in the order of the events as recorded in Scripture.

God's Message to You

"This message is good news for you. You must believe it. You must obey it. It is true. It comes from God. God is a spirit. You cannot see God but He can see you. God never lies. He tells the truth. You must believe what He says. God knows everything. No one knows as much as God knows. God wants to tell you something. You need to know it. God is good. He has good news for you. He tells what that good news is in His Book.

God has a Book. He told good men to write on paper what He wanted you to know. Every word in God's Book, the Bible, is true. There is only one true Book of God. He has many things to say to you in His Book. God wants you to do what this Book says. The words in this book are God's way of talking to you. God wants you to believe what He says in His Book.

God's Book says that God is a Great Spirit who lives forever. He always was and always will be. He is strong. He can do everything. He does many things that people cannot do. Many years ago, He made the earth and the sky. God made everything that you see. He made the first trees, the first fish, and the first animals. He made the sun, the moon, and the stars. Then God made the first man and the first woman. Now there are many trees, many fish, and many animals in the world. There are also many men, women, and children. Only God is strong enough to make all these things.

The name of the first man was Adam. The name of the first woman was Eve. God was good to them. They were not good to God. They did not want to do what God told them to do. They did not listen to what God said.

Adam and Eve ate some fruit that God told them not to eat. God must always be obeyed. He is always right. He never does anything wrong. What He tells us to do is always good for us.

God's home is in heaven. Heaven is above the clouds. We cannot see it, but that is where God lives. God's Book says that this is true. When Adam and

Eve disobeyed God, He came down from Heaven and called to them. Adam and Eve tried to hide from God. It is wrong if we do not do what God wants us to do. Adam and Eve could not hide from God when they did wrong. They thought they could, but God knew where they were. God sees everybody at all times. Nothing we do is hidden from Him. Even the night cannot hide us from Him. We cannot hide in the jungle from Him. He sees all we do. God knew where Adam and Eve were hiding. He found them. He told them what a terrible thing they had done. He was not pleased when they did not obey Him. They listened to a bad spirit called Satan. God's Book tells where Satan came from.

Long ago, a group of good spirits lived with God in heaven. They are called angels. They did whatever God wanted them to do. The leader of the angels was Lucifer. Lucifer rebelled against God. He wanted to be God, too. He did not want to do what God told him to do. He became angry with God. He started a war against God. Many angels joined his group. The angels who joined Lucifer's group became evil spirits. God cast them out of His house in Heaven. He changed Lucifer's name to Satan. Those who followed him are called demons, evil spirits, and powers of darkness. They are very bad spirits.

Satan and his evil spirits are always at war with God. They hate God. They do not want anyone to listen to God. They do not want anyone to love God. They do not want anyone to please God.

Satan told Adam and Eve not to believe what God said. Satan does not want you to believe what God says in His Book. Satan does not tell the truth. He is never to be trusted. Do not believe what he says. He tells many lies. He is present here on earth. You cannot see him because he is a spirit, but he can see you. He tries to make you think and do bad things.

If you listen to Satan, God will not be happy. God loves you. He knows that if you listen to Satan it will hurt you. If you do what it says in God's Book, it will help you. Do not do what Adam and Eve did. They listened to Satan. They did not listen to God. Satan became their leader.

When wrong is done, it must be punished. God is honest. He does what is right. He allowed pain, sickness, and death to come into the world. All people on the earth suffer because Adam and Eve disobeyed God.

A long time ago, Adam and Eve had many children. Their children had children. All people today came from Adam's family. Adam's family did not do what God told them to do. They did what God told them not to do.

God's Book says all people belong to Adam's family as soon as they are born. Because all people are descended from Adam's family, every person needs help to get out of Satan's group. God can help you get out of Satan's group if you ask Him. If you do not ask God to help you before you die, you will have to live with Satan in a burning hole forever. It is a place where people hurt and suffer forever. There is no water there. There is nothing to eat there. People will live forever in the burning hole, always hungry, always thirsty, and always hurting. After death, it will not be possible to leave Satan and his group in the burning hole.

You must turn from Satan today. You must do it now. Speak to God. You cannot see Him, but He can hear you. Tell Him you will do what He tells you to do in His Book.

God loves every person on earth. He loves every white man. He loves every black or brown man. He loves women, too. However, people do not love Him. They do the same thing that Adam and Eve did. They are all in Satan's group.

God wants to show everybody that He loves them. God had a Son. His name is Jesus. God wanted Jesus to come down from His home in heaven and live in a body like we have. God decided that Jesus should come to earth as a baby and grow up to be a man. God wanted His Son to live among people on earth so He could talk to them and help them. God wanted people to see Jesus so they could know that God loves them. Jesus was a very good man. He is just like His Father. He came into the world as a baby, but He was not like other children. He was not a bad man. All the time he lived on earth, He did only good. He always did the right thing. He was strong. He could do anything. He wanted to help people. He especially wanted to help people get out of Satan's group.

A small group of people believed what Jesus said. They loved Him. They did what He told them to do. They left Satan's group. They wanted to live with Jesus in His Father's big house when they died. They did not want to live with Satan in the burning hole.

Many other men and women did not listen to what Jesus said. They did not follow Him. They would not join His group. They hated Him. They did not want to stop doing bad things. They listened to Satan when he told them to kill Jesus. They said they would do it.

When Jesus heard about it, He asked God, His Father, to forgive those who were going to kill Him. Jesus was willing to die for the sins of people to show them that He loved them. He wanted them to believe in Him. He wanted them to follow Him. He wanted to save them from living with Satan in the burning hole.

Jesus could have killed all the people who were going to kill him, but He loved them. Jesus loved His enemies. He loved those who were going to kill Him. He loves you, too.

The bad people put sharp things through his hands and feet. They fastened Him to two tree limbs. Then they lifted the limbs up. Jesus hung there bleeding. The bad people in Satan's group hated Jesus but He loved them. They put a sharp spear into His side. He bled and died. He suffered on the tree to show them that God loved them.

After Jesus died, He was buried in a hole and they put a large stone over it. Satan's group thought Jesus would not be around anymore. Jesus had told them to leave Satan and the evil spirits. They did not like that. These people liked evil spirits, demons, and Satan. They tried to destroy Jesus, but after three days, He left the place where they buried Him. He rose from the dead. This showed that Jesus is God. He rose from the dead because He is the Son of God and can do anything.

Satan and evil spirits do not want you to believe that Jesus died for you. They do not want you to believe that Jesus rose from the dead. Satan and evil spirits do not want you to believe Jesus is God and can do anything, but God's Book says it is true. Jesus wants you to believe it.

When you believe what God says about His Son, Jesus, you join His family. All who believe this truth about Jesus will go to heaven to live with Him in His home after they die. No one can live in God's house unless they do what He tells them to do. They must believe what Jesus says. He said He died on a tree to pay for all the bad things that all the people on earth have done. Jesus is the only one who can save you from the burning hole.

God can hear you when you talk to Him. God wants you to talk to Him. You do not need to see God. God wants to hear you say that you believe Jesus died, was buried, and arose again for you. God wants to hear you say that you love Him and His Son, Jesus. God wants to hear you say that you want to join God's group right now. He wants to hear you say that you want Jesus to be your leader. He wants to hear you say that you want to obey God and His Son, Jesus.

If you say these things to God, He will hear you. He will make you a member of His group. Jesus is the leader of God's group.

God makes His people happy. God is happy when He hears you say you want to belong to His group. He will help you do it. He can do all things. He wants to help you right now. Tell Him you will come into His group right now. He will take you in. You will become a member of God's family.

God's Son, Jesus, is a good leader. He wants His people to be good. He will help you to be good. He will help you do good things. If you asked Him to take you into His group, then you are now in His group, and Jesus is your leader. God wants you to be like His Son, Jesus. He never did any bad things. He wants to help you say no to anything Satan wants you to do. Satan will bother you if you let him, but you do not need to let him.

Satan does not like it when you ask God to take you into His group. The evil spirits and demons do not like it. They want you to do bad things. They will try to make you do bad things. When you are in God's group, it is not right to act like those in Satan's group.

Satan wants you to fight, but Jesus does not fight. He talks to His Father about His enemies. He asks His Father to make them better. When someone wants to fight, you should try to make peace with them. You should tell them about Jesus who died for them. Jesus will help you love those who are mean to you. That will help them. They will want to know about Jesus. Jesus did not become angry with those who did mean things to Him. He did not fight them. He did not kill them. Jesus wants you to be like Him and do what He did. Ask Him to take away the fighting spirit that Satan wants to keep in your heart.

Satan wants you to live with many women. Jesus does not want you to do this. Jesus wants every man to live with only one wife. Jesus will help you do the right thing. Tell Him you want to be a good man, or a good woman, so you can please Him and do what He wants you to do.

Satan wants you to get drunk and to take drugs. You cannot be a good man or woman and do these things. Getting drunk and taking drugs will hurt you. It is not good. Jesus does not want you to do these things. Ask Jesus to help you so you will not do these things. He will help you.

Satan wants you to lie, cheat, and steal. Jesus does not want any of His group to do these things. God does not want us to want something that we have no right to have.

Satan wants you to think about something that will never happen so you will not be thinking about Jesus. He wants you to keep on thinking about that thing until you become afraid. That will not make you feel well. Satan wants to make you feel bad. When you think about what Jesus wants you to think about, you will not be afraid.

Sometimes other people do things you do not like. Satan wants to make you angry about it, but Jesus can help you to love the people who do mean things to you.

Satan wants to make you believe you can do something better than anyone else. He wants to make you feel you do not need anyone to help you. Jesus wants you to ask Him to help you. Then everyone can see it is Jesus helping you do things in His way. We should never want to do anything without Him. He does everything right. He is the only One who can do all things right. You need His help. He is willing to help you. All you have to do is ask Him.

Satan wants to make you feel bad because some one is a better hunter than you are. He wants to make you feel bad because your house is not as nice as the one next to yours. Jesus will help you take care of that evil thinking by filling your heart with love for all people. You will be glad that they have all that they have.

Satan wants to tempt you to do many bad things. He hates God. Therefore, he tempts you to do things that God does not like. If you do any of the things that God does not want you to do, you must not try to hide it from God. God knows everything you do. He wants you to tell Him about it. He wants to hear you say that you did wrong and do not ever want to do it again. When He hears you tell Him that you did wrong, he will forgive you and his blood will wash away the bad things you did. He will never remember it again. His blood washes clean like water. You cannot see His blood, but the blood that poured out of His body on the tree will always be able to wash away the bad things you do.

God does not want you to keep doing wrong. He wants you to be like Him. He never does anything wrong. If you love Him, you will want to do what He wants you to do. He wants you to be good and not do what Satan wants you to do.

God and His Son never want any of Jesus' people to talk to Satan, evil spirits, or demons except to tell them to leave. When one of Jesus' people tells evil spirits to leave, they have to obey. Every time Satan or his group wants you to do something that God does not like, tell them that the blood of Jesus has washed away the bad things in your life. Tell them that you do not want to have anything to do with Satan or any of his group. All of them will have to leave. If you are in the group where Jesus is leader, He will help you send Satan away. Satan will have to leave. Jesus lives with you.

Satan is not as strong as Jesus is. He is afraid of Jesus. Jesus is not afraid of Satan, and He does not want you to be afraid of Satan. Jesus will watch over you. He will not let Satan or evil spirits hurt you when you tell them to leave.

Tell Jesus you are glad you are in God's group. Tell Him you are glad that He is your leader. Tell Him you love Him and always want to do what He wants you to do. He will always help you. He will never leave you. He will never fail to help you.

There are many men, women, and children on the earth. They all need to know about Jesus. They need to know that He died for them and rose from the dead. They need to know that He is in Heaven in His Father's house watching over His people. They need to know that Jesus' blood can wash away all their bad things if they ask Him. If they do not ask Him to take away the bad things in their lives, they will never live with Him in His big house in heaven.

There is enough room in heaven for all who want to live with God. In heaven, there are wonderful rivers and beautiful trees. God and Jesus are there. All people who have asked Jesus to help them will be there. No one will be sick there. No one will have pain. No one will fight. No one will want to leave. People will be happy all the time.

All the people on the earth need to know about Jesus. If they do not ask Jesus to help them, they will have to live forever with Satan in the burning hole. Tell people about all this right away.

Tell as many people as you can about Jesus. Tell them many times, so they are sure to understand. Jesus loves them. He wants to help them. He will help them if they ask Him. He will help them right now."

Courtroom blunder: "You were not shot in the fracas?" "No, I was shot midway between the fracas and the navel."

Chapter 39

Personal Computers

Compared to the human mind, the personal computer is still a primitive machine. However, it can be a useful tool if used wisely. A few years ago, the computer was beyond the financial range of most people. Today a personal computer can reasonably become part of a missionary's equipment. However, there are some important considerations before purchasing one.

The first consideration is the kind of computer that should be bought. There are many kinds available. The PC world is divided into two principle divisions. One division is the standard set by the IBM Corporation. The second is that of the Apple Computer Corporation. This division is slowly being bridged as the Apple computer adopts features that make it more like the IBM computer and vice versa. Now, both companies offer virtually the same features.

The standard that has become accepted worldwide is that set by IBM. Nine-tenths of the computers in the world are IBM (or IBM compatible). IBM computers are more readily available, more readily repairable, and less expensive to buy because of the lower prices of IBM clones.

Should one buy a laptop, a notebook, or a desktop computer? If one will be traveling a lot, the notebook would be best. If one is more settled in one location, the desktop is best. The advantage of the desktop is that it can be repaired more easily than the laptop. To repair a laptop the entire computer must be disassembled. Only the side panel needs to be removed to repair a desktop.

Another consideration is the amount of time one must devote to learning how to use a computer. Apple claims that their computers are easier to learn than IBM's. However, no computer is easy to learn. All manufacturers claim their computers are "user friendly," but unless you are already skilled in the use of a computer, the time needed to learn how to set it up and use it on the mission field will be a waste of time. If you do not have the discipline and time to learn how to use a computer *before* you go to the mission field, you will end up with an expensive time waster and dust collector on your desk.

I recommend that first-term missionaries either take computer training before they go overseas or forget about taking a computer with them on their first term.

Missionaries need to spend the first two years focused on intensive language and culture learning. Too many missionaries are caught up in electronic gadgets like tape recorders, cameras, and now computers and therefore waste the most important years of their missionary career fumbling with a computer. The first two years of a missionary's career is so crucial that he would be unwise to jeopardize it by spending hours and hours learning to use his computer.

This is particularly true of using the internet and e-mail. Unless you know how to use the internet and have a reliable internet service provider with a local telephone number, you could have problems managing your e-mail and internet use. This could waste a lot of valuable time.

If you limit your computer use to writing letters, you may get by without wasting too much of your time. If you want to use your computer for every possible thing it can do, you will be wasting a lot of time. The computer only becomes efficient when used for one or two jobs that you do repeatedly each day.

When you return from your first term, get some computer training and then take your computer back with you. You will be glad you devoted your first term to language and culture learning without the intrusion of a computer.

At Baptist Bible Translators Institute, computers are part of the training throughout the course. Missionaries who go through this training learn how to touch-type, and how to use Microsoft Word. Word processing, desktop publishing, and database programs can serve a missionary well, provided he is trained in the use of them. Knowing how to use a word processing program can save three years in the typing of a New Testament translation.

Do not expect computers to do the actual translating of Scriptures. A translator can use a computer to assist him in the many revisions that will be made to his translation, but he must do the actual translating himself. My wife typed our Sinasina New Testament four times before it was finally printed. We did not have computers in those days, so any changes in the text made it necessary to type the entire manuscript over again. With a computer, this is no longer a problem.

The computer also has some possibilities in the area of educating children. Many educational and recreational programs are available. These programs can help children learn reading, vocabulary, geography, and other subjects. They can even help prepare them for the Standard Achievement Test.

The computer with a modem can be used to keep in contact with the home church and supporting churches via e-mail. This is a great help and involves very little expense or time. Get a modem that has the fastest speed available.

The computer is a powerful tool, but it must be used with understanding. Look before you leap into using a computer, especially in your first term on the mission field.

Chapter 40

A Bible Translator's Goal Sheet

Name of Translator_____

Name of Country_____

Name of Language_____

Book	Chapters	Verses	% of N.T. Completed	Date Completed	Person who checked it
Matt.	28	1071	12.90		
Mark	16	678	8.00		
Luke	24	1151	13.00		
John	21	878	10.20		
Acts	28	1007	13.80		
Romans	16	433	5.40		
1 Corin.	16	436	5.20		
2 Corin.	13	256	3.30		
Gal.	6	149	1.80		
Eph.	6	155	1.70		
Phil.	4	104	1.30		
Col	4	95	1.00		
1 Thess.	5	89	1.00		
2 Thess.	3	47	0.60		
1 Tim.	6	113	1.40		
2 Tim.	4	83	1.00		
Titus	3	46	0.60		
Phile.	1	25	0.30		
Heb.	13	303	3.20		
James	5	108	1.30		
1 Pet.	5	105	1.50		
2 Pet.	3	61	0.90		
1 John	5	105	1.30		
2 John	1	13	0.20		
3 John	1	15	0.20		
Jude	1	23	0.40		
Rev.	22	405	8.50		
Total	260	7954	100.00		

Chapter 41

Bible Translation Course Final Examination

Name_____

Date_____

1. What should be the ultimate objective of a Bible translator?

2. What are the basic elements in any communication between two people?

3. Write a definition of Bible translation.

4. On a separate piece of paper, analyze the semantic components of Acts 4:12. Make a statement of each event and then state the relationships between the events by stating the meaning of the verse. (15 points)

5. Analyze the semantic components of the word *mediator* and state the meaning of it.

6. Analyze the semantic components of the word *offering* and state the meaning of it.

7. State the meaning of the question in Mark 14:6.

8. State the meaning of the question in Luke 13:20.

9. Analyze the semantic components and state the meaning of the genitive structure of *Mount of Olives*.

10. Analyze the semantic components and state the meaning of the phrase, *Cain, who was of that wicked one*. 1 John 3:12.

11. Change the following phrases from passive voice to active voice.

Mark 2:5, "Thy sins be forgiven thee."

Mark 6:14, "John the Baptist was risen from the dead."

Colossians 1:11, "strengthened with all might."

12. What is the implied information in Matthew 26:65a?

13. Change the indirect quote in Acts 23:2 to a direct quote.

14. Supply the ellipsis in John 15:4.

15. Mark 1:1-11.

Find the translation problem areas in Mark 1:1-11 and write out the proper adjustments following the rules of the Mixtupi language structure. The rules of Mixtupi language structure are as follows:

1. There is no passive voice. All passive-voice constructions must be changed to active with an actor and a receiver of the action supplied.

2. All ellipses must be filled in.

3. Abstract nouns are not a part of Mixtupi grammar; so abstract nouns must be changed to verbal phrases.

4. Metaphors are taken literally in this language. They must be changed to similes or spelled out by stating the basis of the comparison.

5. Word elements must be in their proper order. Unusual order of phrases is not used in this language.

6. Many words that go together in English collocationally clash in the Mixtupi language. They must be adjusted.

7. Genitive constructions do not exist in the grammar of Mixtupi, so the word *of* must not be used in your translation adjustments.

8. If a pronominal reference is not clear, as to whom it refers, the name of the person must be put in the place of the pronoun.

9. Mixtupi grammar does not allow indirect quotes. They must be changed to direct quotes.

Make all the adjustments needed in the following verses. Your adjustments must follow the nine rules of Mixtupi language structure listed above.

Verse 1: "The beginning of the gospel of Jesus Christ, the Son of God;"

There are two main problem areas in this verse: ellipsis and genitive structures. Write the verse below with all the problem areas adjusted.

Verse 2: "As it is written in the prophets, Behold, I send my messenger before thy face, which shall prepare thy way before thee."

There are five main problem areas in this verse: transition, ellipsis, abstract noun, metaphor, and pronominal reference. Write the verse below with all the problem areas adjusted.

Verse 3: "The voice of one crying in the wilderness, Prepare ye the way of the Lord, make his paths straight."

There are four main problem areas in this verse: synecdoche, collocational clash, genitive structure, and metaphor. Write the verse below with all the problem areas adjusted.

Verse 4: "John did baptize in the wilderness, and preach the baptism of repentance for the remission of sins."

There are six main problem areas in this verse: transition, implied information, indirect quote, genitive structures, abstract nouns, and order of elements. Write the verse below with all the problem areas adjusted.

Verse 5: "And there went out unto him all the land of Judea, and they of Jerusalem, and were all baptized of him in the river Jordan, confessing their sins."

There are seven main problem areas in this verse: hyperbole, personification, genitive, abstract words, passive voice, order of elements and pronominal reference. Write the verse below with all the problem areas adjusted.

Verse 6: "And John was clothed with camel's hair, and with a girdle of skin about his loins; and he did eat locusts and wild honey;"

There are three main problem areas in this verse: ellipsis, genitive structure, and passive voice. Write the verse below with all the problem areas adjusted.

Verse 7: "And preached, saying, There cometh one mightier than I after me, the latchet of whose shoes I am not worthy to stoop down and unloose."

There are four main problem areas in this verse: comparative, cultural substitute, order of elements, and a doublet. Write the verse below with all the problem areas adjusted.

Verse 8: "I indeed have baptized you with water: but he shall baptize you with the Holy Ghost."

There are two main problem areas in this verse: collocational clash and the word Ghost. Write the verse below with all the problem areas adjusted.

Verse 9: "And it came to pass in those days, that Jesus came from Nazareth of Galilee, and was baptized of John in Jordan."

There are five main problem areas in this verse: collocational clash, implied information, ellipsis, genitive structures, and passive voice. Write the verse below with all the problem areas adjusted.

Verse 10: "And straightway coming up out of the water, he saw the heavens opened, and the Spirit like a dove descending upon him:"

There is one main problem area in this verse: pronominal reference. Write the verse below with the problem area adjusted.

Verse 11: "And there came a voice from heaven, saying, Thou art my beloved Son, in whom I am well pleased."

There are three main problem areas in this verse: collocational clash, abstract words, and synecdoche. Write the verse below with the three problem areas adjusted.

16. Assigned Reading and Homework

Have you read all of Chapters 1 through 40? Yes_____ No_____

Have you completed all the homework assignments in Chapters 1 through 40? Yes_____ No_____

17. Component Analysis

Analyze the components of meaning (T.E.A.R.) in Mark 1:4. Make a statement of the events, and state the meaning of the verse by showing the relationships between the components.

18. Adjustments:

A. Adjust the rhetorical question in Romans 14:10a, "But why dost thou judge thy brother?"

B. Adjust the implied information in John 1:21b, "Art thou that prophet? And he answered, No."

C. Adjust the ellipsis in Matthew 26:5, "But they said, Not on the feast day, lest there be an uproar among the people."

D. Adjust the hyperbole in Acts 17:6, "These that have turned the world upside down are come hither also."

E. Adjust the metonymy in James 3:6, "And it [the tongue] is set on fire of hell."

F. Adjust the synecdoche in Hebrews 3:17, "whose carcases fell in the wilderness."

G. Adjust the irony in Mark 7:9, "Full well ye reject the commandment of God, that ye may keep your own tradition."

H. Adjust the apostrophe in Matthew 2:6, "And thou Bethlehem, in the land of Judah."

I. Adjust the personification in Revelation 20:14, "And death and hell were cast into the lake of fire."

J. Adjust the idiom in Matthew 16:17, "Flesh and blood hath not revealed it unto thee."

K. Adjust the doublet in John 2:19. "Jesus answered and said unto them."

L. Adjust the collocational clash in John 4:1, "The Pharisees heard that Jesus made and baptized more disciples than John."

M. Adjust the pronominal reference in John 5:38, "And ye have not his word abiding in you: for whom he hath sent, him ye believe not."

N. Adjust the abstract noun in Acts 4:12a, "Neither is there salvation in any other."

O. Adjust the genitive structure in John 5:29, "the resurrection of damnation."

Chapter 42

Bible Translation Course Final Examination

(Answers)

1. The ultimate objective of a Bible translator should be to establish New Testament Baptist churches that are reproducing themselves by establishing other churches and who are guided by a New Testament that has been translated into the native language of the people.

2. The basic elements in any communication are the Source, Message, Receiver, Feedback, and Cultural Context.

3. Bible translation occurs when the meaning of the Bible text has been transferred into the nearest formal equivalent meaning in the receiver language in a written form.

4. (1.) Semantic Components of Acts 4:12:

Neither <u>is there salvation</u> in any other
A   (T)E(T)   R A T

For there is none other name under heaven
R   E   A   A   T   R   T

given among men whereby we must <u>be saved</u>.
(T)E(T)   R   T   R   T   A   (T)E(T)

(2.) State the Events:

Someone saves someone

Someone has been given (sent)

The one who was given (by God) is the only one who can save people

He is the one by whom people must be saved.

(3.) State he meaning of the verse:

There is no other person on earth who can save people. God only sent one person to earth by whom people must be saved.

5. Semantic Components of the word *mediator*

(T) E R (T)---(T)

A mediator is a person who mediates between God and people.

6. Semantic Components of the word *offering*

(T)E(T) R (T)

Someone gives something to God

7. Meaning of the Question in Mark 14:1:

Stop troubling her!

8. Meaning of the Question in Luke 13:20:

I will tell you what the kingdom of God is like.

9. Semantic Components of Mount of Olives:

Mount of Olives
   T   R   T

Mount of Olives is equal to a mountain named Olivet (or Olive Trees)

10. The Semantic Components of 1 John 3:12, Cain who was of that wicked one.

Cain   who was   of that wicked one.
T   T   E   R   A   A   T

Cain who obeyed that wicked one.

11. Passive Voice to Active:

Mark 2:5, "I forgive your sins."

Mark 6:14, "God has raised John the Baptist from the dead."

Colossians 1:11, "May God strengthen you with all might."

12. Implied Information in Matthew 26:65a:

Being angry, he tore his garment

13. Indirect quote to direct in Acts 23:2:

The high priest Ananias commanded them that stood by him saying, "Smite him on the mouth!"

14. Ellipsis in John 14:4:

<u>You</u> abide in me, <u>and let me</u> abide in you. As the branch cannot bear fruit of itself, except it abide in the vine; no more can ye <u>bear fruit of yourselves</u>, except ye abide in me.

15. Mark 1:1-11

Verse 1:

Ellipsis: I am writing this book about ...

Genitive: beginning of the gospel is equal to *the gospel began when...*

Genitive: gospel of Jesus Christ is equal to *the gospel is about Jesus Christ.*

Genitive: the Son of God is equal to *He is God's Son.*

Entire verse:

"I am writing this book about Jesus Christ. He is God's Son. This is how the story about Jesus Christ began."

Alternative: "I am writing this book about Jesus Christ, God's Son. The story about Jesus began when..."

Verse 2:

Transition: The gospel began when...

Ellipsis: The gospel began long ago when the prophets wrote in the Bible...

Abstract noun: messenger is equal to *one who is sent by God to tell people His message.*

Behold is equal to *Listen!*

Metaphors: before thy face is equal to *will go ahead of you.*

Prepare thy way is equal to *prepare the hearts of people to receive you.*

Pronominal references: *thy, thee,* and *I* are equal to *God sending John to go ahead of Jesus to prepare the way before Jesus.*

Entire Verse:

"The gospel began long ago when the prophets wrote in the Bible, 'Listen! I, God, send one who will tell people my message. He (the messenger) will come first to prepare people to receive you (the Lord) when you come later.'"

(Note: Even though verse 2 is about Jesus, the name of Jesus should not be introduced into an Old Testament quote.)

(Note: the prophecy is from Malachi 3:1 and Isaiah 40:3)

Verse 3:

Synecdoche: voice is equal to *a person who speaks using his voice*

Collocational Clash: voice of one crying is equal to *a person speaking/preaching loudly.*

Genitive structure: way of the Lord is equal to *receive the Lord.*

Metaphors: prepare ye the way is equal to *get ready.*

Make his paths straight is equal to *Get your hearts right with God.*

Entire verse:

"A prophet wrote in the Bible, 'The one I send will come to the wilderness and preach loudly, Get your hearts right with the Lord! Get ready to receive Him when he comes.'"

Verse 4:

Transition: This prophecy was fulfilled when John went to the wilderness and....

Indirect Quote to Direct Quote: preach the baptism of repentance for the remission of sins is equal to *John preached saying, "Because you have sinned, you must repent. If you repent, God will forgive your sins and I will baptize you."*

Genitive Structures: baptism of repentance, remission of sins is equal to *John preached that people must repent and that he would baptize only those who repented and were forgiven of their sins by God.*

Implied Information: people had sinned.

Order of Events:

1. People had committed sins.

2. John takes up residence in the wilderness.

3. John preaches that people should repent of the sins they have committed.

4. People repented.

5. God forgave people's sins.

6. John baptized those who had repented.

Entire verse:

"This prophecy was fulfilled when John (came to the wilderness) and preached, 'Because you have sinned, you must repent! If you repent, God will forgive your sins and I will baptize you.'"

Verse 5:

Hyperbole: The phrases "all the land of Judea," and "all were baptized" is equal to *many people from Judea province* went to John, *and many were baptized by him.*

Personification: went out unto him all the land of Judea is equal to *many people from Judea province went unto him.*

Genitive Structures: land of Judea, they of Jerusalem, and baptized of him. These are equal to *people from Judea, and Jerusalem and John baptized them.*

Abstract Words: sins, baptized, and confessing are equal to *people sinned, John baptized people and people confessed that they were sinners.*

Pronominal Reference: *him* is equal to *John.*

Passive Voice: were baptized is equal to *John baptized them.*

Entire Verse:

"Many people from Jerusalem city in Judea province went to where John was preaching. They agreed with John when he told them to repent because of their sins. They said, 'We have sinned.' Those who confessed, 'We have sinned' John baptized them in the river named Jordan."

Verse 6:

Ellipsis: clothed with camel's hair is equal to *clothes made from camel's hair*

Genitive Structure: girdle of skin is equal to *a belt made from animal hide.*

Passive Voice to Active Voice: John was clothed is equal to *John wore clothes.*

Entire verse:

"John wore clothes made from camel's hair. He wore a belt around his midsection made from animal hide. He ate grasshoppers and wild bee's honey."

Verse 7:

Comparative: mightier than I is equal to *he is greater than I am.*

Cultural Substitute: latchet of whose shoes is equal to *untie his sandals to wash his feet.*

Order of events: cometh one after me is equal to *after I come, one will come later.*

Doublet: preached saying is equal to *John preached.*

Entire verse:

"John preached, 'After I come, latter one will come who is superior to me. I am not great. He is very great. I am not worthy to even untie his sandals to wash his feet.'"

Verse 8:

Collocational Clash: baptize with the Holy Spirit. Usually, a person is baptized with water. It may be a Collocational clash to speak of a person being baptized with Spirit.

Ghost: This could be a problem if the word *Ghost* in the ethnic language means an apparition of someone who had died. The word Ghost should not mean a phantom of someone who has died.

Entire verse:

"I truly have baptized you with water but the one coming after me will fill you with the Holy Spirit."

Alternative:

"I truly have baptized you with water but the one coming after me will send the Holy Spirit to dwell in you."

Verse 9:

Collocational Clash: It came to pass (Usually people pass, coming and going).

Ellipsis: Jesus came to where John was baptizing people.

Implied Information: a town named Nazareth, a province named Galilee, and a river named Jordan.

Genitive Structures: Nazareth of Galilee, and baptized of John are equal to Nazareth town in Galilee province, and John baptized them.

Passive Voice: was baptized of John is equal to John baptized them.

Entire verse:

"At that time Jesus left the town named Nazareth in the Province named Galilee and when he came to the place where John was baptizing people, John baptized Jesus in the river named Jordan."

(Note: When ethnic people become more familiar with names of places in the Bible, the words *the town named*, and *the Province named* can be deleted.)

Verse 10:

Pronominal Reference: he, him (See John 1:32 for information on this verse)

Entire verse:

"And immediately as Jesus came out of the water, John saw the heavens opened and the Spirit descending like a dove upon Jesus."

Verse 11:

Collocational Clash: came a voice is equal to *God spoke*.

Abstract Words: beloved, and well pleased are equal to *I love you and what you do pleases me much*.

Synecdoche: voice is equal to a person who uses his voice to speak

Entire verse:

"Then God spoke from heaven saying, 'You are my Son. I love you very much. The things you do please me very much.'"

16. Assigned Reading

You should have completed all the assigned reading in Chapters 1 through 40.

You should have done all the Homework assignments in Chapters 1 through 38.

17. Component Analysis:

(1.) Components of Meaning:

John did baptize in the wilderness and
 T   (T)E(T)   R A   T   R

preach the baptism of repentance
(T)E(T) A (T)E (T) R   (T)E
for the remission of sins.
 R   A (T)E(T)   R (T)E

(2.) The Events:

1. People sinned.
2. John preached to people.
3. People repented.
4. God forgave peoples sins.
5. John baptized people who repented.

(3.) The Meaning:

"While John was in the wilderness, he preached to people saying, 'You have sinned! Repent! If you repent, God will forgive your sins and I will baptize you.'"

18. Adjustments:

A. The rhetorical question in Romans 14:10a, "But why dost thou judge thy brother?"

"You should not judge your brother."

B. The implied information in John 1:21b, "Art thou that prophet?"

"Are you the prophet whom God promised to send?" (See Deuteronomy 18:15, and John 7:40 that indicate they were referring to the Messiah?)

C. The Ellipsis in Matthew 26:5, "But they said, 'Not on the feast day, lest there be an uproar among the people.'"

"Let us not arrest and kill him on the feast day, lest there be an uproar among the people."

D. The Hyperbole in Acts 17:6, "These that have turned the world upside down are come hither also."

"These who have caused riots in many places are come here also."

E. The metonymy in James 3:6, "And (the tongue) is set on fire of hell."

"Satan tempts people to speak words that destroy people."

F. The Synecdoche in Hebrews 3:17, "Whose carcases fell in the wilderness."

"God killed them and their dead bodies littered the wilderness."

G. The Irony in Mark 7:9, "Full well ye reject the commandment of God, that ye may keep your own tradition."

"You are really think your doing great by rejecting the commandment of God so you can keep your own tradition!"

H. The Apostrophe in Matthew 2:6, "And thou Bethlehem, in the land of Judah..."

"You people who live in the town named Bethlehem in the province named Judah."

I. The Personification in Revelation 20:14, "And death and hell were cast into the lake of fire."

"And God cast the people who had died and were in Hell into the lake of fire."

J. The Idiom in Matthew 16:17, "Flesh and blood hath not revealed it unto thee."

"No mere human being revealed it unto you."

K. The Doublet in John 2:19, "Jesus answered and said unto them..."

"Jesus said unto them."

Alternative: "Jesus answered, saying unto them."

L. The Collocational clash in John 4:1, "The Pharisees heard that Jesus made more disciples than John."

"The Pharisees heard that Jesus was teaching more people than John was teaching."

Alternative: The Pharisees heard that Jesus had caused more people to follow Him than were following John.

M. The Pronominal reference in John 5:38, "And ye have not his word abiding in you: for whom he hath sent, him ye believe not."

"You Jews do not obey God's Word, for you do not believe in me, the one whom God sent."

Alternative 1: And you (plural) do not have God's word abiding in you, for you do not believe in me, the one whom God sent.

Alternative 2: You are not obeying God's word because you do not believe that God sent me.

Alternative 3: Because you do believe that God sent me, you are not obeying God's word.

N. The Abstract noun in Acts 4:12a, "Neither is there salvation in any other."

"No one else can save people from their sins."

O. The Genitive structure in John 5:29, "the resurrection of damnation."

"People who are dead will be raised to live again so that God can condemn them to damnation (hell)."

End Notes

Chapter 2

1. E. M. Bounds, *Power Through Prayer*, Twenty-sixth edition; London: Marshall, Morgan & Scott, Ltd., 1935, Pg. 9.

2. Andrew Murray, *The Power of the Spirit*, London: James Nisbet & Co., 1896, Pg. 65.

3. Malcom Bowes, *Christianity and Naturalism*, Columbia Bible College, Columbia, South Carolina, 1964. An unpublished M. A. Thesis.

4. F. Deaville Walker, *William Carey*, Chicago: Moody Press, 1951, Pg. 75.

Chapter 10

1. J. Gresham Machen, *The Christian View of Man*, London, The Banner of Truth Trust, 1937, Pg. 108.

2. Charles H. Spurgeon, *The Greatest Fight in the World*, Montville, NJ: Pilgrim Publications, 2001, Pg. 9.

Chapter 14

1. This illustration comes from the book by Eugene A. Nida and Charles R. Taber, *The Theory and Practice of Translation*, United Bible Societies, E. J. Brill, Leiden, Netherlands, 1974, Pg. 57.

Chapter 15

1. Adam Clarke, *A Commentary and Critical Notes*, Abingdon, Nashville, Volume V, Preface to the Epistle to the Romans, Pg. 1. "…and, finding that they consisted partly of heathens converted to Christianity, and partly of Jews who had, with many remaining prejudices, believed in Jesus as the true Messiah, and that many contentions arose from the claims of the Gentile converts to equal privileges with the Jews, and from the absolute refusal of the Jews to admit these claims unless the Gentile converts became circumcised, he (Paul) wrote to adjust and settle these differences."

Chapter 16

1. The Online Bible is now called "The Word" and is available at: www.online-bible.com "The Word" contains hundreds of megabytes of biblical material that totals over $1,000 in value, yet it sells for about $30.00. I highly recommend it!

2. William Barclay, *The Gospel of Matthew*, Volume 1, The Westminster Press, Philadelphia, 1958, Pg. 10. Barclay's commentary is embedded in religious sentiment that without careful scrutiny would pass as sound doctrine, but upon a careful examination of his work, one can see his false doctrine. For example, in his first volume on the Gospel of Matthew, on page 10 he says, "The Virgin Birth is a doctrine which presents us with many difficulties; and it is a doctrine which our Church does not compel us to accept in the literal and the physical sense."

3. The Canadian address of the Trinitarian Bible Society is: The Trinitarian Bible Society, 39 Caldwell Cres, Brampton, Ontario L6W 1A2, Canada. In England, the address is The Trinitarian Bible Society, 217 Kingston Road, London SW 19 4NN, England

4. The addresses to write for further information about Baptist Bible Translators Institute are as follows: **Baptist Bible Translators, PO Box 1450, Bowie, Texas 76230.**

Telephone: 1-940-872-5751.

E-mail: bbti@morgan.net.

Web: http://www.morgan.net/~bbti

End Notes
(continued)
Chapter 29

1. Philip Shaff in his book, *History of the Apostolic Church*, said, "The Jewish feasts had a typical reference to the main facts of gospel history; the Passover to the death and resurrection of Christ, the true paschal Lamb." Pg. 557.

Albert Barnes in his book, *Notes on the New Testament*, said, "In the old Anglo-Saxon service-books, the term Easter is used frequently to translate the word Passover." Pg. 453.

George Fisher in his book, *History of the Christian Church*, said, "The British did not hesitate to hold Easter on the 14th of Nissan, the Jewish lunar month." Note: the 14th of Nissan is the day when the Jewish Passover was observed. Fisher also said, "The first yearly festival generally observed was Easter, standing in the room of the ancient Passover." He further says, "Easter was the Christian name for the Jewish Passover which the Christians spiritualized as the celebration of Christ's death, burial and resurrection. Pg. 64.

The ancient English versions used the word Easter and Passover interchangeably. For example, John Wycliffe transliterates the word Passover as *paske* (A.D. 1380). William Tyndale translates the word Passover as *ester*. (A.D. 1534) The Great Bible translates it as *Ester*.(A.D.1539) The Geneva Bible translates it as *Passover*. (A.D. 1560) The Bishops Bible translates it as *Easter*. (A.D. 1568) The Rheims Bible transliterates it as *Pasche*. (A.D. 1582)

Chapter 33

1. Slocum, Marianna, *Christianization of Vocabulary in the Translation of the Tzeltal New Testament*, The Bible Translator, Vol. 9, Pgs. 49-56, 1958.

Chapter 34

1. Morarie, Maxine, *Outreach*, Number 3, New Tribes Mission, Sanford, Florida, Pg 2, 1981.

2. Gill, Wayne, *Guide to Learning Tribal Languages*, New Tribes Institute, Camdenton, Missouri, Pg. 83.

3. Beekman, John, and Callow, John, *Translating the Word of God*, Zondervan, Grand Rapids, Michigan, 1974, Pgs. 72-73.)

4. There seems to be some doubt about this quote. Some say it is from Samuel Taylor Coleridge, 1772-1834. Others say it is anonymous. If it is from Coleridge, I have not been able to locate it in any of his writings.

Bibliography

The mentioning of a person, book, or organization in this bibliography should not be taken as an endorsement of everything related to that person, book, or organization.

BOOKS

Augsburger, David. *Are They Getting the Message?* Chicago: Moody Press, 1968.

Barnwell, Katharine. *Introduction to Semantics and Translation*, Second Edition and Third Edition, Horsleys Green, S.I.L., England, 1980 and 1986.

Barr, James. *The Semantics of Biblical Language*, Oxford University Press, London, England, 1961.

Beekman, John, and Callow, John. *Translating the Word of God*, Zondervan, Grand Rapids, Michigan, 1974.

Beekman, John., ed. *Notes on Translation: with Drills*, Santa Ana, Calif.: Summer Institute of Linguistics, 1965.

Beekman, John. Notes on Translation, No. 80, *Anthropology and the Translation of New Testament Key Terms*, Summer Institute of Linguistics, Huntington Beach, Calif.

Berlo, David K. *The Process of Communication*, New York: Holt, Rinehart and Winston, 1964.

Blight, Richard C. *Translation Problems From A to Z*, S.I.L., Dallas, Texas, 1992.

Brigance, William Norwood. *Speech*, New York: Appleton Century-Crofts, Inc., 1961.

Bullinger, E.W. *Figures of Speech Used in the Bible*, Baker Book House, Grand Rapids, Michigan, May 1981.

Callow, Kathleen. *Discourse Considerations in Translating the Word of God*, Zondervan, Grand Rapids, Michigan, 1974.

Chase, Stuart and Chase, Marian Tyler. *Power of Words*, New York: Harcourt, Brace, and World, Inc., 1954.

Collett, Sidney. *All About the Bible*, Fleming Revell Co., New York, 1904.

Davis, John. *Westminster Dictionary of the Bible*, Westminster Press, Philadelphia, 1944.

Deibler Jr., Ellis W. *Exercises in Bible Translation*, S.I.L., Dallas, Texas, 1988.

Eisenson, Jon; Auer, J. Jeffery; and Irwin, John V. *The Psychology of Communication*, New York: Appleton-Century-Crofts, Inc., 1963.

Ernst-August, Gutt *Relevance Theory, A Guide to Successful Communication in Translation*, S.I.L., Dallas, Texas and United Bible Societies, New York, NY, 1992.

Fuller, David Otis. *Which Bible?* Grand Rapids International Publications, Michigan, 1975.

Gaussen, L. *The Inspiration of the Holy Scriptures*, Moody Press, Chicago, 1949.

Grady, William P. *Final Authority, A Christians's Guide to the King James Bible*, Grady Publications, Knoxville, Tennessee, 1993.

Gudschinsky, Sarah C. *A Manual of Literacy for Preliterate Peoples*, Summer Institute of Linguistics, Ukarumpa, Papua New Guinea, 1973.

Hall, Edward T. *The Silent Language*, Greenwich, Connecticut: Fawcett Publications, Inc., 1959.

Hayakawa, S. I. *Language in Thought and Action*, Harcourt, Brace and World, Inc., New York, 1964.

Healey, Alan. *Language Learner's Field Guide*, Summer Institute of Linguistics, Ukarumpa, Papua New Guinea, 1975.

Hodges, Zane C. The Greek New Testament According to the Majority Text, Nelson, Nashville, 1982.

Hockett, C.F. *A Course in Modern Linguistics*, New York: McMillan, 1958.

Kraemer, Hendrik. *The Communication of the Christian Faith*, Westminster Press, Philadelphia, 1956.

Kubo, Sakae and Specht, Walter F. *So Many Versions?* Zondervan, Grand Rapids, Michigan, 1983.

Larson, Mildred. *Meaning-based Translation: A Guide to Cross-language Equivalence*, University Press of America, Lanham, Maryland, 1984.

Larson, Mildred. *A Manual for Problem Solving in Bible Translation*, Zondervan, Grand Rapids, Michigan, 1975.

Lawrence, P. and Meggitt, M.J. *Gods, Ghosts and Men in Melanesia*, Oxford University Press, Melbourne, Australia, 1965.

Lawrence, Peter. *Road Belong Cargo*, New York: Manchester University Press, 1964.

Lehmann, Winfred P. *Descriptive Linguistics*, Random House, New York, 1976.

McLuhan, Marshall. *Understanding Media: The Extensions of Man*, New York: McGraw-Hill Book Company, 1965.

McQuilkin, Robertson. *Understanding and Applying the Bible*. Moody Press, Chicago, 1992.

Murray, Andrew. *The Power of the Spirit*, London: James Nisbet and Co., 1896.

Nida, Eugene. *Bible Translating*, United Bible Societies, London, 1961.

Nida, Eugene. *Message and Mission*, New York: Harper and Brothers Publishers, 1960.

Nida, Eugene and Taber, Charles R. *The Theory and Practice of Translation*, United Bible Societies, Netherlands, 1974.

Nida, Eugene. *Toward a Science of Translating*, E.J. Brill, Leiden, Netherlands, 1964.

Orr, James, ed. *International Standard Bible Encyclopedia*, Eerdmans, Grand Rapids, Michigan, 1952.

Perschbacher, Wesley J. Editor. *The New Analytical Greek Lexicon*, Hendrickson Publishers, Inc., Peabody, Massachusetts, 1995.

Pickering, Wilbur N. *The Identity of the New Testament Text*, Nelson, Nashville, 1977.

Pierce, John Robinson. Symbols, Signals and Noise: The Nature and Process of Communication. New York: Harper and Brothers, 1961.

Pyles, Thomas. *The Origins and Development of the English Language*, Harcourt, Brace and World, Inc., New York, 1964.

Rowley, C.D. *The New Guinea Villager*, Melbourne, Australia: F.W. Cheshire Pty, Ltd, 1964.

Schramm, Wilbur, ed. *The Process and Effects of Mass Communication*, Urbana: University of Illinois Press, 1954.

Smalley, William A. *Orthography Studies*, United Bible Societies, London, 1964.

Smalley, William A. *Readings in Missionary Anthropology II*, William Carey Library, South Pasadena, Calif., 1978.

Terry, Milton S. *Biblical Hermeneutics*, Zondervan, Grand Rapids, Michigan, 1981.

Thayer, Joseph H. *Greek-English Lexicon*, American Book Company, New York, 1889.

Trench, R.C. *Synonyms of the New Testament*, Eerdmans Publishing Company, Grand Rapids, Michigan, 1953.

Trinitarian Bible Society. *The Greek Text Underlying the English Authorized Version of 1611*, London, 1976

United Bible Societies. *A Translator's Handbook on Mark*, (also available on other books of the New Testament), Leiden, Netherlands, 1961.

Vine, W.E. *Expository Dictionary of New Testament Words*, Fleming H. Revell Company, Westwood, New Jersey, 1966.

Walker, Deaville, F. *William Carey*, Chicago: Moody Press, 1951.

Warfield, Benjamin B. *The Inspiration and Authority of the Bible*, Presbyterian and Reformed Publishing Company, Phillipsburg, New Jersey, 1948.

Weigle, Luther A., editor. *The New Testament Octapla, Eight English Versions of the New Testament in the Tyndale-King James Tradition*, Thomas Nelson & Sons, New York.

Wiener, Norbert. Cybernetics, or Control and Communication in the Animal and the Machine, New York: Wiley, 1948.

Wiener, Norbert. *The Human Use of Human Beings*, Garden City, New York: Houghton Mifflin, 1956.

Wonderly, William L. *Bible Translations for Popular Use*, New York: United Bible Societies, 1968.

Wright, Charles R. *Mass Communication*, New York: Random House, 1964.

PERIODICALS

Beekman, John. *A Culturally Relevant Witness*, Practical Anthropology, Vol. IV, No. 6 (1957), pp. 83-88.

Bird, George L. and Dean, Lillian Harris. *Christians Can Learn From Communications Theorists*, Christianity Today, Vol. XI, No. 8 (Jan. 20, 1967), pp. 10-11.

Loewen, Jacob. *Bible Stories: Message and Matrix*, Practical Anthropology, Vol. XI, No. 2 (March-April 1964), pp. 49-54.

Loewen, Jocob. *The Question in the Communication of the Gospel*, Practical Anthropology, Vol. XIII, No. 5 (Sept.-Oct. 1966), pp. 213-226.

Longacre, Robert E. *Items in Context--Their Bearing on Translation Theory*, Language, No. XXXIV, 1953, pp. 482-491.

Morarie, Maxine. *Outreach, Number 3*, New Tribes Mission, Sanford, Florida, June 1981.

Nida, Eugene A. *Christo-Paganism*, Practical Anthropology, Vol. VIII, No. 1 (Jan.-Feb., 1961), pp. 1-14.

Nida, Eugene A. *Communication of the Gospel to Latin Americans*, Practical Anthropology, Vol. VIII, No. 4 (July-August, 1961), pp. 145-156.

Richert, Ernest, L. *Indigenous Reaction as a Guide to Meaningful Translation*, Bible Translator, Vol. XVI, No. 4 (October, 1965), pp. 198-200.

Slocum, Mariana. *Christianization of Vocabulary in the Translation of the Tzeltal New Testament*, Bible Translator, Vol. IX, No. 2 (April, 1958), pp. 49-56.

Turner, Charles V. *Cultural Change and the Sinasina Church*, Practical Anthropology, Vol. XIII, No. 3 (May-June 1966), pp. 103-106.

Turner, Charles V. *The 'Grease' Complex of New Guinea*, Practical Anthropology, Vol. XV, No 1 (1968), pp. 16-23.

Turner, Charles V. *The Sinasina 'Big Man' Complex: A Central Culture Theme*, Practical Anthropology, Vol. XV, No. 1 (1968), pp. 16-23.

Turner, Charles V. *The Sinasina Stone Bowl Cult*, Practical Anthropology, Vol. XVII, No. 1 (Jan.-Feb. 1970), pp. 23-32.

Turner, Charles V. *The Socio-Religious Significance of Baptism in Sinasina*, Practical Anthropology, Vol. XI, No. 4 (July-Aug. 1964), pp. 179-180.

Wonderly, William L. *Some Factors of Meaningfulness*, Bible Translator, Vol. XIV, No. 3 (July 1963), pp. 114-125.

PAMPHLETS AND ARTICLES

Gill, Wayne, "Guide to Learning Tribal Languages," New Tribes Institute, Camdenton, Missouri, 1981.

Nida, Eugene A, "*How the Word Is Made Flesh*", Princeton Pamphlets No. 7. Princeton, N.J.: Princeton Theological Seminary, 1952.

Young, Bill, "God's Message to You," New Tribes Mission, Sanford, Florida.

REPORTS

Bowman, Robert H, "Research and Evaluation of Christian Communications," Reports of the 16th Annual Mission Executives' Retreat, Winona Lake, Indiana, Oct. 2-5, 1967. Washington, D.C.: E.F.M.A., 1967.

UNPUBLISHED MATERIALS

Bowes, Malcom Edgar, "Christianity and Naturalism," unpublished M.A. thesis, Columbia Bible College, Columbia, SC, 1964.

Culberson, James Olin, "A Survey of Cultural Factors Relevant to Differential Reception of the Gospel in Primitive Societies," Unpublished M.A. thesis, Columbia Bible College, Columbia, S.C. 1957.

Kornfield, William J., "Anthropology--An Effective Key to Pioneer Work," unpublished M.A. thesis, Columbia Bible College, Columbia, SC, 1962.

Turner, Charles V., "Effective Communication: The Principles and Procedure for Developing It Across Cultures," unpublished M.A. thesis, Columbia Bible College, Columbia, SC, 1971.

Turner, Charles V., "Personal Bible Translation Notes" from United Bible Societies Translation Institute, Lae, Papua New Guinea, 1964.

Turner, Charles V., "Personal Bible Translation Notes" from Summer Institute of Linguistics, Ukarumpa, Papua New Guinea, 1973.

Index of Subjects and Scripture References

1

1 Corinthians 1:1 85
1 Corinthians 1:12 108
1 Corinthians 1:21 23
1 Corinthians 12:17 111
1 Corinthians 13:4 106
1 Corinthians 14:8-9 26
1 Corinthians 15:29 138
1 Corinthians 15:55 132
1 Corinthians 2:14 .... 28, 33
1 Corinthians 2:9 132
1 Corinthians 3:10 8
1 Corinthians 4:9 18
1 Corinthians 5:6 136
1 Corinthians 6:16 112
1 John 1:1-3 145
1 John 3:12 200
1 John 3:12-13 151
1 John 3:17 33
1 John 3:9a 44
1 John 4:9 178
1 Peter 124 126
1 Peter 3:21 138
1 Thessalonians 1: 25
1 Thessalonians 1:3 .... 88, 89, 93, 108
1 Thessalonians 1:6 89
1 Thessalonians 1:9 88
1 Thessalonians 2:6 17
1 Timothy 2:15 138
1 Timothy 3:1-5 18
1Corinthians 1:17 129
1Corinthians 3:1-8 128

2

2 Corinthians 10:5 6
2 Corinthians 11:4 131
2 Corinthians 12:13 131
2 Corinthians 13:1 172
2 Corinthians 5:14 .... 24, 146
2 Corinthians 5:21 143
2 Corinthians 6:15 114
2 Corinthians 8:23 17
2 Peter 1:21 .... 1, 53
2 Thessalonians 1:3-
10 94
2 Thessalonians 2:10 108
2 Thessalonians 2:8-9 143
2 Timothy 1:2 87
2 Timothy 2:7 9

A

Abram 11
Abstract Words 105
Abstracts 82
active voice 116
Acts 1:21- 17
Acts 1:22 108
Acts 1:25 129
Acts 1:6 116
Acts 1:8 6
Acts 12:2 150
Acts 12:4 .... 146, 178
Acts 13:1-5 18
Acts 13:3 16
Acts 13:36 129

Acts 14:14 .... 17, 140
Acts 15:4 136
Acts 17:6 .... 130, 204, 210
Acts 2:15 122
Acts 2:17 125
Acts 2:25 146
Acts 2:30 133
Acts 20:12 130
Acts 20:28 24
Acts 20:32 132
Acts 21:21 130
Acts 21:39 130
Acts 21:8 107
Acts 22:22 129
Acts 23:2 201
Acts 3:25 149
Acts 4:12 .... 106, 200
Acts 4:12a 211
Acts 4:12A 205
Acts 4:30 130
Acts 4:32 122
Acts 5:28 135
Acts 7:18 131
Acts 7:26 87
Acts 8:1-2 143
Acts 8:30 135
Acts 8:30, 31 22
Acts 8:31 33
Acts 9:31 79
adding to Scripture 34
Adjustments
   record those made 152
Agnostics 3
agreement among

5,000 Biblical
   manuscripts 53
Ambiguity 145
American Bible
   Society 32
An Objection
   answered 23
Anachronism 146
Apocrypha
   not Scripture 118
apocryphal books
   rejected by faithful
     churches 54
apostle 16
   defined 16
   emotional meaning
     of 16
   identity of 18
apostle, church
   apostle defined 17
apostles
   church sent ones 17
apostleship
   an office 18
   of the Twelve 17
apostolos, Greek
   word for
     missionary 16
Apostrophe 132
Arabic 153
Ask Questions
   to find words 169
Aswan Dam
   in Egypt 10

Australia
    the word "bum" 67
Author of the Book
    quoted
        Jesus testimony of
            the Scriptures 54
Authority
    erosion of 46
authority of God's
    Word 46

B

B.T. Westcott, and
    F.J.A. Hort
        the openers of
            "Panddora's
            box." 50
Baal 155
back translation 99
Back Translation
    why make one 174
Backtranslation 117, 173
baptism
    as sprinkle 20
    changed to a verb 105
    in relation to
        repentence 86
Baptist Bible
    Translators
        Institute
            address of 212
            of Bowie, Texas 101
            where we stand 55
Baptist churches

New Testament
    ones 22
Baptists
    inconsistent with
        claim to love
            Bible 21
baptize
    double reference to 24
    meaning of 24
    why transliterated 24
Barnabas 17
Baruya people 181
Bearing Precious
    Seed
        Scripture
            distribution 101
bedoubted and
    becriticized
        words chosen by
            Spurgeon 51
best way to learn
    Bible translation
        do some 37
biased interpretation
    avoid it 24
Bible
    inanimate until
        taught 23
Bible believers 3
Bible Commentaries
    use of 97
Bible Inspiration,
    implications of 3

Bible is not a Book
of religious-
magical powers 22
Bible Translating
and doctrinal
persuasion 20
biblical philosophy
of 5
Bible translation
"tricks of the
trade" 30
biblical basis of 26
inspired or not 4
proper prospective
of 23
Bible Translation
definition of 26
device for teaching
it 37
objective of 22
Bible Translator
requirements for 28
Bible Translators
faithful ones
needed 14
Bible Translators
Institute
BBTI 15
Bible Words
conditioning of 158
Bibleless languages
3,000 of them 25
Biblical Definition of
a nation

implications of 12
Bibliography 214
bicultural 31
bilingual 31
birth of Jesus
a holy birth 1
blaspheme 80
blood
Sinasina word for 29
Body by Fisher 105
bone 157
Boot Heel
of Missouri 66
born again 158, 163
Borrow Words 169
Bounds, E.M. 5
bowels 80
bowels of
compassion 33
brain surgeon
training needed
equal to 15

C

Cameron Townsend 32
Canaanite 155
Canon
the standard for a
book of the
Bible 54
canon of the New
Testament
formally decided in
397 A.D. 54

Canon of the New Testament 118
Centurion 123
change in the form
  of grammar 62
Charity 106
Charles H. Spurgeon
  against a horde of
    little popelings 50
Check Your
  Translation
    8 ways to do it 175
Checking the
  Translation 172
Checking Your Own
  Translation 175
Chiasmus 142
children
  of the
    bridechamber 149
Chronological
  Bible teaching 182
chronological events
  of the Bible 183
church
  Greek word for 156
  meaning of 79
  meaning of it 78
church planting
  experience
    translator must be
      a part of 23
circumcision 17

Coleridge 171
Collocational Clash 139
Colossians 1
  9-17
    all one sentence 145
Colossians 1:11 .... 116, 200
Colossians 1:13 26
Colossians 1:14 47
Colossians 1:18 132
Colossians 1:8 106
Colossians 2:8 6
Colossians 4:16 49
Comanche Code
  Talkers 57
combine old words 163
commentaries
  useful to
    translators 99
communication
  laws of 8
  natural laws of 10
Communication
  elements of 61
companied 17
Comparatives 148
Componential
  Analysis 85
Components of
  Meaning
    in a single word 92
components of
  referential meaning 82
Computers 197

Concordance 147
Connotative Meaning 76
constructive criticism
   of a Bible
      translator 26
contextual
      conditioning 157
Contextual Meaning 77
conversion.. 8
correcting variant
      texts 48
Cotton Patch Version............................. 179
Council of Carthage
   AD 397... 118
Council of Trent
   AD 1545... 118
Critical Text....................................... 118
Critical text 1881,.................................... 4
cultural bias.. 62
Cultural Context................................. 62
Cultural Substitutes 140

D

Danny Leahy... 150
Decapolis 151
Decode... 116
Deity
   of Christ 1
deletions
   examples of 47
depend upon native
   speakers
      reason for it 31
descriptive analysis

   of any language 8
Desiderius Erasmus
   Publisher of the
      first Greek New
      Testament in
      1516...50
Deuteronomy 18:15................................210
Deuteronomy 8:3 54
Dictionaries
   useful to translators..........................99
Direct Quotations 119
Discourse Structure 174
doctrinal persuasion 20
Doublet...136
doubts 3
Dr. Charles V. Turner............................101
Dr. D. M. Fraser....................................101
Dr. George Anderson 101
Dr. Gresham Machen
   great American
      theologian......................................50
drawers in the dresser
   dictionary meaning..........................73
Dynamic
   Equivalence
      errors of...32
dynamic equivalent
   the wrong
      approach to
      Bible translation 32

E

eardrums... 8
earth-apple...163

Easter 146
ecumenical 98
Elizabethan English 47
Ellipsis 123
empiricist 2
Encode 116
End Notes 212
England
   the word "bugger" 68
Enoch 26
   was translated 26
Epaphroditus 17
Ephesians 1: 7-12 94
Ephesians 1:13 115
Ephesians 1:15 88
Ephesians 1:7 .... 90, 134, 135
Ephesians 1:7-12 94
Ephesians 2:8 103
Ephesians 2:8,9 91
Ephesians 4:30 108
Ephesians 5:18 3
Ephesians 5:23 79
Ephesians 5:25 .... 24, 146
Esau 178
Ethiopian 33
   needed guidance 22
ethno-centricism 13
ethnology 5
Eugene Nida 32
Euphemisms 129
Events 82
every creature 13
Examination

Final 200
Final--answers 206
Exegesis 117
exegete of the Bible
   translator must be
     an accurate 24
Exodus 20:4 20
Exodus 22:31 160
Exodus 24:12 11
Exodus 32:13 12
experts
   1, 881 years
     without them 51

F

faith 8
   reasonable 2
Faithful Translation
   5 barriers to 177
Faithfulness in
   Translation 177
Farmer Smith 50
Feedback 62
Figurative (Extended)
   Meaning 80
figure of speech 81
Figures of speech 125
Figures of Speech 105
final source of all
   truth 6
Find Words
   through teaching 170
First Baptist Church
   of Milford, Ohio 101

first Greek New
   Testament
      printed in 1516 49
first textual critical
   edition 50
first two years
   the most critical 155
Flashback 137
Flashforward 137
Flemish language 105
flesh
   meaning of 125
Focus 136
Four Biblical
   Principles
      for Bible
         translating 5
fox 80
French word marche 75
friend
   in Sinasina 106

G

Galatians 1:13 78
Galatians 2:8-9 17
Galatians 2:9 .... 123, 126
Galatians 3:2 109
Galatians 3:8 130
Galatians 6:14 126
Gee and Haw
   meaning of 67
generic and specific
   chart of 79
Generic Words
   to find specific
      words 167
Generic-Specific
   Meaning 78
Genesis 1 191
Genesis 1:28 7
Genesis 12:2 11
Genesis 12:7 .... 11, 12
Genesis 14:13 11
Genesis 22:18 12
Genesis 3:15 183
Genesis 38:22 160
Genesis 39:9 .... 104, 110
Genesis 4:1 129
Genitive Structures 107
Gnosticism 2, 6
Gnostics 3
Goal Sheet
   for Bible
      translators 199
God loved the world
   so much 178
God's Message to
   You
      by William B.
         Young 191
God's method 5
good shepherd
   I am the good 40
Gospel Presentation
   by William B.
      Young 191
government cabinet 73
grafow biblon

I am writing a
  book 40
Grammatical
  Matching 104
Grammatical or
  Structural Meaning 81
Greek classics 49
Greek idiom
  with stomach
    having 43
Greek sentence in
  order 1
Greek word
  Lord (Kurios) 156
Greek word pneuma 75
Greek word
  splanchna 80

H

Hamtai people 169
harlot qedeshah 160
Hebrew 11
Hebrew word
  holy 155
Hebrew word qadosh 155
Hebrews 1:5 113
Hebrews 10:26 151
Hebrews 11:5 26
Hebrews 11:6 191
Hebrews 12:17 177
Hebrews 3:17 .... 205, 211
Hebrews 4:12 .... 23, 132
Hebron 11
Helps
  for interpreting text 94
Herod 80
higher knowledge 6
Historical Context 134
Holy 1
holy men 1
Holy Spirit, the mark
  of 3
human mind
  how it works 35
humanist-intellectual 2
Hyperbole 129
Hypothetical
  Situations 168

I

I Corinthians 3:5 112
I John 3:17 .... 122, 133
I John 3:8 151
idiom 117
Idiom 133
Idiomatic Meaning 80
II Peter 3:15, 16
  Peter says Paul's
    epistles are
    Scripture 48
II Tim. 3:16 191
implied information
  chart of 123
Implied Information 121
in Matthew 16:17 205
Including Implied
  reasons for
    including 122

inclusive
  inclusive or
    exclusive 59
  or exclusive 150
Indirect Quotations 119
Inerrant.. 117
information
  explosion 8
Inspiration of
  Scripture 117
inspiration of the
  Bible 2
intellectualism 2
Intellectualism 9
Interpreting
  the Biblical text 94
Irony 131
Isaiah 30:1,2 10
Isaiah 31:1 9
Isaiah 36:6 21
Isaiah 40:3 207
Isaiah 53:6 80
Isaiah 7:14 96
Iwam people 61

J

J. Beekman 98
James 1:1 69
James 1:13 116
James 1:15 106
James 2:2 156
James 3:6 .... 130, 205, 211
Jehovah's Witnesses 36
Jesus

being a textual
  critic 3
John 1:21b 210
John 1:21B 204
John 1:29 .... 134, 141
John 1:32 210
John 10:11 .... 25, 41, 42
John 10:17 139
John 10:35 55
John 10:9 127
John 11:50 137
John 12:19 130
John 12:30 139
John 13:12 112
John 13:33 149
John 14:6 6
John 15:16 148
John 15:4 201
John 16:22 139
John 16:6 139
John 17:12 149
John 18:14 137
John 18:32 121
John 18:35 .... 111, 113
John 19:20 116
John 19:30 143
John 2:19 .... 136, 211
John 2:19 205
John 20:19. 148
John 21:25 130
John 3:16 178
John 3:19 106
John 3:3 69
John 3:3. 163

John 3:5 136
John 3:6 75
John 3:8 75
John 4:1 .... 139, 205, 211
John 4:10 106
John 4:39 137
John 5:29 .... 108, 205, 211
John 5:38 .... 144, 205, 211
John 6:53 127
John 6:63 5
John 6:70 114
John 7:19 114
John 7:21 123
John 7:40 210
John 8:15 .... 125, 126
John 8:39 149
John 8:44 149
John 8:51 139
John 8:52 133
John Beekman 168
John F. Kennedy
   Berlin Wall speech 5
John the Baptist
   sprinkling water 21
John the Methodist 20
Joseph
   and Potiphar's wife 104
Judaism 18
Judges 17:6 47

K

Kaka people 161
Karl Lachmann
   a German
      rationalist 49
Katharine Barnwell 176
Khmu People of Laos 14
King James Version 25
   not correcting 25
   only reliable
      version 47
   why the 46
kingdom of God 147
Kinship Terms 149

L

Lachmann
   the rationalist 48
language
   all borrow words 59
   all distinct in
      grammar 60
   all have vocabulary
      focus 61
   none perfect 59
   none primitive 57
language and culture
   must know both 29
Language and
   Culture
   inseparable and
      inter-dependent 58
Language focus 61
Language Focus 153
language, all is
   structured 8
leadership 5

Lenski 98
Limiting Meaning 157
linguistic training 28
linguistics 5
Linguistics
  phonetics,
    phonemics, etc 28
listen for words used
  by Christians 163
Literal translation 117
Litotes 130
Living Context 162
Loan Words 149
Local Church
  Context 162
long time ago
  a Sinasina word 66
love
  meaning of 72
Luke 1:12 135
Luke 1:27 107
Luke 1:42 135
Luke 1:47 75
Luke 1:66 131
Luke 1:9,10 123
Luke 10:34 105
Luke 11:11 140
Luke 11:12 111
Luke 12:14 111
Luke 12:3 .... 140, 141, 146
Luke 13:20 200
Luke 13:21 108
Luke 13:32 .... 80, 125
Luke 13:34 132
Luke 15:22 149
Luke 15:24 130
Luke 16:11 111
Luke 16:17 54
Luke 16:29 132
Luke 18:13 140
Luke 2:5 129
Luke 2:7 144
Luke 22:1
  unleavened bread 147
Luke 24:49 107
Luke 4:34 108
Luke 7:37 129
Luke 8:26 - 30 142
Luke 9:51 134

M

majority text 49
Majority text 117
Malachi 3:1 207
Manobo people 168
Marianna Slocum 163
Mark 1:1 108
Mark 1:11 131
Mark 1:1-11 201
Mark 1:14 116
Mark 1:17 132
Mark 1:2,3 151
Mark 1:26 75
Mark 1:4 .... 86, 89, 151, 204
Mark 1:5 130
Mark 1:9 115
Mark 10:5 133
Mark 11:8 121

Mark 12:30	56
Mark 13:2	112
Mark 13:5	116
Mark 14:24	137
Mark 14:4	112
Mark 14:43	137
Mark 14:6	112, 200
Mark 16:15	13
Mark 16:3-4	143
Mark 2:1-6	173
Mark 2:19	133
Mark 2:4	122
Mark 2:5	115, 116, 149, 200
Mark 2:7	112
Mark 3:17	109
Mark 3:19	137
Mark 3:23	111, 131
Mark 3:9-10	119
Mark 4:38	122
Mark 4:41	113
Mark 5:18	119
Mark 5:20	119
Mark 5:25	129
Mark 6:14	200
Mark 6:16	137
Mark 7:26	120
Mark 7:9	131, 205, 211
Mark 8:15	127
Mark 8:17	104
Mark 8:34	130
Mark 8:37	114
Mark 8:8	144
Mark 9:10	119, 120
Mark 9:48	138
Mark 9:49	138
Mary mother of His humanity	1
Masoretic Hebrew text	4
Masoretic Hebrew text	4
Masterbuilder	8
Matthew 1:1	107
Matthew 1:18	42, 43
Matthew 1:20	1
Matthew 1:21	152
Matthew 1:23	134
Matthew 1:6	122
Matthew 1:6b	43
Matthew 10:2	16
Matthew 10:28	143
Matthew 10:42	108
Matthew 11:16	112
Matthew 11:18	129
Matthew 11:7	112
Matthew 12:31	108
Matthew 12:48	112
Matthew 13:15	142
Matthew 13:18	140
Matthew 13:55	114
Matthew 13:55.	114
Matthew 13:56	112
Matthew 13:8	152
Matthew 14:21	152
Matthew 15:31	107

Matthew 15:37 131
Matthew 16:14 121
Matthew 16:17 211
Matthew 18:12 110
Matthew 18:6 148
Matthew 19:24 136
Matthew 2:11 137
Matthew 2:6 .... 132, 205, 211
Matthew 20:30 107
Matthew 22:13 129
Matthew 23:14 105
Matthew 23:28 107
Matthew 24:35 54
Matthew 26:2 150
Matthew 26:5 .... 123, 204, 210
Matthew 26:55 111
Matthew 26:65A 201
Matthew 26:66 106
Matthew 27:25 132
Matthew 27:53 137
Matthew 28:17 122
Matthew 3:14 112
Matthew 3:16 122
Matthew 3:8 86
Matthew 4:4 54
Matthew 5:10 106
Matthew 5:13 113
Matthew 5:4 60
Matthew 5:40 141
Matthew 5:46 .... 113, 114
Matthew 5:6 132
Matthew 6:10 139
Matthew 6:13 47
Matthew 6:26 140
Matthew 6:28 123
Matthew 6:30 111
Matthew 6:31 112
Matthew 7:3 112
Matthew 7:6 142
Matthew 8:21,22 121
Matthew 8:26 112
Matthew 8:4 136
Matthew 8:8 .... 131, 135
Matthew 9:13, ... 145
Matthew 9:15 149
Matthew 9:6 123
Maxine Morarie, ... 166
meaning
   generic-specific 29
   referential 29
Meaning
   a person tells
     himself the
     meaning 67
   by one word or
     many 75
   cannot be told to
     someone 67
   different grammar
     can be same
     meaning 69
   does not have a
     location 66
   expressed by
     different
     grammars 68

expressed by several grammars 73
in terms of old words 70
in terms of situations 72
is something that occurs 65
not always in dictionary 73
not fixed and unchanging 71
overlap of 72
should be in terms of receiver 70
Similar grammar can be different meaning 68
Meanings
  many expressed by one grammar 74
merely a Bible Translator should be a church planter as well 22
Methodist 20
Methodist missionary 20
Metonymy 130
Milan
  a confused translation helper 84
missio, Latin for missionary 16
missionary
  qualifications for 18
Missionary
  mandate of 22
missionary, 3 reasson not in Bible 16
Missionary, identity and place in church 16
modern textual critics
  no two of whom agree 51
morphology 28
Moulton and Milligan 160
Murray, Andrew 212

N

Name for God 157
Names 151
nation
  biblical definition of 11
Nation
  four criteria of 11
  geo-politically defined 12
  Land 12
  Language 11
  Laws 11
  Lineage 11
Nation of Israel 12

National language
   words 169
Nations in the world 13
native speaker
   as co-translator 31
Native Text Material............................. 165
natural laws
   world governed by 7
Naturalism
   four beliefs of 6
nearest formal
   equivalence
      defined 33
nearest formal
   equivalent
      the right approach
         to Bible
            translation.. 32
New Testament
   church
      focal point of
         God's work 24
nine witnesses
   eight of them agree 54
Numbers.. 152

O

Obligatory grammar 150
old words in new
   ways 160
Order of Elements 142
original autographs
   of Scripture.. 4
original Greek New
   Testament
      same as in the
         manuscripts
            today 54
Other Objectives of
   This Book 25
outward trappings of
   Christianity 23

P

Papua New Guinea 95
      languages of 145
Passive voice.. 115
Paul... 18
pays a bride price 58
Pennsylvania Dutch............................... 46
personal computer 197
Personification 132
Peter 17
Pharisee 123
Philemon 5 142
Philemon 7 80
Philippians 2:25 17
Philippians 4:9 108
Philippines 95
phonemic analysis
   an accurate one................................ 179
Pidgin English.. 95
Plutarch.. 169
post translation 181
preservation
   of the Bible 55
Preservation

by faithful
  churches 46
preservation of
  Scripture 54
presupposition
  of textual critics 49
pre-translation 181
primitive language
  a myth 57
Principles for
  Successful Bible
  Translatin 189
Procedure for
  Analyzing
  semantic
  components 85
Pronominal
  Reference 143
Propositional
  Outlines 100
Proverbs 11:4 172
Proverbs 19:20 174
Proverbs 2:2 10
Proverbs 3:5 9
Proverbs 3:5,6 9
Psalm 23 14
publican
  connotative
  meaning of 77

Q

Quotation Marks 120

R

reasonable faith 3
Receiver Language 117
Referential Meaning 76
Reformers
  and second
  commandment 20
Relate to God
  Three ways to 7
Relationals 82
Relationship,
  miraculous 7
Relationship,
  religious-magical 7
Relationship,
  supernatural-
  natural 7
repentance 105
repented 169
restatements
  of the King James
  Version 25
Revelation 1:1 109
Revelation 1:13 79
Revelation 11:8 132
Revelation 12:1 108
Revelation 16:20 132
Revelation 20:14 .... 132, 205, 211
Revelation 21:14 16
Revelation 22:18 34
Revelation 22:18, 19 14
Revelation 22:18,19 106
Rhetorical Questions 110

    meaning of 111
righteousness 106
Roman Catholicism
    Hocus Pocus 7
Romans 1:5 .... 88, 90
Romans 10:14 5
Romans 10:15 5
Romans 10:17 8
Romans 10:9 134
Romans 10:9,10 8
Romans 11:13 18
Romans 11:14 125
Romans 12:20 133
Romans 14:10 112
Romans 14:10a 210
Romans 14:10A 204
Romans 15:33 87
Romans 2:15 119
Romans 2:4 107
Romans 3:15 131
Romans 3:23 168
Romans 3:9 113
Romans 5:1 12
Romans 6:15 113
Romans 6:3 .... 24, 117, 146
Romans 7:5 126
Romans 8:1 47
Romans 8:22 132
Romans 8:31 114
Romans 9:17 139
rules followed by
    textual critics
        vague 52

S

salvation 106
    a possible word for 168
Samaritan
    connotative
        meaning of 77
santo
    meaning images 169
Sawi people
    Judas a hero 77
scholars or Jesus 55
second
    commandment
        left out 20
Second Corinthians 97
semantic system 8
Semantics 56, 117
Señor 162
Sentence Length 145
several kinds of
    contexts 161
shorter and shorter
    texts
        result of textual
            criticism 51
sign in Japan
    drive sideways 15
Silvanus 17
Simbari language 150
Simile and Metaphor 126
sin 170
Sinasina people 58
Since 1881

controversy and
confusion 51
smaller and smaller
New Testament
the result of textual
criticism 51
smoogle 161
Son
of perdition 149
sound system 8
sound waves 8
Source Language 116
Source Text
basis of the
translation 30
stone
meaning of 78
Summer Institute of
Linguistics 99
synagogue 156
Synecdoche 131
synonyms
none total 60
syntax 28

T

T.E.A.R. 85
Tagalog 95
taking away from
Scripture 34
Tense of Verbs 151
text material 31
Text material
definition of 31

Text Material
recording it 165
textual criticism 2
the old Gnosticism
in new garb 52
Textual Criticism 2
development of 48
textual critics
biased, subjective 4
textual history 48
Textus Receptus 47
Greek text 4
the apostles, of the
churches 18
The Funeral of Kua
a Sinasina text 166
the word santo 169
Things 82
Things, Events,
Abstracts, and
Relationals 82
Timotheus 17
tittle 55
Transitions 151
translated us into the
kingdom 26
translating, without a
native speaker 14
translation
best comes from
N.T. situation 22
pre-translation 180
Translation 116

literal 103
priorities of 189
Translation Blunders
humorous 15
Translation
Development 181
translation handbooks
on Mark, Luke,
Acts, etc. 99
translation mistakes
all translators make
them 36
Translation Principles
books on 98
Translation
Procedure 179
translation process
best context in
which to
develop 22
translation proper 181
Translations
8 in one volume 95
translator and a
church planter
objection to this 23
transliterating 24
Transliteration 117
transmission of the
Scriptures 53
Trinitarian Bible
Society 100
address of 212
two choices

text of faithful
churches or text
of scholars 51
two watches
not sure of time 46
tyranny of the experts 50
Tzeltal people 163

U

uncertain sound
speaking into the
air 26
uncertainty of
modern art 53
uncircumcision 17
Understanding
in the way
intended 56
United Nations
200 of them 13
Urias 44

V

Verbal Context 161
Verbal Meanings 76
virgin birth of Jesus 1
vocabulary
development of 22
Vocabulary
development of 154

W

Wayne Gill 166
well of salvation 3
Westcott and Hort

openers of the evils of rationalism 51
Where did I come from?
   a little girl's question 70
Wichita Eagle Newspaper 14
widen the focus of words 160
William Barclay 98, 212
William Carey
   "I can plod." 31
Woodlark Island 104
Word Hunting 153
word of God
   discerns when taught 23
Word, living 1
Word, written 1
Words
   meaning of in terms of cultural context 56
   mutually delimit each other 78
Words are pliable 157
work ethic 8
wrest the Scriptures 48
write out the meaning to state meaning clearly 25
Written Context 161
written style 31
Written Style 145
Wycliffe Bible Translators 32

Y

Yagaria 169
Yagaria people 173
Yanamamo people
   Jesus a coward 77
Young
   William B. 191

Z

Zulu language 58

www.ingramcontent.com/pod-product-compliance
Lightning Source LLC
Chambersburg PA
CBHW080553090426
42735CB00016B/3216